THE *AMERICAN* CATHOLIC LAND MOVEMENT

Past, Present, and Future

THE *AMERICAN* CATHOLIC LAND MOVEMENT

Past, Present, and Future

EDITED BY
JASON M. CRAIG &
R. JARED STAUDT, PHD

TAN Books
Gastonia, North Carolina

Cover design by David Ferris, www.davidferrisdesign.com

Cover image: *Carmel Mission*, Jules Tavernier (1844–1889), 1875, oil on canvas. *Jules Tavernier, Artist & Adventurer* by Claudine Chalmers, Scott A. Shields, and Alfred C. Harrison Jr., Pomegranate Communications, Portland, Oregon, 2014 / Public Domain via Wikimedia Commons.

ISBN: 978-1-5051-3412-4
Kindle ISBN: 978-1-5051-3824-5
ePUB ISBN: 978-1-5051-3823-8

Published in the United States by
TAN Books
PO Box 269
Gastonia, NC 28053

www.TANBooks.com

Printed in the United States of America

IN MEMORIAM

John Senior (1923–1999)

"The great analogy of delving in the earth is prayer—elevation of mind and heart in praise—united in the single root of cult and cultivation. *Ora et Labora*. Work, from erg, en-erg-y, the force which moves the universe, finds its highest physical point in man who in labor transforms matter into praise as God through grace transforms both matter and spirit to glory. According to the Gospel, *Deus agricola est*, God is a farmer."

—*The Restoration of Christian Culture*

CONTENTS

Commander John F. Sharpe, U.S. Navy (retired)

CDR Sharpe is a 1993 distinguished graduate of the United States Naval Academy at Annapolis, Maryland, where he earned a Bachelor of Science degree with honors in English and emphases in political thought and history. Following graduation, he served for six years with the United States Navy Submarine Force and thereafter for two-plus decades as a Navy Public Affairs Officer. In 2000, he and a colleague founded IHS Press to bring back into print classics of Catholic Social Doctrine by major Catholic thinkers of the early twentieth-century, and since then, he has remained Chairman and Managing Director of the Press. Simultaneously, he received his Master of Arts in History from Old Dominion University and completed all but the dissertation towards a PhD in History as a Hagley Fellow at the University of Delaware. He currently serves as Senior Legal Assistant at the Law Offices of Jeffrey E. McFadden, raises sheep and chickens with his wife and children on his homestead, Bold Venture Farm, and directs and occasionally teaches Gregorian chant and classical polyphony at chapels and other venues around the United States. CDR Sharpe is also currently a first-year JD student with the part-time evening program at the University of Baltimore School of Law.

FOREWORD

"The only step forward is the step backward."

—G. K. Chesterton, What's Wrong With the World, 1908

"Each man who desires the success of an ideal should keep its enthusiasm with certitude in his own mind, and trust through this to inspire others."

—Hillaire Belloc, Essays in Liberalism 1897

"As a rule, only that stability which is rooted in one's own holding makes of the family the vital and most perfect and fecund cell of society."

—Pius XII, La Solennità della Pentecoste 1943

The policy of history's greatest statesmen, from the classical to our contemporary age, says political economist Charles Devas in his article on "agrarianism" for the old *Catholic Encyclopedia*, has been to encourage in their states a flourishing population of small farmers—call them what you will: yeomen, peasants, homesteaders, smallholders, or, perhaps less precisely, just the "middle class." In making this observation, and noting its consonance with what the Catholic Church has taught, from the beginning of her formal commentary upon and, I dare say, *correction and critique* (if not outright denunciation) of the social disorder that arose at the dawn of the modern age[1] owing to the confluence of several historical trends—rationalist developments in philosophy (and, accordingly, economic thought); centralizing and machine-based developments in industrial technology; and the ever-growing complexity, abstraction, and "unreality" of methods and entities employed by governments and financial actors for the manipulation and increase of token wealth, which rationalism permitted, and which enabled the industrial developments—Devas admits what is perhaps obvious after a moment's serious reflection. To advocate a rural, agrarian, or yeoman ethos as the ideal foundation upon which both to ideologically envision and to practically construct social, political, and economic order—whether in its smallest manifestation, i.e., the family, or, writ large, as and where relevant, across the legal, political, social, and economic machinery of the state—is to utter a proposition that is essentially *natural*, insofar as the proposition both concerns and derives from the natural order, rather than being an aspect of revelation (as touching upon doctrines that are intelligible but without divine assistance effectively unknowable) or of grace (as in, relating to the participation of the human soul in the life of the Blessed Trinity by means of the sacramental system that Our Lord established while on earth).

---

[1] Broadly speaking, the modern period follows the Renaissance and the revolt known as the "Reformation" which then gave us the so-called "Enlightenment" and everything that that entailed. The opposition between its doctrine and that of the Catholic Church is perhaps most easily, if not best, grasped from a review of the chief encyclicals of Pope Leo XIII, whose writings—in, again, the words of Charles Devas—"form a manual of social politics."

Support for this assertion comes in many forms. In terms of the personalities known to have advocated ruralism, numerous are the virtuous pagans of the pre-Christian era who had no connection with revealed religion. We need only think of Aristotle who insisted upon the "mean" as (one of) his ethical rules of life—such as the mean between concentrations of wealth and extreme poverty—and who decried the proliferation of unproductive middlemen to the eclipse of genuine agricultural and craft producers. Likewise, Virgil, whose pastoral sympathies and predilection for rural life are so well known as to need no extended elaboration. Devas mentions Solon of Athens as another. Likewise, post- or non-Christian pagans, such as, if you will excuse the claim,[2] Jefferson and many of the founding fathers of the United States, were equally drawn—as adverted to in so many words by Harrelson's essay in this volume on the Southern Agrarians—to a concept of an ideal "yeoman republic" where the cultivation and maintenance of civic virtue depended upon the character traits and ways of thinking nourished and developed by one's management of a farmstead or smallholding rather than upon participation in great economic enterprises that necessarily concentrate wealth in a few hands and reduce the great many others to the status of non-owning workers.

Closer to our day, numerous perceptive and rigorously thoughtful individuals, such as the architect Ralph Adams Cram, the political thinker and essayist Richard Weaver, the poet T. S. Eliot, and the social critic Arthur J. Penty, have

---

2 Assuming the claim needs excusing!

advanced the proposition that human society, to be healthy and sane, should both practically—in its laws, customs, and habitual and typical ways of doing and thinking—and philosophically—that is, in the core, shared vision that sits as the bedrock foundation that works, often just imperceptibly, to give society its color, unity, direction, and expression, i.e., what Weaver has called the "metaphysical dream"—comprise, among other things, concrete ethical standards that guarantee and defend the right of owners of small productive properties to remain secure in that ownership and in their status as independent owners. Penty, having studied the medieval guild system in depth, becoming in the process what many Distributists, to include G. K. Chesterton, thought of as the chief thinker and theorist of that movement, insisted that the role of law (again, among other things) and of the accompanying guild rules and customs was to make it feasible for the small owner and the poorer economic actor to survive independent and free in the face of pressure from the rich and powerful whose almost inevitable influence intrinsically conspires to undermine that independence and small ownership. These men, however, being non-Catholics and of various and even eclectic religious persuasions,[3] came to the conclusion we have been discussing

[3] Indeed, Penty himself was not even much of a Christian, spiritually or theologically speaking, perhaps akin to the position of another notorious (in some circles) non-Catholic, turn-of-the-century thinker who saw the Church as (or, rather, admitted that she was) the source of European cultural and political order. Which is not to say that Penty was hostile to Christianity or, as an aficionado and genuine lover of the medieval world and the art and culture it produced, to Catholicism or to

without any strictly religious guidance, and without reading *Rerum Novarum*—though read it they assuredly did—as a command demanding the submission of the intellect as to a binding religious decree.

Offering yet another of many possible examples, modern scholarship, for all its failings, has established more or less definitively that in the pre-national and early-republic phases of American history—I reference this in view of the fact that the present volume purports to be about an *American* movement even if the idea it elaborates is not the property of a single nation—there was a concept today referred to as the "moral economy," somewhat of a species of "little-r" republicanism. As a quick point of orientation or reference, Gordon Wood comes to mind as one of the most familiar names from among the diffuse school of historians attempting to see and understand in early-American economic behavior, with an inevitably contemporary and capitalist lens, what a reader familiar with the social ethics of the Middle Ages—which all Catholics are or at least should be—will quickly recognize as the workings of concepts such as justice, fairness, frugality, independence, fortitude, self-reliance, and sacrifice in economic no less than in other affairs.[4] Outside the intellectual fold from within

---

the Church. His papers as well as his published writings establish with certainty his sympathy with the Catholic ideological position, and his daughter, whom I had the good fortune to meet in England, told me directly of both the fervor of his wife's Catholicism and his full support for her having raised their children in the Church.

4 While Wood's is perhaps the most well-known name, at least from among those I studied during a period both intense and now admittedly

dated by fifteen-or-so years while a doctoral candidate in history at the University of Delaware, it is not the most relevant among those seeing in the early American republic vestiges of medieval economic, and therefore (*pace* the contemporary "free marketeers" of the Salamanca school) anti-capitalist, thought and practice. Even given the obvious absence of a fully Catholic worldview informing their work, some of Wood's fellow historians have done exceptional work pointing out the moral limits that many if not most early Americans envisioned as applicable to economic behavior. The arguably most interesting among dozens of relevant works are the following: Michael Merrill, "The Anticapitalist Origins of the United States," *Review* 13, no. 4 (Fall 1990): 465-97, and "Putting 'Capitalism' in Its Place: A Review of Recent Literature," *The William and Mary Quarterly* 52, no. 2 (Apr 1995): 315-26; Rowland Berthoff, *Republic of the Dispossessed: the Exceptional Old-European Consensus in America* (Columbia: University of Missouri Press, 1997); Mary Roys Baker, "Anglo-Massachusetts Trade Union Roots, 1130-1790," *Labor History* 14, no. 3 (Summer 1973): 352-96; James L. Huston, "The American Revolutionaries, the Political Economy of Aristocracy, and the American Concept of the Distribution of Wealth, 1765-1900," *The American Historical Review* 98, no. 4 (Oct 1993): 1079-1105, and "Economc Landscapes Yet to Be Discovered: The Early American Republic and Historians' Unsubtle Adoption of Political Economy," *Journal of the Early American Republic* 24 (Summer 2004): 219-31; Drew R. McCoy, *The Elusive Republic: Political Economy in Jeffersonian America* (New York: Norton, 1982); Allan Kulikoff, *From British Peasants to Colonial American Farmers* (Chapel Hill, NC: University of North Carolina Press, 2000); Daniel Vickers, "Competency and Competition: Economic Culture in Early America," *The William and Mary Quarterly* 47, no. 1 (Jan 1990): 3-29; Ronald Schultz, "The Small-Producer Tradition and the Moral Origins of Artisan Radicalism in Philadelphia 1720-1810," *Past & Present*, no. 127 (May 1990): 84-116; Barbara Clark Smith, "Food Rioters and the American Revolution," *The William and Mary Quarterly* 51, no. 1 (Jan 1994): 3-34; Richard Stott, "Artisans and Capitalist Development," *Journal of the Early Republic* 16, no. 2 (Summer 1996): 257-71; Gary J. Kornblith, "The Artisanal Response to Capitalist Transformation," *Journal of the Early Republic* 10, no. 3 (Autumn 1990): 315-2; and Michael J. Thompson, "The Radical Critique of Economic Inequality in Early American Political Thought." New Political Science 30, no. 3 (Sep 2008): 307-24. This list—which omits mention, at least which Devas extols the ideal population of small farmers, historians have struggled to situate the ideal, referring variously (and quite interestingly, as Our Lord says in Luke 9:40, sometimes even the very stones, as in, the atheist historians, will cry out in praise of evident truth) to "artisan republicanism," "small proprietorship," the "producer economy," and other constructs, to identify a socio-economic vision that puts family scale, productive land, and craftsmanship at the center of economic life, in contradistinction to the capitalist and socialist behemoths bequeathed to us by our post-Reformation, post-World War, and post-Cold War history.

Coming a bit closer to home, but still prescinding from a purely religious and certainly from a uniquely Catholic idea, the roots in "natural" ethics of the importance to society of a critical mass of independent producers who wrest, through their own labor, some if not most of their livelihood from productive property managed under their free and sole control are apparent in a number of ways. To note just one of these: the classical understanding of prudence, queen of the cardinal virtues. Among its many parts is "providence." While certainly analogous to the name and character a religious soul assigns to God the Father, the philosophers, leaving theology aside, understand that "how to *provide* for the future" derives from "remembrance of the past and understanding of the present," which three forms of insight work together to enable an intelligent being—like man—to

for context, of the works Gary Nash, Joyce Appleby, Eric Foner, James Henretta, and numerous others who have made relevant contributions to this area of study—is admittedly abbreviated and highly selective.

govern things wisely and direct them toward an end.[5] Aquinas remarks, in fact, in his short manual of advice to the ruler of Cyprus, following *not* a dogmatic decree but only "the Philosopher"—i.e., Aristotle—that a sufficiency of material goods is *necessary* for an individual to practice virtue.[6] Only a minute's reflection is needed to answer the question that this remark raises: What kind of material good requires, to bring it to its specific end (hint: creation of wealth for the meeting of man's material needs): knowledge and observation of the past (learning from one's mistakes, or, better, from one's ancestors); understanding of the present (the sky's the limit); and a resultant ability to provide for the future (whether this be ensuring the animals are fed, preparing for the frost, or harvesting and storing grain and vegetables)? More provocatively: Can a man who is not faced with these and the thousand-and-one other duties, tasks, and burdens of the active homestead (whether full or partial) ever come authentically to know providence and prudence, or even in their fullness to exercise them?

Given the upshot of the foregoing excursus, touching briefly upon the reality that the rural or agrarian social ideal, as the preferred inspiration for family and broader social organization, is, strictly speaking, a creature of the natural order, how, then, do we have before us a book on the "Catholic" land movement? Our editor's introduction makes clear that Catholic authorities—from popes to activists to scholars to social workers—have all adverted to the sanity and

---

5 St. Thomas Aquinas, *Summa theologiae* I, q. 22, a. 3, c.

6 St. Thomas Aquinas, *De regno*, no. 118, https://isidore.co/aquinas/DeRegno.htm.

necessity of a social order that facilitates the maintenance and defense of Devas's "flourishing populations of small farmers or peasants." But the question that arises is whether those authorities, coincidentally Catholic, promote Devas's vision as mere custodians and spokesmen of his essentially natural and political conception, alongside other brilliant and sane non-Catholic thinkers like Penty, Weaver, Eliot, and so many others, or whether they do so as integral Catholics promoting an integrally Catholic ideal. And why does it matter?

For a quarter century, inspired by my partner,[7] Deric O'Huallachain, IHS Press has endeavored, in amateur fits and starts that pale in comparison with the legacy of our friend Tom Nelson, founder of TAN Books, which has published the anthology you now hold in your hand, to draw to the attention of those who have ears to hear the reality that, however controversially, Hilaire Belloc belligerently asserts as the final line of *Europe and the Faith*: "The Faith is Europe. And Europe is the Faith."[8] The point for IHS, of course, not

[7] Deric O'Huallachain is a London-born Irishman, my senior in age as well as in wisdom, experience, and general knowledge, with whom I founded IHS Press in June of 2001. His health is very poor, and as of this writing, we can only, humanly speaking, pray for a holy and happy death. As with many mentors I have known over a very blessed lifetime that started early on with driving American submarines behind Russians in the North Atlantic, and soon thereafter developed into a near obsession with reading the works of Catholics and other authorities on all the burning questions of the twentieth century, my only regret is failing to squeeze that last drop of knowledge and wisdom out of my friend before Divine Providence made it impossible to do so. I have no way of knowing, by the time this volume will be in print and circulating, whether my friend, as St. Paul says, will be in or out of the body. In any case, I do ask readers' prayers for the welfare of his soul. *Oremus et vigilemus.*

[8] Hilaire Belloc, *Europe and the Faith* (London: Constable & Co. Ltd., 1924), p. 331.

to take away from the literal (and defensible) meaning of Belloc's premise, has been that if the Word was indeed made flesh, His cult would quite obviously become incarnate in a whole host of ways: law, customs, habits, fashion, architecture, music, liturgy, cuisine, literature, folklore, and, finally, political economy—and that, following the Incarnation, man must not put asunder what God has joined.

In other words, just as, for Belloc, Europe can be nothing other than the Faith, during that period of human history following the Incarnation in time and on the earth of the Second Person of the Blessed Trinity, so for us, as for St. Thomas, the purpose of men living together in society is for the purpose of living *well*; and living well is living the *good* life, which is the *virtuous* life.[9] And yet living the virtuous life is not an end in itself but, rather, "through virtuous living, man is further ordained to a higher end, which consists in the enjoyment of God."[10] St. Thomas, accordingly, sums up the height, breadth, width, and depth of the doctrine of the Social Kingship of Our Lord Jesus Christ as follows: "It is not the ultimate end of an assembled multitude to live virtuously, but through virtuous living *to attain to the possession of God*."[11]

Thus the *Catholic* land movement. The *anima naturaliter Christiana* of Tertullian instinctively realizes that there can no longer, on this side of Calvary, be a radical separation (without obliterating *distinctions*) between grace and nature, faith and reason, Church and state, knowledge and inquiry, authority and vindication, justice and preference, equanimity

---

[9] St. Thomas Aquinas, *De regno*, no. 106.
[10] Aquinas, no. 107.
[11] Aquinas, no. 107.

and power, apportionment and acquisition. All power must serve justice, and, as Maritain famously remarked before the disorientation in the *Action Française* affair, "The human city fails in justice and sins against itself and against its members if, when the truth is sufficiently proposed to it, it refuses to recognize Him Who is the Way of beatitude."[12] For the vindication of this and no other principle was IHS Press established.

In our time, however, one problem seemed to need more attention than any other—and this probably because of the uniquely *American* contribution to capitalism, and hence the unique glory of this volume on the American Catholic back-to-the-land effort. Historically, capitalism sundered the laborer from his property. By doing so, it ushered in the "wage system," where mere employees—"hands," as the English masters had it, rather than heads, hearts, and souls—were reduced, as Pius XI reminds us, to a proletarian state, referencing not so much Marx as classical antiquity. In response, it was not only the Knights of Labor, rescued from destruction by the good offices of a figure no less than Henry Cardinal Manning himself, who agitated for the destruction of the "wage system," but also Father Vincent McNabb, OP, who insisted contrarily upon the "ownership system," and the American bishops in conference, who, in 1918, under the intellectual leadership of John Ryan, also mentioned herein later on, insisted that the "majority must somehow become owners, or at least in part, of the instruments of production"

---

[12] Jacques Maritain, *Three Reformers: Luther, Descartes, Rousseau* (Sheed & Ward, 1928), 37.

even though such a radical change would involve "to a great extent the abolition of the wage system."

IHS, therefore, embarked on a program to publish tracts by Catholic thinkers that would, ideally, appeal to a twin track of reader: first, the Catholic who was docile to the teaching of the Church, and who could be rescued from economic error and ignorance by simple exposure to the reality that the Church—read Sheen's *Communism and the Conscience of the West* if this proposition is hard to swallow—disfavored capitalism as much as she disfavored communism and socialism. Second, the non-Catholic who, following Eliot, Weaver, Penty, Cram, and others, instinctively knew that there was something ruthless, inhumane, unjust, and unnatural about capitalism that was no less bad than socialism, and that a sane alternative, sanctioned by—as Weaver puts it, in a different setting—the wisdom of the Greeks and the mercy of Christianity, necessarily existed—but who did *not* know that this alternative was, saving the distinction between temporal and spiritual affairs, sacred doctrine and philosophy, and the other analogous dualities, in modern (i.e., post-Renaissance) times, uniquely defended by the Catholic Church and her chief exponents and apologists. Fritz Schumacher is perhaps the easiest example, alongside Douglas Hyde, of a thinker who all along was looking for the Church's social doctrine and, when he found it, joined her. For this reason, I humbly beg to differ with at least the word choice of the illustrious Dr. Carlson who suggests below how "unlikely" it is that agrarianism emerged among American Catholics. His point—that Catholic immigrants were concentrated in urban centers—is well-enough taken.

But his intellectual and ideological point is incorrect: from the time Our Lord walked the earth, the ethos of the Church has been rural; His parables are agrarian; He first revealed Himself in the flesh to an ox, an ass, and sheep; The Church's liturgy favors, by reference, rural, real, natural life; the classical authors at the root of her philosophy are of a pastoral temperament; her ethics are Distributist; and her thinkers, to a man, *pace* Michael Novak,[13] defend the wide distribution of ownership of productive property. As Fanfani says in his study of capitalism, though examples be adduced *ad infinitum*, no evidence is available to make us change our conclusion that there is an unbridgeable gulf between the Catholic and capitalistic conception of life.

At the end of the day, the value of this volume, as of the few historical gems (we hope and pray there are many more to come) that IHS has been privileged over the years to circulate, is the testimony to the immortality of truth—and, in this particular case, of the permanence of the socio-economic ideal represented by whatever name one wishes to give it: Distributism, agrarianism, ruralism, small proprietorship, solidarism, synarchism ("Google" this term and "Mexico" for a primer), corporatism, the guild system, etc. The vision comes to us not from the Church as a matter of faith to be believed by virtue of an *ex cathedra* pronouncement, though, I would argue, it has equivalent intellectual authority. Rather, it comes to us as part of the human patrimony—i.e., the unchangeable nature of man and society, upon

---

[13] His neo-conservative capitalism is definitively dealt with in our introduction to Fanfani's *Catholicism, Protestantism, and Capitalism* (Norfolk, Va.: IHS Press, 2003).

which Christianity has built, placing grace atop the natural order to confirm, defend, uplift, rectify, and inspire what was already good and true in our civilization. Though it does not constitute fully decisive evidence, I offer anecdotally the fact that long before, in 1926, the term "Distributism" came to be as a result of a blessed or ill-fated evening in a London pub—thirty years before, as it happens—Belloc was decrying the divorce of personality and production and again in 1907 affirming that "the sentiment of property is normal to and necessary to a citizen."

The Catholic land movement, accordingly, is *Catholic* essentially and incidentally—the latter because Catholicism is not strictly necessary for vindicating a principle of natural reason which makes ownership of productive property by a man and his family one of the primary social and political rights, and which no revelation is necessary to reveal; but the former because, given humanity's darkened intellect, it is the unique role of the Church, as guarantor and custodian of all that is true and good, to not only teach men the truth as revealed, as it were, in secret, by the Holy Ghost, but to confirm and affirm and vindicate those sane, natural principles without service to which human civilization will not survive. For this reason, Pope St. Pius X, in his definitive and arguably unsurpassed work on the duty of the Catholic laity to combat the forces working to eliminate the influence of the Faith on public life, observes, with characteristic clarity and precision, that while the Church has no *direct* role in promoting the good of the temporal order, such good flows naturally from her divine and supernatural mission, because, the pope says—in terms we might even call Bellocian—"*The civilization of the world is Christian.* The more completely Christian it is, the more true, more lasting and more productive of genuine fruit it is."[14]

With the foregoing in mind, perhaps readers will better appreciate the profundity and significance of the words that close Belloc's *Europe and the Faith*, in which—with his unparalleled concision and forthrightness, and obvious if not intentional reference to the spirit, if not the words, of the remark St. Pius X made fifteen years earlier—he sets before his readers the specters of communism and capitalism, and adverts to the reaction thereto within the remains of Christendom.

> Against both, the pillar of reaction is peasant society, and peasant society has proved throughout Europe largely coordinate with the remaining authority of the Catholic Church. For a peasant society does not mean a society composed of peasants, but one in which modern Industrial Capitalism yields to agriculture, and in which agriculture is, in the main, conducted by men possessed in part or altogether of their instruments of production and of the soil, either through ownership or customary tenure. In such a society all the institutions of the state repose upon an underlying conception of secure and well-divided private property which can never be questioned and which colors all men's minds. And that doctrine, like every other sane

[14] *Il fermo proposito* § 4 (1905) (my emphasis).

> doctrine, though applicable only to temporal conditions, has the firm support of the Catholic Church.[15]

Let us hope, by God's grace and the efficacy of the present volume, that He will continue to conserve His Church in holy religion, such that from the housetops she will preach, in and out of season, her true and traditional social doctrine and the social reign of her Lord, and that the reaction of peasant society will increase and multiply unto the salvation, temporal and eternal, of mankind.

Commander John F. Sharpe, USN (ret.)
Director and Chairman, IHS Press
B.S., United States Naval Academy
M.A., Old Dominion University
Ph.D. (ABD) University of Delaware
L1, University of Baltimore School of Law

---

15 Hilaire Belloc, *Europe and the Faith*, (the Paulist Press, 1921), 260.

INTRODUCTION

THE STORY OF THE AMERICAN CATHOLIC LAND MOVEMENT

R. Jared Staudt

¡Tierra!

This word of promise and opportunity, spoken from the Pinta on October 12, 1492, contained within it seeds of both encounter and conflict. Land lies at the heart of American colonization and the opening of the new world to the spread of the Catholic faith. Even within the United States, which grew out of predominately Protestant colonies on the Eastern seaboard, Catholics played a central role. Coming to this "new" world mixed up spreading God's glory and a quest for man's own in a way inextricably bound together.

Tierra . . . This is how the drama of European settlement of the Americas began. Columbus was not the first European to discover America, for the Vikings and perhaps the Irish monks preceded him, but this first fateful voyage drastically altered the course of human history. We cannot forget the great human tragedy that accompanied this settlement, displacing the Indigenous population and a horrific outbreak of disease, but from a Catholic perspective, we can also recognize the work of providence under the guidance of Our Lady of Guadalupe.

Catholics came to America for the promise of land and opportunity, extending the culture of their homelands, seeking to sanctify their new home in faith, and build something new. Every human story involves tragedy, the brokenness of sin, conflict, and promises falling short. Yet despite the failures of some Catholics, the martyrs sanctified the American continents with their blood. Could we say that despite human sin, God wanted His people to come to this new land? October 12 is the feast of Our Lady of Pillar, the apparition marking the farthest westward journey of any of the apostles, St. James in Spain. And it was from Spain that European immigration to America began.

This book will explore the spiritual promise of Catholic life in the land of North America. It is not primarily a historical account, even though we will begin there, setting up the story of the American Catholic Land Movement as an unfolding reality. Looking to the movement of Catholic settlement, we can ask: Does the land still contain a promise for Catholics today? What does God want us to do to continue the sanctification of the land, to promote reconciliation in faith, and to live in a way that truly gives Him glory?

The Drama of the American Catholic Land Movement

The story of the American Catholic Land Movement constitutes a drama in five acts. This introduction will examine some of the protagonists who advanced this unfolding story, both earthly and heavenly, particularly Our Lady. Each bears its own inner tension, a drama to be worked out with its lessons for us to learn.

Act 1: The Missions

Unity or conflict; spiritual purification or physical destruction?

We find both of these dynamics at work in the Catholic settlement of America.[1] Within both the Spanish and French territorial incursions into North America, the establishment of missions served as the initial social organization, setting up a spiritual frontier acting as a vanguard beyond the few colonial settlements. Certainly, colonial officials viewed them pragmatically as a means of spreading European civilization through the Catholic faith and European means of farming and economic development. The missions, however, became spiritual and agricultural centers in their own right, leading to genuine inculturation of the Catholic faith and the stimulation of native culture in significant, though temporary, ways, such as music and the arts.

The first mission in the present territory of the United States was Nombre de Dios in St. Augustine, Florida, with missions radiating from there up the Atlantic coast to the Chesapeake Bay and along the Gulf Coast. Distinct mission-founding ventures would enter New Mexico

---

[1] For the most comprehensive overview of Catholic settlement in North America, see Kevin Starr, *Continental Ambitions: Roman Catholics in North America: The Colonial Experience* (San Francisco: Ignatius Press, 2016).

beginning in 1598, Arizona in 1687 (led by Ven. Eusebio Kino, the geographer and rancher), Texas in 1698, and California in 1769 (led by St. Junipero Serra).[2]

The National Park Service has acknowledged the economic impacts of their efforts in the nation's history:

> The work of the missionaries was pioneering and varied. The natives learned trades, came to know new technologies, and provided indispensable manual labor to construct the churches, which mark the paths of the missionaries. Grains, vegetables, and fruits from Spain were cultivated for the first time in the missions. Cattle, sheep, and rams were also raised. Irrigation ditches were constructed to carry water to

---

[2] See John Kessell, *Spain in the Southwest: A Narrative History of Colonial New Mexico, Arizona, Texas, and California* (Norman, OK: University of Oklahoma Press, 2002). In addition, French Jesuits established less agriculturally based missions off the coast of Maine in 1613, in upstate New York in 1656, and on the site of the future cities of Green Bay in 1634, Biloxi 1699, Detroit 1701, Mobile 1702, New Orleans 1718, Baton Rouge 1720, and St. Louis 1764. That is not to say the Jesuits did not seek to advance agriculture in their missions. For instance, at Saint-Joseph de Sillery in Quebec, "Algonquin and Montagnais nomads were provided with medical services. . . . They were also provided with food, homes, tools for farming and artisanal production, and end-of-life-care." Bronwen McShea, *Apostles of Empire: The Jesuits of New France* (Lincoln, NE: University of Nebraska Press, 2019), 96. In the later territory of the United States, "several French colonial villages based on agriculture emerged. These included St. Genevieve, Missouri (1735), Vincennes, Indiana (1732), and Fort Duquesne (1754; later Pittsburgh, Pennsylvania)." Jeffrey Marlett, "Strangers in Our Midst: Catholics in Rural America," in *Roman Catholicism in the United States: A Thematic History*, ed. Margaret M. McGuinness and James T. Fisher (New York: Fordham University Press, 2019), 158.

> the dry fields; water, more precious than gold or silver. The friars, with the labor of the natives, created new landscapes. Wheat complemented the native corn. Grapevines and wine are today hallmarks of California. Friars were loyal to the Christian principle of "ora et labora," pray and work.[3]

There is much both to praise and critique in the missions, as they provided protection from colonial abuses but also often brought about a reduction[4] of the population in a paternalistic setting of the padres' care. Within these enclaves, there was a flowering of economic, artistic, and spiritual life that many times was too successful for envious European colonists. Speaking of the California missions, Stephen Binz notes that "after serving in this kind of apprenticeship," in "farming, spinning and weaving, blacksmithing, cattle raising, and masonry, Indians would be given land to own. Fully competent in the ways of 'civilized' living, they would set up their own small farms near the mission, assembling each Sunday at the mission church."[5] Noting the last-

---

[3] Dr. Alfredo Jiménez, "Spanish Missions in the United States: Cultural and Historical Significance," *National Park Service*, accessed 4/28/24, https://www.nps.gov/subjects/travelspanishmissions/spanish-missions-in-the-united-states-cultural-and-historical-significance.htm.

[4] Reduction means the gathering of the native population into mission centers, whether voluntarily or not, giving the name "reduccion" as an alternative to mission, though "congregacion" was also used.

[5] Stephen Binz, *Saint Junipero Serra's Camino: A Pilgrimage Guide to the California Missions* (Cincinnati, OH: Franciscan Media, 2017), 36. There is, of course, an irony in lands that were once owned by the tribes being distributed to individuals again through colonial settlement. Serra himself, however, related how the Indians responded to the missions: "Every day Indians are coming in from distant homes in the Sierra. . . .

ing impact of the missions in Latin America, Felipe Valencia Caicedo documented that when they invested in education and manual training, "significant long-lasting effects . . . on education and income" can be seen in these communities even today.[6]

Beyond the enduring agricultural and political legacy of the missions, we can also recognize them as places of conversion and martyrdom. Men like Antonio Cuipa, an Apalachee martyr and future saint, truly represent the jewels of the missions. An educated layman, a carpenter, and musician, he assisted both in the governance of his native

---

They told the padres they would like them to come to their territory. They see our church which stands before their eyes so neatly; they see the *milpas* with corn which are pretty to behold; they see so many children as well as people like themselves going about clothed who sing and eat well and work. All of this, together with the way Our Lord God touches their souls—who can doubt that He will win their hearts?" Quoted in Binz, *Saint Junipero Serra's Camino*, 47.

[6] Felipe Valencia Caicedo, "The Mission: Human Capital Transmission, Economic Persistence, and Culture in South America," *The Quarterly Journal of Economics* (2019), 507–56. doi:10.1093/qje/qjy024. Robert Archibald meticulously details the economic life of the California missions, noting that, despite initial hardships, they laid the foundation for agriculture in the region. "Unlike the English colonies, the Spanish colonization of California was not prompted by economic motives but by a combination of religious zeal and defensive strategy. Given the peripheral interest of Crown and missionary in solvency the economic achievements of the California missions are all the more remarkable. The eventual despoliation of the California Indian points to an apparent failure of the missions: However, the missions were unqualified successes in providing the basis for the agricultural industry for which California has subsequently become justly famous. Both in agriculture and in livestock raising the missions provided the foundations for future prosperity." *The Economic Aspects of the California Missions* (Washington, DC: Academy of American Franciscan History, 1978), 185.

village and helped the friars in their missionary work, giving his life when English colonists from Carolina destroyed the mission of San Luis near present-day Tallahassee. Despite their own greed and acts of oppression, the Spaniards' stated intention in pushing further north in America was to spread the Faith.[7] We can find glimpses of what was possible even from the first settlement in St. Augustine, settled in the "name of God." The area became a refuge both for Indians, who coalesced as the Seminoles, and for escaped slaves fleeing oppression in the English colonies who established the first free black settlement at Ft. Mose, just north of St. Augustine.

This spiritual settlement may ultimately have failed to live up to its full realization, but the missionary endeavors of Spain and France still point to the reality of the land meant as a place for the meeting of peoples. A proper stewardship of the earth from this perspective seeks to order its resources to the glory of God for the good of all. The lands of the Americas are inextricably bound to Our Lady, who has overseen the growth of the Church there, overcoming the sins that would have impeded the spread of the Faith. Our Lady

---

[7] See, for instance, this contract of Don Juan de Oñate y Salazar from the Spanish Crown for the settlement of New Mexico, which bears its own problems, stated: "Your main purpose shall be the service of our Lord, the spreading of His Holy Catholic faith, and the reduction and pacification of the Natives of said providences. You shall bend all your energies to his object, without any other human interest interfering with this aim." Quoted in Donna Blake Birchell, *New Mexico Mission Churches* (Charleston, SC: The History Press, 2021), 14. Unlike mission territory, the missions of New Mexico were not reductions, with the Native population leaving their habitations to move into them, but consisted of churches attached to existing pueblos.

of Guadalupe, especially, marked a turning point, showing that all the peoples of the Americas are invited to recognize Our Lady as Mother, making the Western Hemisphere a place of unity in the Catholic faith.

This is our legacy as Catholics: the first settlements in America were made by missionaries seeking to extend God's kingdom in this land. The United States literally counts saints, such as St. Junipero Serra and Bl. Eusebio Kino, as founders of parts of its territory. The missionaries and martyrs sanctified the land, beginning a project of claiming this land "in the name of God." We know from Scripture that the land can become polluted by sin, but that He calls His people to purify and sanctify it. We can pick up today where the missions left off, bringing the unrealized promise of America to fruition. Taking up their legacy, we are now the stewards of this land, and our actions will affect our neighbors and our country as a whole.

Act 2: A Place for Freedom?

Jamestown versus Plymouth Rock: Profit plantation or refuge of freedom?

We see these two major thrusts of profit and freedom in the British colonies along the Atlantic Seaboard. When it comes to the English colonies, it would be easy to think of them as a solely Protestant endeavor, especially since they destroyed the Spanish and French missions whenever they could.[8] Though

8 Catholics who concealed their identity did participate in the settlement of Jamestown, and the Puritans encountered a baptized Catholic, Squanto, who greatly assisted in the initial success of their foundation.

largely Protestant, whether Anglican or Non-Conforming, we do find some White Anglo-Saxon Catholics (to use Walker Percy's term) at their center in Maryland, who united these two thrusts, finding a temporary refuge from religious persecution in England while participating in a plantation economy. Maryland was founded by a Catholic peer of England, Cecil Calvert, 2nd Baron Baltimore, who sent two Jesuits to accompany his brother who arrived there on the feast of the Annunciation in 1634 to found St. Mary's City. Catholics did find freedom there, though eventually only in their own homes, but would never become a majority.

Settlers often viewed America as a "virgin" land of promise, an "almost infinite expanse of arable land."[9] Though named for Queen Elizabeth, the colonial name "Virginia" spoke to the great promise of this land of unrealized potential. Though not a vacant waste, as often portrayed at the time, America offered a land of promise to countless Europeans. Next to the virgin colony, one more explicitly named for the Blessed Virgin, though via her patronage of the Catholic Queen Henrietta Maria, spoke more to the spiritual promise of this land. Catholics came from England seeking religious freedom, but it would take time for them to feel at home in the colonies and future United States. The Jesuits who settled in Maryland to care for the first Catholics initially sought to minister to the Native Americans, though they quickly turned their attention to Africans imported as slaves. Unfortunately, Catholics, too, owned slaves, though

---

[9] Henry Nash Smith, *Virgin Land: The American West as Symbol and Myth* (Cambridge, MA: Harvard University Press, 2007), 6.

they focused more attention on their education and faith than their Protestant neighbors. Even the Jesuits ministering to them came to own slaves on their own plantation lands, such as at Priests Point at St. Inigoes, for, without them, they thought they could not survive in a plantation economy.[10] Even the places founded for freedom displaced others and resorted to bondage in an effort to preserve their agrarian life focused on growing tobacco.

Initial areas of settlement quickly populated, straining the soil, but seemingly endless tracts of land awaited on the frontier. One Frenchman, J. Hector St. John de Crèvecœur, settled in Upstate New York after serving in the French and Indian War, becoming a successful farmer and helping to found the first Catholic Church in New York City. His *Letters from an American Farmer* found enormous success in Europe, speaking of the boundless opportunity waiting in America: "Let him go to work, he will have opportunities enough to earn a comfortable support, and even the means of procuring some

---

10 Walker Gollar describes how this came about: "In about 1636, Leonard Calvert sold to the Jesuits the slave Jowett, along with a few parcels of land in the newly laid-out Saint Mary's City in what was called Saint Mary's County. In 1637 Jesuits acquired three thousand additional acres that they christened Saint Inigoes in honor of the founder of the Jesuits, Ignatius Loyola. The Jesuits entrusted Saint Inigoes to a local Catholic, Cuthbert Fenwick, who rented out some of the property to former indentured servants. Jesuits relied on income from Saint Inigoes (augmented by donations from Europe) to allow them to pursue their primary reason for coming to America, namely, the conversion of indigenous peoples. But Jesuits did not have much success in bringing natives to Catholicism." *American and Catholic: Stories of the People Who Built the Church* (Cincinnati, OH: Franciscan Media, 2015).

land; which ought to be the utmost wish of every person who has health and hands to work."[11] And further:

> After a foreigner from any part of Europe is arrived, and become a citizen; let him devoutly listen to the voice of our great parent, which says to him, "Welcome to my shores, distressed European; bless the hour in which thou didst see my verdant fields, my fair navigable rivers, and my green mountains! If thou wilt work, I have bread for thee; if thou wilt be honest, sober, and industrious, I have greater rewards to confer on thee: ease and independence. I will give thee fields to feed and clothe thee; a comfortable fireside to sit by, and tell thy children by what means thou hast prospered; and a decent bed to repose on."[12]

Crèvecœur strongly advocated for religious tolerance, something important to American settlers seeking to leave behind the religious controversy and persecution of Europe. This was true of Catholics, who were less than 5 percent of the population in the early days of the Republic.

> Let us suppose you and I to be travelling; we observe that in this house, to the right, lives a Catholic, who prays to God as he has been taught, and believes in

[11] Hector St. John de Crevecoeur, *Letters from an American Farmer: Describing Certain Provincial Situations, Manners, and Customs, and Conveying Some Idea of the Late and Present Interior Circumstances of the British Colonies in North America* (London: T. Davies, 1782), Letter III, https://avalon.law.yale.edu/18th_century/letter_03.asp.

[12] Hector St. John de Crèvecœur, *Letters from an American Farmer*, Letter III.

> transubstantiation; he works and raises wheat, he has a large family of children, all hale and robust; his belief, his prayers offend nobody. About one mile farther on the same road, his next neighbour may be a good honest plodding German Lutheran, who addresses himself to the same God, the God of all, agreeably to the modes he has been educated in, and believes in consubstantiation; by so doing he scandalises nobody; he also works in his fields, embellishes the earth, clears swamps, etc. What has the world to do with his Lutheran principles? He persecutes nobody, and nobody persecutes him, he visits his neighbours, and his neighbours visit him.[13]

The long-term effects of this approach, however, became apparent enough: "A very perceptible indifference, even in the first generation, will become apparent; and it may happen that the daughter of the Catholic will marry the son of the seceder, and settle by themselves at a distance from their parents."[14] Thus, a distinctive American culture would form from diverse European ethnicities and religious traditions.

Another Frenchman, Alexis de Tocqueville, also observed the life and practices of Americans for Europeans in his *Democracy in America*. In the second volume, he likewise spoke of American Catholics losing the practice of their faith, but also the attraction of Catholicism for other Americans,

---

13 Hector St. John de Crèvecœur, *Letters from an American Farmer*, Letter III.

14 Hector St. John de Crèvecœur, *Letters from an American Farmer*, Letter III.

who by overcoming their excessive attachment for freedom came to value the unity of the authority of the Church:

> Roman Catholics are seen to lapse into infidelity, and Protestants to be converted to Roman Catholicism. If the Roman Catholic faith be considered within the pale of the church, it would seem to be losing ground; without that pale, to be gaining it. Nor is this circumstance difficult of explanation. The men of our days are naturally disposed to believe; but, as soon as they have any religion, they immediately find in themselves a latent propensity which urges them unconsciously towards Catholicism. Many of the doctrines and the practices of the Romish Church astonish them; but they feel a secret admiration for its discipline, and its great unity attracts them. If Catholicism could at length withdraw itself from the political animosities to which it has given rise, I have hardly any doubt but that the same spirit of the age, which appears to be so opposed to it, would become so favorable as to admit of its great and sudden advancement.[15]

Catholics may have sought freedom in America, but they would also have to face the consequences of embracing greater freedom within a liberal system of democracy, with its inevitable relativization and prioritization of the individual over community and authority. The Church would serve as a balance to radical American principles, though

---

[15] Alexis De Tocqueville, *Democracy in America*, vol. 2, trans. Henry Reeve, Chapter VI, https://www.gutenberg.org/files/816/816-h/816-h.htm.

Catholics would continue to live in tension between the economic benefits of America and their religious traditions.

While Crèvecœur spoke of the boundless opportunity of agriculture in America, de Tocqueville already saw industry as replacing it in the "American dream" for those too impatient to realize its potential.

> The cultivation of the ground promises an almost certain result to his exertions, but a slow one; men are not enriched by it without patience and toil. Agriculture is therefore only suited to those who have already large, superfluous wealth, or to those whose penury bids them only seek a bare subsistence. The choice of such a man as we have supposed is soon made; he sells his plot of ground, leaves his dwelling, and embarks in some hazardous but lucrative calling. Democratic communities abound in men of this kind; and in proportion as the equality of conditions becomes greater, their multitude increases. Thus democracy not only swells the number of workingmen, but it leads men to prefer one kind of labor to another; and whilst it diverts them from agriculture, it encourages their taste for commerce and manufactures.[16]

The Northeast in particular would abound in this transfer of labor from agriculture to industry, with others seeking profit elsewhere:

---

[16] Alexis De Tocqueville, *Democracy in America*, vol. 2, trans. Henry Reeve, chapter XIX, https://www.gutenberg.org/files/816/816-h/816-h.htm.

> It seldom happens that an American farmer settles for good upon the land which he occupies: especially in the districts of the Far West he brings land into tillage in order to sell it again, and not to farm it: he builds a farmhouse on the speculation that, as the state of the country will soon be changed by the increase of population, a good price will be gotten for it. Every year a swarm of the inhabitants of the North arrive in the Southern States, and settle in the parts where the cotton plant and the sugar-cane grow. These men cultivate the soil in order to make it produce in a few years enough to enrich them; and they already look forward to the time when they may return home to enjoy the competency thus acquired. Thus the Americans carry their business-like qualities into agriculture; and their trading passions are displayed in that as in their other pursuits.[17]

Restlessness and the demand for profit would continue to haunt the American farmer throughout history, while agriculture moved further westward to new lands and opportunities.

From Maryland, Catholics sought greater freedom in Pennsylvania, settling in Emmitsburg on the border and Philadelphia, but they also looked further west, joining the first settlers in Kentucky. The institution of the Catholic Church would remain rooted in Maryland, with the first

---

[17] Alexis De Tocqueville, *Democracy in America*, vol. 2, trans. Henry Reeve, chapter XIX, https://www.gutenberg.org/files/816/816-h/816-h.htm.

bishop of the United States, John Carroll, coming from one of its oldest Catholic families, but from there would expand north, with dioceses founded in 1808 in Philadelphia, New York, and Boston, but also west with Bardstown, Kentucky.

The last of these sites may strike us as an odd choice, but the first inland, frontier diocese arose around the homesteads and farms of Catholics who sought new land in Kentucky, growing up to be called an American "Holy Land" with two new American religious orders, the Sisters of Nazareth and the Sisters of Loretto, a seminary, and a Trappist monastery at Gethsemane. But the Church arose slowly there, with Catholic families, such as the Howards, Fenwicks, and Haydens, offering the famous missionary and accumulator of land, Fr. Stephen Badin, land and a simple cabin as his first church at Pottinger's Creek, which became known as Holy Cross. Inevitably, property also creates conflicts, with these founding families, Fr. Badin, and numerous bishops squabbling over land rights. From Kentucky, missionary priests would push into Ohio, Indiana, and Illinois to serve immigrants and to begin acquiring land for churches.

The two highest density areas of Catholics, however, arose in areas that became incorporated into the United States only later. Though there was some French missionary activity and settlements in northern New England, many French Catholics were forcibly removed from the Atlantic seaboard, particularly Acadia, by the British and resettled in Louisiana in 1764.[18] This would be incorporated as territory of

[18] See Fr. Sébastien Rale's mission to Maine, for instance, where he founded an Indian school in the early 1700s and was martyred by Massachusetts colonists.

the United States following the Louisiana Purchase in 1803, which also had the unintended consequence of making the federal government the primary agent of western settlement. After that, New Mexico had the largest rural population of Catholics, becoming part of the United States, along with Texas, Arizona, and California, with the forceable seizure of vast western lands in 1848, following the Mexican-American War. Willa Cather beautifully describes how the American Southwest became a melting pot of cultures in *Death Comes to the Archbishop*, accurately depicting the dynamics of French missionaries encountering Native and Mexican cultures at the time of the arrival of American settlers.

Act 3: Waves of Immigrant Homesteaders

Opportunity or destitution?

The voice of America, so aptly personified in Crèvecœur's letters, reached many ears in Europe. Poverty and famine in Ireland, the forceable breakup of the Holy Roman Empire, and a greatly increased industrial population all put enormous pressure on Europe. To the dismay of American Protestants, waves of Catholic immigrants entered the United States in the nineteenth century, taking the Catholic population from a few percentage points to a quarter of the population by 1900. The Irish could not own land in their own country unless they abandoned the faith of their fathers, while many German farmers found their traditional way of life turned upside down by the upheavals of the Napoleonic Wars and consequent revolutions. The Irish tended to settle in cities, though some did find their way onto homesteads and farms,[19] especially later in the century, while Germans tended to form their own rural communities, especially in the German triangle in the area between Cincinnati, Milwaukee, and St. Louis.

German Catholics began moving Westward from Philadelphia to Goshenhoppen and Conewago, served by German Jesuits coming north from Maryland. Even further to the west, in the mountains of Pennsylvania, Captain Michael McGuire of Maryland was given a land grant for his service in the Revolutionary War in 1787. He invited a settlement of Catholic families, which also attracted a Russian aristocrat who converted to the Catholic faith and became a priest, Prince Demetrius Augustine Gallitzin. The prince-priest founded the town of Loretto, where he built the church of St. Michael the Archangel, now a basilica. Religious orders followed, with the Franciscans establishing St. Francis University and Benedictines founding St. Vincent Archabbey nearby.[20] Similar clusters of German Cath-

---

[19] "The first Catholics to settle in rural New England were Irish immigrants who, between 1815 and 1845, landed at St. John, New Brunswick, and then traveled south by land or sea. Initially, most of the participants in this 'second colonization of New England' worked as itinerant laborers on canals and railroads or in factories, but eventually a number of them found homes on the land. Of the diverse immigrants into New England later in the century, a small percentage, among whom French Canadians were prominent, also joined that region's always small Catholic rural population." David S. Bovee, *The Church and the Land: The National Catholic Rural Life Conference and American Society, 1923-2007* (Washington, DC: Catholic University of America Press, 2010), 2.

[20] Kevin Schmiesing describes the area's development: "From this modest headquarters, Fr. Gallitzin orchestrated the development of one of

olic settlement arose in Ohio, such as around the shrine of Maria Stein under Fr. Francis Brunner in 1843.

Bishops and priests sometimes facilitated the movement of Catholics out of the cities and into new rural communities:

> From 1827 to 1836, Boston bishop Benedict J. Fenwick counseled Irish immigrants in Maine to pursue agriculture as the best vehicle to prosperity. A product of rural Catholic Maryland, Fenwick purchased land in Maine for an Irish Catholic colony in 1834. Christened "Benedicta" by Fenwick, it came to play an important role in establishing potatoes as northern Maine's cash crop. In the mid-1830s, Bishop Mathias Loras established Dubuque, Iowa, as a new agricultural center for Catholic immigrants struggling in eastern cities. Father Ambrose Oschwald established St. Nazianz, Wisconsin, in 1854, as a quasi-monastic community. Father Jeremiah Trecy founded St. John's City, Nebraska, in 1857. Occupying a prominent location atop a Missouri River bluff, the community erected an enormous crucifix to signal home for later arrivals. Around the same time but further south, Father Joseph Hogan

---

the country's most enduring Catholic enclaves. Over the course of his career, Gallitzin purchased more than twenty thousand acres of western Pennsylvania, with the purpose of reselling to Catholic pioneers. Several other Catholic settlements sprang from Loretto, some during Gallitzin's lifetime and others during the tenure of his collaborator and successor, Peter Henry Lemcke. The towns of St. Benedict, Gallitzin, and Carrolltown, with their respective parishes, were progeny of Loretto Catholicism." *A Catholic Pilgrimage through American History: People and Places that Shaped the Church in the United States* (Notre Dame, IN: Ave Maria Press, 2022).

> established a small rural Catholic community between the Eleven Point and Current rivers in the Missouri Ozarks. The town "Wilderness" provided refuge from the urban drudgery of St. Louis.[21]

The United States government, however, directly oversaw and facilitated the settling of the Upper Midwest and Western Plains. This entailed forcing Indian tribes into reservations, making land grants to new States and railroad companies, and directly encouraging settlers through a series of Homestead Acts beginning in 1862. Settlement reached Wisconsin by 1833, with other territories following. German and Irish settlers advanced west, followed by Eastern European Catholics later in the nineteenth century. Life in the West proved harsh, and not all homesteaders made it or could prove up on their homestead claims. Agents eventually began brokering immigration for entire communities of Catholics, such as Simon Peter Paul Cahensly for Germans and Jan Barzyński for Poles.

> Around 1880 Jan Barzyński negotiated an agreement with the Burlington Railroad. The railroad designated him its agent for Polish colonization, and Barzyński committed himself to settling four hundred Polish families on Burlington land in the Nebraska counties of Howard, Greeley, Sherman, and Valley. The railroad promised to reserve three townships for the colonists,

21 Marlett, "Strangers in Our Midst," 159–60.

provide free passage for them, and donate land for a Polish church and cemetery.[22]

Priests successfully supported these colonization efforts, as well as Catholic land agents cooperating with the railroads. The rail companies, seeking to divest their large land holdings and build up a clientele, "also recognized that settlers with the support network that came from living among friends and neighbors were less likely than the unattached to become discouraged and leave. This was especially true of immigrants, strangers in a strange land who could not return to their homes as readily as could people with families in the United States."[23] Although the Plains could lead settlers into isolation and failure, "local networks were easier to construct when neighbors had kin connections, shared an ethnic or religious identification, or had migrated to the area as part of a group," giving close-knit Catholic communities a better chance of survival.[24]

Densely Catholic communities would spring up further north as well, with communities clustering across Indiana, Missouri, Kansas, Wisconsin, Minnesota, Nebraska, and the Dakotas. "One priest in particular, Father Francis Pierz, worked tirelessly to create rural ethnic enclaves. His signature project made Stearns County, Minnesota, 'probably the most rural Catholic county in the United States.'"[25] This

---

[22] David B. Danbom, *Sod Busting: How Families Made Farms on the 19th-Century Plains* (Baltimore: Johns Hopkins University Press, 2014), 30.

[23] Danbom, *Sod Busting*, 30.

[24] Marlett, "Strangers in Our Midst," 73.

[25] Marlett, "Strangers in Our Midst," 161.

area, "outside St. Cloud, Minnesota . . . was almost entirely rural Catholic. This included the towns of Collegeville and St. Joseph, where Saint John's College (for men) and the College of Saint Benedict (for women), the epicenter of Virgil Michel's liturgical work, were located."[26] Though rooted in a predominately Protestant country, Catholic enclaves formed both in cities and rural communities where Catholic religious orders served immigrants and many thousands of Catholic churches were built.

Like her concern for the indigenous population of Mexico, Our Lady was also solicitous for the salvation of Catholic immigrants. When Adele Brise was twenty-four years old, her family emigrated from Belgium in 1855, purchasing land to the northeast of Green Bay, where other French-speaking Belgians had settled. As she was making the long walk home from church, Our Lady of Champion appeared to her on October 9, 1859, telling her, "Gather the children in this wild country and teach them what they should know for salvation. . . . Teach them their catechism, how to sign themselves with the sign of the Cross, and how to approach the sacraments; that is what I wish you to do. Go and fear nothing, I will help you."[27] Catholics on the land must remain engaged with their faith, staying engaged in parish life despite the distance and prioritizing religious formation and prayer.

---

[26] Marlett, "Strangers in Our Midst," 164–65.

[27] Susan Ciancio, "The Miracles of Our Lady of Champion," *Celebrate Life Magazine*, 2024 Spring-Fall, https://clmagazine.org/post/the-miracles-of-our-lady-of-champion/.

Our Lady was a main actor in the drama of American settlement, but so, also, was government, whether foreign monarchies, local colonial or state legislatures, or the federal government, all of which sponsored settlement on the plains. Though we often associate agriculture and homesteads with rugged American individualism, we see from the beginning of colonization that the government often orchestrated the settlement of land and created economic conditions for farmers to sell their products (such as by cooperating with railroads); though, as we will see in the next act, this would come back to bite many farmers.

Act 4: Catholic Agrarian Witness

Capitalism, Communism, or a Catholic way?

The year 1920 marked a major shift in American society when a majority of its population became urban.[28] We could even describe this as part of a broader epochal change in human history because, since the dawn of civilization, a majority of the human population engaged in agriculture. This transfer of population occurred as a result of the Industrial Revolution and a fundamental reorganization of society by the modern state, shifting the nature of property ownership for farming families, especially through inheritance laws, resulting in the primacy of the individual over traditional societal structures. Massive change brought massive unrest, with an upsurge in impoverishment, labor exploitation, alcoholism,

---

28 "History: Urban and Rural Areas," United States Census Bureau, accessed May 12, 2024, https://www.census.gov/history/www/programs/geography/urban_and_rural_areas.html.

and divorce, alongside a decline in church attendance. Communism, ushered in by Marx and Engel's famous manifesto of 1848, offered a compelling answer for many, but the Church proposed its own response.

Pope Leo XIII flatly condemned socialism as unjust in its denial of the legitimacy of private property, materialism, and intrusion into the rights of both Church and family. His 1891 watershed encyclical, *Rerum Novarum*, marked the dawn of the Church's modern social teaching. It laid out an ideal of localism and agrarianism for the spiritual and material well-being of Catholic families. Rather than abolishing ownership, Leo argued that "the law, therefore, should favor ownership, and its policy should be to induce as many as possible of the people to become owners."[29] If this were to happen, three consequences would follow:

> If working people can be encouraged to look forward to obtaining a share in the land, the consequence will be that the gulf between vast wealth and sheer poverty will be bridged over, and the respective classes will be brought nearer to one another. A further consequence will result in the great abundance of the fruits of the earth. Men always work harder and more readily when they work on that which belongs to them; nay, they learn to love the very soil that yields in response to the labor of their hands, not only food to eat, but an abundance of good things for themselves and those that are

[29] Leo XIII, *Rerum Novarum*, https://www.vatican.va/content/leo-xiii/en/encyclicals/documents/hf_l-xiii_enc_15051891_rerum-novarum.html, §46.

> dear to them. That such a spirit of willing labor would add to the produce of the earth and to the wealth of the community is self evident. And a third advantage would spring from this: men would cling to the country in which they were born, for no one would exchange his country for a foreign land if his own afforded him the means of living a decent and happy life.[30]

In the early years of the Great Depression, Pope Pius XI furthered Leo's vision forty years later in his own social encyclical, *Quadragesimo Anno*, likewise arguing for a just distribution of goods through fair wages and greater ownership of property. The popes raised the question: Could a back-to-the-land movement help solve the "social question"?

Concerns about urbanization and labor greatly intensified with the onset of the Great Depression in 1929. With a growing Communist movement in Europe following the Bolshevik Revolution in 1917, many Catholics wondered if a third way was needed that navigated between the Scylla and Charybdis of socialism and capitalism. The latter threatened agricultural communities through the consolidation of family farms through an excessive focus on efficiency and profit. The Distributist Movement in England, spearheaded by Fr. Vincent McNabb, OP, Hilaire Belloc, and G. K. Chesterton, sought to implement the teaching of Leo and Pius by encouraging a Catholic back-to-the-land movement in England.[31] Though often accused of pushing socialism

---

30 Leo XIII, *Rerum Novarum*, §47.

31 See Vincent McNabb, *The Church and the Land* (Norfolk, VA: IHS Press, 2003); G. K. Chesterton, *The Outline of Sanity* (New York: Dodd,

under another guise, distributism advocated for the opposite effect: not the consolidation of property in the hands of a few, which occurs both under communism and corporate capitalism, but the widest distribution into the hands of families, small local businesses, and voluntary cooperatives.

The Church's social teaching led to lesser-known developments in the United States as well, with the Depression, Dust Bowl (happening in three waves from 1934 to 1940), and Franklin D. Roosevelt's New Deal (which included back-to-the-land provisions[32]) providing ample opportunity for bishops to speak about social matters. In particular, as people abandoned agriculture as their livelihood, the Church began addressing it more directly than ever before, because the issue could no longer be taken for granted. The importance of agriculture, not only as a profession but also a way of life, had to be considered and defended. Pope Pius XII spoke out on a number of occasions in support of

---

Mead & Co., 1926); Hilaire Belloc, *The Servile State* (London: T.N. Foulis, 1912).

32 Edward S. Shapiro, "Catholic Agrarian Thought and the New Deal," *The Catholic Historical Review*, vol. 65, no. 4 (Oct. 1979): 583–99. Catholics largely welcomed the New Deal's Agricultural Policy, though they began to see some negative effects quickly. Key components of government action beginning in 1933 included the Commodity Credit Corporation (CCC) that offered loans to farmers, the Agricultural Adjustment Administration (AAA), which sought to boost prices by paying farmers to plant conservation grasses instead of crops, and the Farm Credit Administration (FCA), which refinanced mortgages. The Agricultural Adjustment Act of 1938 made the Farm Bill a permanent fixture of government policy.

Catholic farmers and encouraged the agrarian movement in the United States.[33]

The United States had its own agrarian moment in the early twentieth century, made up of various strands that intersected but never coalesced into a single movement. We can organize them into five major groups.

1. Social Activism. The Church's social teaching found its strongest advocate in the United States in Fr. John Ryan, a professor of moral theology and social theology at the Catholic University of America. He focused primarily on the condition of workers, writing extensively on issues like a living wage and the distribution of property.[34] He also drafted the "Bishop's Program of Social Reconstruction" in 1919 and headed the Social Action Department of the National Catholic Welfare Conference. Its agrarian influence would come through tasking one of Ryan's former students, Msgr. Edwin O'Hara, to establish the Rural Life Bureau within the conference to study the status of Catholics in rural America.[35] Ryan often partnered with the German Roman Cath-

---

[33] Pope Pius XII, "The Pope Speaks on Rural Life: Speech to the delegates at the Convention of the National Confederation of Farm Owner-Operators," Nov. 15, 1946. In 1948, he appointed Msgr. Luigi Ligutti of the National Catholic Rural Life Conference as Vatican Observer to the Food and Agriculture Organization of the United Nations.

[34] See his books: *A Living Wage: Its Ethical and Economic Aspects* (New York: Macmillan Co., 1906); *Distributive Justice: The Right and Wrong of Our Present Distribution of Wealth* (New York: Macmillan Co., 1916).

[35] For a history of his remarkable life, see Timothy Michael Dolan, *Some Seed Fell on Good Ground: The Life of Edwin V. O'Hara* (Washington, DC: Catholic University of America Press, 2012). O'Hara's work in the land movement led also to his establishment of the Confraternity of Catholic Doctrine (CCD) in the United States, as well at the Catholic

olic Central Verein of North America, which had formed to support rural Catholics, and which took a turn toward social activism in the twentieth century.

2. Catholic Rural Life. O'Hara, through his own extensive research of Catholic education in rural America, founded The National Catholic Rural Life Conference in 1923.[36] Initially, he sought to support rural families, which often suffered from a lack of pastoral support and educational opportunities, by offering workshops for priests, retreats, educational materials, and summer vacation Bible schools. Over time, in light of the country's economic struggles, the conference addressed policy issues and sought to help urban families relocate to the country. It offered well-attended annual conferences, uniting thousands of Catholic farmers, especially in the Midwest, encouraging the development of rural cooperatives[37] and credit unions, appointing diocesan representatives, and publishing a number of periodicals, such as *St. Isidore's Plow, Catholic Rural Life Bulletin, Landward, Christian Farmer News Letter*, and *Catholic Rural Life Page* for syndication in diocesan papers.

Bible Association.

[36] For an extensive history of NCRLC, see David S. Bovée's *The Church and the Land: The National Catholic Rural Life Conference and American Society, 1923–2007* (Catholic University of America Press, 2010).

[37] The NCRLC defines cooperatives in its Manifesto on Rural life as "voluntary associations of farmers organized with the prime purpose of giving greater stability and better security to their farming enterprise. There are consumer, production, purchasing, marketing, and credit cooperatives" (no. 145). The Grange (The National Grange of the Order of Patrons of Husbandry), founded in 1867, demonstrated the power of united action by farmers.

Two other key priests in the conference partnered to write *Rural Roads to Security* in 1940. Its first author, Fr. John Rawe, SJ, became a prominent spokesman for the back-to-the-land movement, directing the Omar Research Farm in Elkhorn, Nebraska. The second, Monsignor Luigi G. Ligutti, became the conference head in 1940 as its first full-time executive director, infusing new life into its initiatives and extending its reach worldwide. He began his work on rural matters by establishing the Granger Homesteads for low-income families in Iowa, showing, along with Fr. Rawe, that the conference's ideals were rooted in more than mere theory.

The NCRLC stood as the primary organizational force of the American Catholic Land Movement in the twentieth century. Its 1939 "Manifesto on Rural Life" expresses the dynamics of the movement more clearly and succinctly than any other document. Drafted by a group called the "Fargo Trio" of Bishop, later Cardinal, Muench, Fr. William Mulloy, and Fr. Vincent Ryan, the manifesto's chapters provide a clear overview of its scope and priorities:

I. The Rural Catholic Family
II. Farm Ownership and Land Tenancy
III. Rural Settlement
IV. Catholic Rural Education
V. Rural Catholic Youth
VI. Catholic Culture in Rural Society
VII. Rural Community
VIII. The Rural Pastorate
IX. Rural Church Expansion
X. Rural Health

XI. Rural Social Charity
XII. The Farm Laborer
XIII. Farmer Cooperatives
XIV. Rural Credit
XV. Agriculture in the Economic Organism
XVI. Rural Taxation

The manifesto boldly proclaims that "the time is opportune for an extensive program to re-establish families on the land" (no. 26). But NCRLC was founded to address spiritual and educational problems in rural Catholic life. Therefore, to succeed in drawing Catholics to land, it needed to reinvigorate rural parishes as the center of a vibrant community: "A rural parish with a social and educational program, in which cultural and economic activities are integrated with religion and centered in the parish hall or school, will be effective in developing among its members a spirit of neighborliness and a helpful sense of solidarity" (68). Catholic villages, it somewhat idealistically argued, would strengthen this community and mutual support even further (71).

3. A Liturgical Connection. Benedictine monks also played a role in supporting the Church's new agrarian focus. Dom Virgil Michel, OSB, a monk of St. John's Abbey in Collegeville, MN, united his work pioneering the liturgical movement in the United States to the land movement. The move from the city to the country "is really a question of restoring the natural basis of Christian living for the greater flourishing of the supernatural Christ-life among men."[38]

---

[38] Virgil Michel, OSB, "Timely Tracts: City or Farm?" 368, quoted in Michael J. Woods, *Cultivating Soil and Soul: Twentieth-Century Catholic*

Another Benedictine, Edgar Schmiedeler, who taught sociology at the Catholic University of America, headed the NCRLC for a number of tumultuous years. Monasteries also remained important centers of Catholic culture, uniting a life of prayer, agricultural work, education, and the arts. Many examples could be offered, such as the controversial brewery at St. Vincent's Archabbey (shuttered by Prohibition), cattle ranching at Assumption Abbey in North Dakota, egg production at Mepkin Abbey in South Carolina, and timber harvesting at Gethsemane.

4. Apostolic Farms. In the face of material and spiritual poverty, various groups founded apostolic farms to use agriculture for educational, social, and spiritual renewal. The French peasant Peter Maurin, who guided Dorothy Day in the founding of the Catholic Worker Movement, placed farming at the center of his vision for a Green Revolution. Although the Catholic Worker newspaper and hospitality houses came first, the first Worker Farm arose in Easton, Pennsylvania. There is no unemployment on the farm, Peter would often say during the Depression, and he saw the farm setting as the perfect place for the exchange of ideas, which he described as agronomic universities. He dreamt of a society where it would be easier for people to be good, building around the principles of cult, culture, and cultivation (prayer, education, and work) in integrated fashion. Though many of the Worker Farms struggled for decades, the vision

---

Agrarians Embrace the Liturgical Movement (Collegeville, MN: Liturgical Press 2009), 83.

continues today with over two dozen farms throughout the United States.[39]

Catherine Doherty (née Ekaterina Fyodorovna Kolyschkina), who knew Dorothy Day when they both opened hospitality houses in New York City in the 1930s, founded the Madonna House in Ontario in 1947.[40] Having grown up on the land in Russia, when not traveling for her father's business, she had always conceived farming as an aspect of the apostolate. Doherty emphasized poverty, subsistence, and charity on her first farm, "St. Benedict's Acres," which became the model for other Madonna House farms around the world. She describes her approach to engaging "in farming because we want to spread the Good News by bringing God to everyone who sees or hears of our farm. We bring the Good News by living the gospel, and there is no better place to live the gospel than on a farm."[41] This happens by "feeding and teaching. These the farmer utilizes by loving the earth and loving the work he does. He learns what the best food is and how to grow it. He delights in gospel poverty

---

[39] Eric Anglada, "Taking Root: The history and new growth of Catholic Worker farms," *America: The National Catholic Review*, May 6, 2013, https://www.americamagazine.org/issue/taking-root.

[40] On a rural community of families, she could look to Fr. Francis McGoey, who started a successful community dedicated to the Sacred Heart north of Toronto to give families a new start on the land during the Depression. See Francis McGoey, *Back to the Land: Turning an Ancient Slogan from a Bit of Counsel into a Remarkable Reality*, https://qspace.library.queensu.ca/server/api/core/bitstreams/b1278fb6-f1ca-49da-b615-52a9e8b15dde/content.

[41] Catherine Doherty, *Apostolic Farming: Healing the Earth* (Combermere, Ontario: Madonna House Publications, 2001), 36.

and simplicity, in producing all that is needed for the family at the lowest price, yet for greatest health."[42]

5. Southern Agrarians and *Free America*. The Southern Agrarians, centered at Vanderbilt University, who gathered to defend the traditions and agrarianism of the Southern United States against industrialism, might not seem to fit within the story of the American Catholic Land Movement. The group of twelve writers took some inspiration, however, from the British Distributists and other regionalist groups in Europe.[43] One of the group's central editors, Allen Tate, sympathized with the Catholic tradition and would eventually convert in 1950. He and his wife, Carolyn Gordon, mentored Flannery O'Connor, who rooted her fiction in the agricultural South and influenced another Southern writer, Walker Percy. Tate co-wrote the introduction to the group's 1930 manifesto, *I'll Take My Stand: The South and the Agrarian Tradition*, which argued that "the theory of agrarianism is that the culture of the soil is the best and most sensitive of vocations, and that therefore it should have the economic preference and enlist the maximum number of workers." Along with the Northerner Herbert Agar, he edited a follow-up volume to *I'll Take My Stand*, titled *Who Owns*

---

[42] Doherty, *Apostolic Farming*, 41–42.

[43] The agrarian historian Jeffrey Marlett makes this connection: "The Catholic Revival turned American Catholics toward the social criticism of the English decentralists and their American followers. American decentralist intellectuals, such as Herbert Agar, Ralph Borsodi, and the "Vanderbilt Agrarians," followed Catholic intellectuals Hilaire Belloc and G. K. Chesterton in their condemnation of mass production and intrusive bureaucracies." "Strangers in Our Midst," 171.

America? A New Declaration of Independence, in 1936, which included contributions from Hilaire Belloc and Fr. Rawe.[44] The Catholic philanthropist Chauncey Stillman drew in writers such as Tate and Agar and others, such as the famous agrarian Ralph Borsodi, to contribute to an agrarian journal he founded, *Free America* (1937–47), that would build upon and broaden the reach of many of the principles of the Southern Agrarians.[45]

Only in the early twentieth century do we find the formation of an explicit American Catholic Land Movement, made up of these various strands, arising in response to fundamental changes and challenges in American society. In an age of economic distress, Catholics might have been inclined to focus primarily on practical means of recovery. Our Lady of Fatima, however, appearing in the very year of the Russian Revolution, pointed to prayer and sacrifice as the means of saving souls and renewing Christian society.

The key question, however, of government involvement in agriculture lingered. Government had been involved from the beginning, sponsoring initial colonization, purchasing or seizing Western lands, opening up homesteads, building infrastructure and financial mechanisms to bolster farms,

---

[44] Herbert Agar and Allen Tate, *Who Owns America: A New Declaration of Independence* (Wilmington, DE: ISI Press, 1999). The University of Notre Dame Press has also finally released a lost economic volume from another key member of the group, John Crowe Ransom, *Land!: The Case for an Agrarian Economy* (Notre Dame: University of Notre Dame Press, 2017).

[45] The Wethersfield Institute has published the most important contributions of *Free America* in a single volume: *Land & Liberty: The Best of Free America*, ed. Allan C. Carlson (Amenia, NY: Wethersfield Institute, 2019).

and controlling prices during wartime. This involvement would only increase further into the twentieth century.

Act 5: A Countercultural Movement

Backwards or forwards; technological progress or cultural decline?

The frontier was gone. In 1936, John Senior fled to North Dakota to experience the last gasp of the untamed West as a cowboy, in imitation of Teddy Roosevelt's similar flight from New York City in 1884. That wouldn't be an option for the following generations. America had been domesticated, suburbanized, and increasingly dominated by technology.

Agriculture in the twentieth century took a sharp turn toward industrial consolidation. Stalin oversaw the mass collectivization of Soviet farms, leading to starvation for millions. In America, consolidation happened in the name of capitalism, seeking greater efficiency and profits. Christopher Dawson in the 1930s had already recognized there were different means to the same end in Russia and the United States as both nations similarly undermined faith and family in their own way.[46]

The rise of the Mass State, of either variety, has led to declining birthrates, indoctrination through government schools and biased media, and weaker families through collectivized living, whether in Soviet high-rises or more spacious but stale suburban neighborhoods. Archbishop

---

[46] See his essay, "Christianity and Sex," in *Enquiries in Religion and Culture* (Washington, DC: Catholic University of America Press, 2009), 214–40.

O'Hara's "rural ideology" had already proposed rural living to strengthen family life and fertility and to bolster democracy through a self-sufficient and invested citizenry.[47] Catholics have continued to advocate for their own version of the Jeffersonian ideal, bolstered by faith.

A common objection to distributism, arguing for the availability of productive property for families, is that it unjustly depends upon the agency of the government for the process of distribution. As we have seen, the government largely oversaw the settlement of the West and the rise of industrial farming, and, likewise, it engineered the rise of suburban culture in America by regulating and propping up long-term mortgages, allowing the deduction of mortgage interest, controlling zoning to favor the rise of these neighborhoods, and establishing the highway systems to facilitate commuting.[48] If growing food could be accomplished more efficiently through supersized farms, then the population could be freed up to bolster a consumer-driven economy, no longer needing the productive property advocated by the

---

[47] See Timothy M. Dolan, "The Rural Ideology of Edwin V. O'Hara: Analyze, Publicize, Organize," *U.S. Catholic Historian* 8, no. 3 (Summer 1989): 117–29.

[48] Allan Carlson describes how federal subsidies shifted from the country to the suburbs: "Homesteading also fell out of favor. For example, federal support for new villages of subsistence homesteads—introduced as an early part of the New Deal in 1934—ended during the war. After 1945, federal subsidies shifted to the support of tract housing outside of city centers, on lots far too small for any form of subsistence gardening or farm animal care." "Introduction," in *Land & Liberty: The Best of Free America*, xxiv. See also his *From Cottage to Work Station: The Family's Search for Social Harmony in the Industrial Age* (San Francisco: Ignatius Press, 1993).

Land Movement. The government has been heavily involved in the distribution of property, but it has fostered the acquisition of non-productive over productive property, ensuring the ability of home loans to encourage most of the population to settle in the new suburban-style home. The government will facilitate some economic policy, so why should it not aim through law and tax policy to enable families to become owners of productive property and businesses?

In the process of achieving a new American dream, families have lost their ability to sustain themselves, becoming dependent on consumerist products, food chains, and entertainment. Interestingly enough, the hippies were the first to throw off the new, technocratic, and suburbanized order, setting off a countercultural movement of rebellion. Catholics must reject the embrace of drugs and "free love" but can also credit them for inspiring a new return to the land with a natural, organic approach to growing food.[49] Likewise, some Catholics embraced bio-dynamic farming, such as John Thomas and James McShane, who saw in it a method to "conserve the health and fertility of the soil."[50] A new American order would pose challenges to bodily health, with increasingly unhealthy food, and spiritual health through constant distraction and immoral entertainment.

No one, however, has influenced the fifth act of the dramatic history of the American Catholic Land Movement more than Wendell Berry. He took up the voice of the Southern Agrarians, leaving his academic career to return to

---

[49] The new wave of the back-to-the-land movement also was inspired by Helen and Scott Nearing's 1954 book *Living the Good Life*.

[50] Quoted in Marlett, "Strangers in Our Midst," 175.

his family's Kentucky farm as the stage for his poetry, essays, and novels detailing the Port Williams community. Berry, while not a Catholic, has guided many diverse groups in the United States to address the crisis of agriculture and food afflicting our nation: The rise of industrial farms displacing family traditions and practices; pollution from artificial fertilizers; massive soil erosion; declining nutrition of food which leaves many Americans deficient; inhumane treatment of animals; toxic pesticides and herbicides; and the genetic modification of plants and animals.[51] Berry points out that the average American has become fundamentally disconnected from the origin and production of his food. While advocating for a return to traditional farming practices, he also encouraged Americans to shape food production through their lifestyle and purchasing power.

Are Americans helpless in the face of economic and social changes in America? Enormous threats to bodily and mental health have emerged in the last few decades. The documentary *Food Inc.* (2008) woke up many Americans to the unhealthy food they daily consume. Chronic gut problems, autoimmune disease, and fatigue have become common occurrences. Joel Salatin, featured in the documentary, has provided an example, among others, that the self-sufficient life still offers a realistic and healthier alternative.[52] The year 2007 marked the beginning of a decline in the nation's mental health, with the launching of the first iPhone, marking

---

[51] See Wendell Berry, *The Unsettling of America: Culture & Agriculture* (New York: Counterpoint, 2017).

[52] See Joel Salatin, *You Can Farm: The Entrepreneur's Guide to Start & Succeed in a Farming Enterprise* (2015).

a turn to life behind a screen. Greater isolation, depression, sexual confusion, and general distraction have followed, along with what Matthew Crawford artfully captured in his book *Shop Class as Soulcraft* (2010), a growing inability to do things for oneself in an information-saturated culture. People have been more passive and abstracted from the fundamental realities of human life.

The COVID-19 crisis served as a breaking point for many families: fed up with city life, including its growing costs, crime, traffic, and ideological schooling. One positive, however, flowed along with its restrictions: the rise of remote work that has driven families to the exurbs. Despite rising land costs and inflation, many families have entered into a new phase of the back-to-the-land movement, embracing homeschooling and moderate homesteading. In a culture uncertain about the nature of humanity, faced with the threat of transhumanism, and confused about sexuality, a return to the land has offered a dose of reality. Families can become more self-sufficient, leading a healthier lifestyle without having to go to the gym or buy expensive organic food. Dona Brown contrasted more contemporary homesteading with its "romantic longing for a rural life in close contact with nature" with past movements focused "a great deal more on the rising cost of food, job insecurity, and the desire for independent work."[53] In light of recent developments, we can affirm that things have come full circle, and the romantic ideal has once again taken on economic urgency.

---

[53] Dona Brown, *Back to the Land: The Enduring Dream of Self-Sufficiency in Modern America* (Madison, WI: University of Wisconsin Press, 2011), 11.

There is a "new" Catholic Land Movement afoot, pushing back against what the popes have called the dominant technocratic paradigm.[54] It has arisen as a grassroots movement of homesteaders but also responds to the teaching of recent pontiffs who have pointed out a divorce between faith and life in modern culture.[55] With a fraction of 1 percent of the United States population working in agriculture, the battle now focuses on the loss of the fundamental goods of human life—faith, family, work, leisure, and community. In seeking to overcome the fracture between faith and life, Pope St. John Paul II taught that the dignity of work must be rediscovered in his encyclical *Laborem Exercens*, going back to Genesis as a frame of reference to overcome the lingering difficulties of the ongoing struggle between communism and capitalism in the modern world:

> And yet, in spite of all this toil—perhaps, in a sense, because of it—work is a good thing for man. Even though it bears the mark of a *bonum arduum,* in the terminology of Saint Thomas, this does not take away the fact that, as such, it is a good thing for man. It is not only good in the sense that it is useful or something to enjoy; it is also good as being something worthy, that is to say, something that corresponds to man's

---

[54] See Pope Francis's frequent use of the term in *Laudato Si'*, 2015.

[55] The Church has continued to address issues related to the land. Pope Benedict XVI, *The Garden of God: Toward a Human Ecology* (Washington, DC: Catholic University of America Press, 2014), Pope Francis, *Laudato Si'* (2015), Pontifical Council for Justice and Peace, "Towards a Better Distribution of Land: The Challenge of Agrarian Reform," Nov. 23, 1997.

> dignity, that expresses this dignity and increases it. If one wishes to define more clearly the ethical meaning of work, it is this truth that one must particularly keep in mind. Work is a good thing for man—a good thing for his humanity—because through work man not only transforms nature, adapting it to his own needs, but he also achieves fulfilment as a human being and indeed, in a sense, becomes "more a human being."[56]

Too many people found their work pointless and draining, pulling them away from the meaning of work and their fundamental cultural vocation as human beings made in the image of the Creator. Pope St. John Paul II situated work within the context of the family, something that speaks to the hearts of many fathers who feel drawn out of the home and their primary vocation by their work in the office.

> Work constitutes a foundation for the formation of *family life*, which is a natural right and something that man is called to. These two spheres of values—one linked to work and the other consequent on the family nature of human life—must be properly united and must properly permeate each other. In a way, work is a condition for making it possible to found a family, since the family requires the means of subsistence which man normally gains through work. Work and industriousness also influence the whole *process of education* in the family, for the very reason that

[56] John Paul II, *Laborem Exercens*, https://www.vatican.va/content/john-paul-ii/en/encyclicals/docments/hf_jp-ii_enc_14091981_laborem-exercens.html, §9.

> everyone "becomes a human being" through, among other things, work, and becoming a human being is precisely the main purpose of the whole process of education.[57]

The reintegration of work and family life forms the center of the Catholic homesteading movement, seeking to reunite what has become fractured in our experience in the great search to recover our humanity and to become saints. This entails a flight from the oversaturation of technology, the overwhelming demands that pull families in too many directions, and the never-ending consumerism that sucks in our attention and wealth.

John Senior's *The Restoration of Christian Culture* has served as a touchpoint for many seeking to recover a lost way of life. Senior's vision begins with the first things first—consecrating our lives to the Immaculate Heart of Mary—then relocating to the land, and following the Benedictine approach to integrating *ora et labora*. Senior looks back on the settlement of America, the missed opportunity to order it properly, and the work that can still be done to recapture a lost ideal:

> Take a look at your city, suburb, town, or even factory-in-the-fields still anachronistically called farm. Ask honestly if the place has been improved since its purchase from the Indians or if you have been improved by living there. . . .

---

[57] John Paul II, *Laborem Exercens*, §10.

You can see with your own eyes that there is no inevitability in the suicide of civilization. If America had been governed by its farmers and craftsmen supplying their real needs and nothing more, as Jefferson hoped, not catering to lust and the agitated sloth which masquerades as lust, without the waterbeds and cyclotrons but obedient to the Christian religion and the rough philosophy of frontier common sense, New York, Chicago and Los Angeles would be as beautiful as Assisi, Chartres and Salamanca and its sons strong, generous and free as cavaliers, and not the fat cats jamming the freeways in their red Corvettes, puffing joints in the college dorms, drunk on the undistilled bilge they get from the entertainment industry which manages the courses and produces the textbooks from its headquarters at Princeton and Yale. Flee, for God's sake, flee from the sapped ramparts of success. Go home to the ruined neighborhoods and villages of your childhood and rebuild them. They will accuse you of nostalgia. In Greek, nostalgia means "home-sickness." Our hearts have been pierced like the sad heart of Ruth, sick for home amid the alien corn. Contrary to the famous verse, home is something you have very much to deserve. In fact you must sacrifice your life for it. If we all went home, any village in America today could be . . . beautiful, good, strong and free.[58]

---

[58] John Senior, *The Restoration of Christian Culture* (Norfolk, VA: IHS Press, 2008).

In a similar vein, Rod Dreher's *The Benedict Option* (2017) also looked toward monasticism as a model for restoring Christian culture. It resonated with many by relating how our institutions have become hollow and that new intentional communities need to be formed, both in rural areas and cities, in order to communicate and live the faith more robustly. Christian community has become a central issue in a time of growing isolation and mental illness.

We can point to concrete examples of the American Catholic Land Movement today. Our Lady of Clear Creek Abbey has embraced the principles of permaculture in growing fruits and vegetables and the raising of livestock. American monks in Italy have settled into the mountains outside of St. Benedict's hometown of Norcia where they have established a successful brewery. Boarding schools, inspired by John Senior's vision, have embraced work and farming as key elements of education, especially St. Gregory the Great Academy in Pennsylvania and St. Martin's Academy in Kansas. On the collegiate level, Ave Maria University has initiated a new agriculture and sustainability program, and many new Catholic post-secondary trade schools have been founded in the last few years to meet a growing demand for practical skills. The Santiago Trade School in Orange County, California, for instance, includes a working farm. Catholic Worker Farms have taken on new life, and the Southwest Indian Foundation has founded a new mission farm, San Isidro & Three Sisters Farm, in the Zuni Mountains of New Mexico. There are also new apostolates, some which focus on the outdoors like Creatio and COR Expeditions, while others have embraced an agricultural vision, like St. Joseph's Farm in North Carolina, led by Jason Craig, John Cuddeback's Life Craft, The Healing Land in Ohio, Our Lady's Ranch in California, and Sanctus Ranch in Texas, among others. Recent books testify to the influence of the most recent wave of the movement, especially Shawn and Beth Dougherty's *The Independent Farmstead* (2016) and Craig and Van Horn's *Liturgy of the Land* (2024). Building on these initiatives and attempting to recapture the lost momentum of the twentieth century, a new group, the Catholic Land Movement, founded by Michael Guidice and Andrew Ewell, has started over thirty local chapters, programs, and events aimed at promoting an agrarian vision.

The American Catholic Land Movement will continue, but its full impact remains to be seen. Will Catholics be able to fulfill the hope of the first settlers in sanctifying the land in the Name of God? Will rural America become a place to unify like-minded people in the pursuit of freedom in virtue? Can the country help America to overcome the spiritual and cultural problems it faces? These questions can only be answered in the next act of the movement (which I will address in chapter twelve). We must continue to turn to Our Lady to oversee the growth of the Catholic faith in the Americas and to guide us in sanctifying the land. Perhaps, like Scarlett O'Hara, we will find our way back to Tara, harkening back to the fateful cry of *tierra* with which we began, healing our wounds in the soil from which we all come.

This Volume

The mission, plantation, pioneer homestead, immigrant colony, mission farm, and remote job-homeschooling homestead—this is the story of the American Catholic Land Movement. With the general playbill laid out with its *dramatis personae*, we now will explore the intricacies of this history, how it shapes current dynamics, and the way it can open up future prospects. This is not simply a book about the past. It seeks to reclaim a distinctively American agrarian heritage for Catholics in order to move forward with a clearer vision.

For the first time, the contributors of this volume have laid out the contours of the American Catholic Land Movement in one coherent account, portraying the contributions of its key figures while exploring its essential themes. Past legacy, present dynamics, and future prospects form the organizing principle uniting the chapters. The contributors lay out the historical contributions of its major figures and movements such as the Southern Agrarians, Catholic Rural Life Conference, and Catholic Worker Movement. The volume continues to explore its present dynamics under the influence of figures such as Wendell Berry and the move to form local, family-based economic initiatives. From addressing current challenges, the authors lay out aspirational solutions for sanctifying the home and, through it, the soil of America itself, uniting Catholics in the pursuit of an integrated life of prayer, work, and community.

Works Cited

Agar, Herbert and Allen Tate. *Who Owns America: A New Declaration of Independence.* Wilmington, DE: ISI Press, 1999.

Anglada, Eric. "Taking Root: The history and new growth of Catholic Worker farms." *America: The National Catholic Review.* May 6, 2013. https://www.americamagazine.org/issue/taking-root.

Binz, Stephen. *Saint Junipero Serra's Camino: A Pilgrimage Guide to the California Missions.* Cincinnati, OH: Franciscan Media, 2017.

Birchell, Donna Blake. *New Mexico Mission Churches.* Charleston, SC: The History Press, 2021.

Bovee, David S. *The Church and the Land: The National Catholic Rural Life Conference and American Society, 1923-2007.* Washington, DC: Catholic University of America Press, 2010.

Brown, Dona. *Back to the Land: The Enduring Dream of Self-Sufficiency in Modern America.* Madison, WI: University of Wisconsin Press, 2011.

Caicedo, Felipe Valencia. "The Mission: Human Capital Transmission, Economic Persistence, and Culture in South America." *The Quarterly Journal of Economics* (2019): 507–556. doi:10.1093/qje/qjy024.

Crevecoeur, Hector St. John de. *Letters from an American Farmer: Describing Certain Provincial Situations, Manners, and Customs, and Conveying Some Idea of the Late and Present Interior Circumstances of the British Colonies in North America.* London: T. Davies, 1782. https://avalon.law.yale.edu/subject_menus/letters.asp.

Danbom, David. *Sod Busting: How Families Made Farms on the 19th-Century Plains.* Baltimore: Johns Hopkins University Press, 2014.

Doherty, Catherine. *Apostolic Farming: Healing the Earth.* Combermere Ontario: Madonna House Publications, 2001.

Gollar, Walker. *American and Catholic: Stories of the People Who Built the Church.* Cincinnati, OH: Franciscan Media, 2015.

"History: Urban and Rural Areas." United States Census Bureau. Accessed May 12, 2024. https://www.census.gov/history/www/programs/geography/urban_and_rural_areas.html.

Jiménez, Alfredo. "Spanish Missions in the United States: Cultural and Historical Significance." National Park Service. Accessed May 28, 2024. https://www.nps.gov/subjects/travelspanishmissions/spanish-missions-in-the-united-states-cultural-and-historical-significance.htm.

John Paul II. *Laborem Exercens.* https://www.vatican.va/content/john-paul-ii/en/encyclicals/documents/hf_jp-ii_enc_14091981_laborem-exercens.html.

Leo XIII. *Rerum Novarum.* https://www.vatican.va/content/leo-xiii/en/encyclicals/documents/hf_l-xiii_enc_15051891_rerum-novarum.html.

Marlett, Jeffrey. "Strangers in Our Midst: Catholics in Rural America." In *Roman Catholicism in the United States: A Thematic History.* Edited by Margaret M. McGuinness and James T. Fisher. New York: Fordham University Press, 2019.

McShea, Bronwen. *Apostles of Empire: The Jesuits of New France.* Lincoln, NE: University of Nebraska Press, 2019.

Michel, Virgil. "Timely Tracts: City or Farm?" Quoted in Michael J. Woods, *Cultivating Soil and Soul: Twentieth-Century Catholic Agrarians Embrace the Liturgical Movement.* Collegeville, MN: Liturgical Press 2009.

Pius XII. "The Pope Speaks on Rural Life: Speech to the delegates at the Convention of the National Confederation of Farm Owner-Operators." November 15, 1946.

Schmiesing, Kevin. *Catholic Pilgrimage through American History: People and Places that Shaped the Church in the United States.* Notre Dame, IN: Ave Maria Press, 2022.

Senior, John. *The Restoration of Christian Culture.* Norfolk, VA: IHS Press, 2008.

Shapiro, Edward S. "Catholic Agrarian Thought and the New Deal." The Catholic Historical Review, vol. 65, no. 4 (Oct. 1979): 583–599.

Smith, Henry Nash. *Virgin Land: The American West as Symbol and Myth.* Cambridge, MA: Harvard University Press, 2007.

Tocqueville, Alexis De. *Democracy in America*, vol. 2. Translated by Henry Reeve. https://www.gutenberg.org/files/816/816-h/816-h.htm.

William Edmund Fahey, PhD

William Edmund Fahey, PhD, (Fellow of Thomas More College of Liberal Arts, Merrimack, New Hampshire) has lived in the Midwest, the South, Scotland, and New England, but admits with affection that he is at home in two little known places (one in New Hampshire and one in Maine). He is a descendant of doughty explorers who first came to New England in 1616. He has pursued a professional vocation for over three decades teaching classical languages, history, natural science, and anything else he finds interesting--which is most of the Catholic and Western intellectual tradition. For some years, he has enjoyed and tried caring for the natural world of New Hampshire, just outside of a tiny village, and takes consolation and joy in life with his wife, children, and grandchildren.

CHAPTER 1

CAN YANKEES BE AGRARIANS? HOW NEW ENGLAND REVEALS THE DIVIDED HEART OF AMERICA

William Edmund Fahey

The four-hundredth anniversary of the arrival of Pilgrims at Plymouth Rock, the signing of the Mayflower Compact, and the mythic birth of colonial New England occurred in November 2020. Though its observation was disrupted more by COVID-19 than by the kind of protests and historical revisionism that mark the 1619 movement, which reviles the celebration of the Jamestown Colony and all aspects of what the man of letters Russell Kirk once called "America's British Culture." To the "Woke," the seventeenth-century New World means slavery and genocide. And so, to diminish public consternation, the organizers of Plymouth 400, Inc.—the non-profit created to celebrate the occasion—long ago chose the safer route of incorporating the Wampanoag Tribe in the event, to the extent of rolling in references to the fiftieth anniversary of "The National Day of Mourning," which the United American Indians of New England annually observe in lieu of a celebratory Thanksgiving Day. Our current moment in history scarcely seems attuned to the kind of natural patriotism of my youth, when even in the wake of the fall of Saigon, the United States mustered considerable unity for the two-hundredth anniversary of the Declaration of Independence. But now, a common American identity seems so fragile and so potentially divisive that most Americans appear content to chart a course of quiet ignorance and polite non-observance of this day, apart from perhaps taking advantage of a paid holiday and consuming turkey. So, with the day, so with the culture.

But let us ask, why should one bother to think about the jumble of historical facts and embellishments that fill the national holiday brought into prominence not by the British colonists of Virginia or New England but Abraham Lincoln and Franklin Roosevelt? Do we need founding myths? Why, in particular, would a Catholic of Irish lineage care what the English pioneers did—after all, is this not an enforced bit of mythology foisted on us by the WASP (white Anglo-Saxon Protestant) establishment, the same establishment that enforced an "Irish [read Catholic] Need Not Apply" policy in most sectors of the American economy apart from mills, railroads, and military service for decades?

As a boy, my own family dutifully and cheerfully celebrated Thanksgiving in the standard fashion, as if we had tumbled into a Pepperidge Farm commercial. But from my college years on, I wondered—what did this have to do with us? And yet there is a family story, as there always is, and that story provides a response. My great-grandmother, Margaret Fahey, was a McKenney. Her father, Thomas McKenney, came from a long and well-established Protestant family. After his first wife died, Thomas fell in love with an Irish mill girl, Hannah O'Hare. They were married by Fr. John Colbert of St. Peter's Catholic Church in Lowell, Massachusetts, on October 1, 1882. Their marriage certificate, family daguerreotypes, a lock of hair, and other relics are wedged between the pages of a Douay-Rheims Bible published in Boston. Thomas took Hannah back to where his family had lived for a century near Auburn, Maine, where their daughter Margaret would marry my great-grandfather Joseph Fahey, a surgeon, graduate of Bowdoin College, third generation Irish-American, whose grandfather, Michael Fahey, had come over in 1836 to work on the Montreal-Portland railroad.

Unlike the upstart O'Hares and Faheys, McKenney's family boasted officers in the War of 1812 and the American Revolution; they were Baptists and Congregationalists—in other words, Yankee and fully WASP. I often wonder what Thomas McKenney and Honora O'Hare spoke about when they looked at that Douay-Rheims Bible sitting in the parlor, and what Thanksgiving looked like for them.

What Thomas McKenney, proud descendant of patriots who fought at the siege of Boston, Saratoga, Valley Forge, and Monmouth Court House did not know was that his first ancestor on these shores, John McKenney—my great-grandfather of nine generations ago—was a recruit from the Isle Skye—in all likelihood Catholic—who fought with his clan and was captured at the battle of Worcester (1651) while protecting his king, the Stuart claimant to the throne of England, Scotland, Wales, and Ireland. McKenney, whose name was a garbled transliteration of the Gaelic now commonly written as "Mackenzie," was among thousands of Scots put in internment camps, then marched ragged to London and sold into slavery. Unlike other Scottish prisoners from the battles of Dunbar and Worcester, who were sent to plantations in the Caribbean or North America and died, John toiled under a foreign sun and worked his way back into freedom. After years of fueling the furnaces at the Puritan Iron Works near Saugus, Massachusetts, John McKenney was granted his liberty and traveled as far north as he could in British territory—to the pro-Royalist frontier of what is now Maine. John McKenney lived and died in Scarborough, close to where I spent every summer as a boy and young man. He arrived in time to fight in King Philip's War (1675–78), to find himself on the wrong side of the law for brawling and drinking, and to establish a long line of Yankees.

When I dwell on my lineage of colonial ancestors, I am confronted by a rich irony. On the surface, I am of a rather typical blend of nineteenth-century Catholicism—with Irish, German, Austrian, Romanian, Slovak, and Mexican blood. I am ladled out from that quintessential melting pot like so many, yet through one chance romance in New England, my forefathers are also British, colonial, and . . . WASP.

When the New England worthies behind Plymouth 400, Inc. began their polite debate and tolerant planning of the 1620–2020 celebrations (as if the doughty Pilgrims flashed "Coexist" stickers on their flat-topped capotains), I took interest, but already knew I had 1620 "beat" with my tenth generation grandfather John Winter (1595–1645), who is documented to have operated from Monhegan Island, Maine, in 1616, as master of the good ship *David*, which sailed from Plymouth, England. John Winter was of the seafaring Wynter family, men who sailed to the Straits of Magellan with Francis Drake, who organized defenses against the Spanish Armada, who converted back to Catholicism under the Stuarts, and who represent a long line of Englishmen from Bristol and Plymouth who had been exploring the coast of what is now Canada and New England since 1498, at least, when Cabot sailed and claimed lands in America for Henry VII. In my view, the haggard Puritan Separatists of Leiden who were saved by Indians in 1620–21 were late arrivals. And yet, I felt a bond with these bright-eyed pursuers of "the Moses Option," perhaps irrational, but sincerely felt. The sense of their hardship, trial, the quashing of the dreams, the experience of toil in building a community in a hostile world—all this had a resonance and called forth sympathy.

As I dug deeper, I found that I too had Puritan blood. Again, no surprise to anyone who has by fortune descended from an East-coast family prior to the Potato Famine. Nine generations back, I find grandparents of that very Puritan colony which I viewed as the enemy of all things Catholic: Edward Bangs (1591–1677), John Doane (1590–1686), and John Woodbury (1579–1641). All three were committed to the Puritan project and stood as officers in the governments of Massachusetts and were founders of Salem, Cape Ann, Eastham, and other early colonies in that dour Commonwealth. Woodbury, in particular, is connected to the Puritan heritage of New England. When John Endicott, Puritan firebrand, arrived in 1628, his ship ran aground on a sand bar.

According to the local tradition, my forefather John Woodbury wadded out and carried Endicott on his back safely to shore. I often say at the dinner table, our family once held in its hands the power to stop militant Puritanism. If John had but stumbled . . .

Balancing this Puritan side, my Maine ancestors seem all to be, in the early years, staunch Royalists and High Church Anglicans. Robert Jordan (1611–1679), another ninth-generation grandfather, was a graduate of Balliol College, Oxford, and ministered to the Anglicans between Falmouth, Maine, south to Portsmouth, New Hampshire. He married John Winter's daughter Sara, and from Cape Elizabeth, presided over an estate of some six thousand acres. He was an ardent defender of King Charles II's interests and held offices in the now vanished Royal Province of Lygonia (northern New England). For celebrating the Anglican Mass and baptizing infants, he was arrested numerous times by Puritan militia sent up from Massachusetts. As a minister and judge, Jordan was also known for his patient inquiries into natural and human causes of misfortunes, and by such helped to keep witch trials out of Maine.

The Maine side of the family seems to be marked by such a contrary tendency toward monarchy, High Church sentiments—if not commitments—and a certain degree of liberality. Among the shining examples: my grandmother of ten generations Anne Downing (c. 1610–1670), who with her husband ran a tavern on Crooked Lane in Kittery, Maine. Anne has a place in the legal documents of the period for a lawsuit wherein she was accused by one Sarah Trickey of drunkenness and monarchism. To quote the court documents: "She [Anne Downing] did stand upon her head until a cup of wine was taken off the heels of her shoows and that the King's health was drunke." The accusation may appear to cast light only on riotous behavior, but the papers are dated to 25 June 1656, the height of Cromwell's military rule in England and the tightest grip of Puritan conformity in North America. Mere mention of crown and wine were code for loyalties to throne and altar.

Perhaps the most iconic blender of new and old traditions, William Pepperell, a fiercely self-made man of a bumptious self-made family whose fortunes started with one small boat and whose activities became emblematic of a Yankee maritime entrepreneur. Pepperrell rose to become the only American who commanded both British Regulars and American Militia simultaneously and commanded the successful siege of Louisbourg, New France's greatest fortress which fell in the summer of 1745, bringing safety to the empire and confidence to the thirteen colonies. Massachusetts would name a town in his honor and create a charming square on Beacon Hill to remember his victory; the city of London presented Pepperell with a silver plate; and King George II granted Pepperell, now Sir William, a hereditary Baronet. Not bad for the son of poor Welsh immigrants.

Strangely, the news of Louisbourg's fall would have been a cause for sorrow and concern to one of my and Pepperell's distant cousins—Arabella, Mme. de Boulanger de Saint-Pierre. Arabella had been born Mary Anne Jordan (c. 1687) to my eighth-generation grandfather Dominicus. Dominicus was a tradesman to the Abenaki tribesmen who migrated seasonally to the Maine coast. Although relations with

Native Americans had been largely peaceful with Stuarts on the English throne, the Glorious Revolution brought with it near perpetual war. In the summer of 1703, Dominicus met with Indians who indicated their desire for peaceful trading. He was scalped, and his family farm ransacked and his little brother, his wife, and his six children were dragged away into the wilderness. Those who survived the journey were ransomed by French authorities; some of the children returned, but Mary Ann was not among them; she—like scores of Puritan women—chose to stay in Canada. She converted, married, took the name Arabella, and was after many years granted French citizenship by Louis XV. Meanwhile, over the course of her life, Catholic forces under the leadership of Jesuits like Fr. Sebastien Rale were conducting a bloody conflict against the seaboard English colonies. Three wars were waged against Rale and his Catholic Abenakis, culminating in Rale's martyrdom with scores of faithful Native Americans at Norridgewock, Maine, in 1724.

Such strange divisions are regular, if not the norm, in any long genealogy. My relatives among the Pepperrels and the Sparhawks were among proud Americans rewarded and then punished for their belief that Americans had a place within the British Commonwealth. They were opposed by cousins whose descendants proudly call themselves by names such as the Sons of the American Revolution. Thus, sitting cheek by jowl around the groaning board of history, I have stiff Puritans and jovial Anglicans (and perhaps some Recusant Catholics), Republicans and Monarchists; Separatists and Empire men. This is true of every American whose ancestry touches our deep past.

The tension arises from that particular moment in Western history. To understand it, we need only turn to two contemporary accounts of Englishmen gazing upon the New World. Many are familiar with William Bradford's account of the Pilgrim's arrival along the shores of Massachusetts:

> Being thus passed the vast ocean, and a sea of troubles . . . , they had now no friends to welcome them nor inns to entertain or refresh their weather-beaten bodies; no houses or much less town to repair to, to seek for succour. . . . What could they see but a hideous and desolate wilderness, fall of wild beasts and wild men—and what multitudes there might be of them they knew not.[1]

Yet the same culture produced a man like Thomas Morton, who wrote in his *New English Canaan*:

> I did indeavour to take a survey of the Country: The more I looked, the more I liked it. And when I had more seriously considered of the bewty of the place, with all her faire indowments, I did not thinke that in all the knowne world it could be paralel'd . . . the Land to mee seeme paradice: for in mine eie t'was Natures Masterpeece; Her cheifest Magazine of all where lives her store: if this Land be not rich, then is the whole world poore.[2]

---

1 William Bradford, *Of Plymouth Plantation*, ix.

2 Thomas Morton, *The New English Canaan* (Society, 1883), bk. 2, ch. 1, 179.

Morton became an icon of the other seventeenth-century model, royalist and Anglican, warmer to relations with the Indians, conscious and proud of the British Anglican *and* Catholic past. Indeed, there were several attempts to establish Catholic colonies in the British new world, some in New England, the most enduring being in the Chesapeake—but Thomas Morton (who like his friend Ben Jonson was accused of Catholicism), established a colony for Anglicans and Catholics named Mare Mount in Massachusetts—to the classically trained Morton, "Mare Mount" was the hill of mirth, the hill by the sea, and the hill of Our Lady. In time, the name was simplified to Merry Mount. But such projects are largely effaced by the turns of history and our tendency to simplify accounts of the past. In the case of Merry Mount, it was destroyed by Puritan military action.

One writer who could not accept such a simplification was Nathaniel Hawthorne. He remains America's most vivid observer of the New England character. He was fully aware of the two sides of its British culture—the Puritan and the Anglican. He was attracted to both and even saw the beauty and superiority of the Anglican and Catholic. He painted the life of Thomas Morton's suppressed colony in his early story "The May Pole of Merry Mount" (1832).

After opening pages depicting the gay beauty of Merry Mount, Hawthorne's pen shifts to doom:

> Unfortunately, there were men in the new world of a sterner faith than those Maypole worshipers. Not far from Merry Mount was a settlement of Puritans, most dismal wretches, who said their prayers before

> daylight, and then wrought in the forest or the cornfield till evening made it prayer time again. . . . When they met in conclave, it was never to keep up the old English mirth, but to hear sermons three hours long, or to proclaim bounties on the heads of wolves and the scalps of Indians. Their festivals were fast days, and their chief pastimes the singing of psalms.[3]

Hawthorne knew much of the Puritan spirit, but not fully of its history—several of my Puritan ancestors were, in fact, licensed to sell strong wine and liquor; and I do not think it was to restore throats flagging from the singing of psalms. Still, Hawthorne does seize upon that drive to take seriously the whole Pauline injunctions like that in Galatians 5, not merely the brighter parts of the Christian message. For these fierce Englishmen, the command to "Stand fast in the liberty wherewith Christ hath made us free" (Gal 5:1) required not (as in the current Lectionary) that Paul's words be broken and hidden in "optional readings," but (like the traditional Lectionary) regularly considered so that "the works of the flesh are manifest" (Gal 5:19) and put into place. Hawthorne knew that his ancestors forsook the easy grace that can come in a Catholic culture and sought to understand and seek the harder graces of mortification and suffering. Hawthorne saw it, honored it, feared it, and could sense but not quite put a finger on the inadequacy of it.

At its core, Hawthorne's struggle between the grizzled saint and the gay sinner is not a struggle between a religious

---

[3] Nathaniel Hawthorne, "The Maypole of Merry Mount" in *Twice-Told Tales* (Philadelphia: David McKay, 1889).

path versus a libertine path; nor yet a struggle over the choice between Calvinism and Anglicanism (and Catholicism). The struggle he depicts is deeper and older. It is the perpetual struggle, the strain of which echoes in the American heart according to a hereditary trait.

In many of his works, Hawthorne conjures for our imagination *the* American struggle. It is undeniable in reviewing our history that this one of our earliest and greatest voices has discovered *the* strain in our culture. He discovered it because he explored constantly his own mind and heart. The opening sentences of "The Maypole of Merry Mount" is, for me, one of the most prescient and painful of all to be found in American literature:

> Bright were the days at Merry Mount, when the Maypole was the banner staff of that gay colony! They who reared it, should their banner be triumphant, were to pour sunshine over New England's rugged hills, and scatter flower seeds throughout the soil. Jollity and gloom were contending for an empire.[4]

If we look with honesty, how can one *not* see our history as but a contended empire pitted between jollity and gloom? This is no simplistic view. I do not think we are *merely* to see the innocents of Merry Mount and their Puritan foes represented by cavalier versus roundheads, or one side versus the other in any of the contentious moments that mark the epic history of the United States (the founding, the Civil War, the reconstruction of the Union and the modern state,

---

[4] Hawthorne, "The Maypole of Merry Mount."

the civil rights movements, etc.). Still less would I think this image allows us lightly to condemn one side or the other in the current mayhem and frivolity that churn upon the surface of contemporary America. The brutalization of human life, the brutalization of human memory, the brutalization of truth makes it very hard to condemn any one side fully, because it has become very hard to discern *a simple* divide between the forces of jollity and the forces of gloom. And it is because the problem lies deeper.

Several years after "The Maypole of Merry Mount," Hawthorne wrote "Endicott and the Red Cross" (1837). Again, he opens with a meditation upon a symbol, a banner: the English Colors, the Cross of St. George, which flies above the Colony of Salem and reminds all beneath its shadow of the United Kingdoms under the Stuart monarchs and the vision of a united Church and State. Endicott appears again at this moment to rally the stalwart Puritans of Massachusetts and to reveal to them that King Charles I and his primate William Laud, the archbishop of Canterbury, are tightening their political and ecclesial control over the Puritan colonies in North America. Endicott's goal in speaking is to put steel into the veins of his coreligionist, to resist the Crown and preserve their freedoms.

Hawthorne now more willingly calls attention to the irony of history. Endicott speaks before a Puritan house of prayer—"with neither steeple nor bell," but "the grim head of a wolf," nailed to the church porch, its "blood was still plashing on the doorstep."[5] To the sides of the village green, close

[5] Nathaniel Hawthorne, "Endicott and the Red Cross" in *Twice-Told Tales* (Philadelphia: David McKay, 1889).

to Endicott, are the whipping post and sinners in stocks and at the pillory, most noticeably "the head of an Episcopalian and suspected Catholic" and "the Wanton Gospeller" who was being punished by the Puritan separatists because "he had dared to give interpretations of Holy Writ unsanctioned by the infallible judgement of the civil and religious leaders." Before an assembled body—among which are a motley array of stoic Indians and private sinners, who have been put on display with public instrument of shame—Endicott speaks passionately of the political and religious freedoms won in the American wilderness. He urges to rebellion his "fellow soldiers—fellow exiles," now threatened by King Charles—"This son of a Scotch tyrant—this grandson of a Papistical and adulterous Scotchwoman."

His peroration is interrupted by the quiet presence of Roger Williams, who councils him to hold his peace. In response, Endicott merely increases his steam, condemning especially Archbishop Laud, who "shall kiss the Pope's toe, as cardinal of Rome, [so that] he may deliver New England, bound hand and foot, into the power of his master." The king and his prelate will, Endicott continues, force high altars and tapers, and soon New England will hear "the sacring bell, and the voices of the Romish priests saying the mass." This Endicott will not permit. To make clear his zeal and what must be done by all, he orders the banner of St. George lowered, and "brandishing his sword, Endicott thrust it through the cloth, and, with his left hand, rent the

Red Cross completely out of the banner,"[6] compelling the soul of New England to a future without Pope or Tyrant.

Hawthorne was haunted by his own family's Puritan past (Hawthorne's great-great grandfather was one of the most dogged persecutors of witches in Salem). Hawthorne sifted history to see what motives of the human heart he might uncover, the hearts of his very ancestors. In this, Hawthorne was moved rightly by the natural virtue of piety. And here I draw to my meditation's end.

What a thorough jumble my family, our American family is. Which side shall we separate and condemn; which shall we join and applaud? How are we to understand the past sufficiently to purify our memory? All Americans face this agonizing problem. Perhaps a quiet reflection on our own past and that of our own families would help. Family life and social life reveal what Augustine once wrote grandly about in describing the nature and reality of history—there are two communities in a final sense, the City of Man and the City of God. Each will, in the end, be filled with citizenry who are distinguished by their loves: One city will be filled with those whose pursuit of self-love is at the cost of their love of God; the other is filled with those willing to put aside self-love for their love of God. In time, in history, it is not possible to discern clearly the two cities. Grave errors and bloodshed have happened when men try. *Perplexae quippe sunt istae duae civitate in hoc saeculo invicemque permixtae donec ultimo iudicio dirimantur*. "In point of fact, these two

---

[6] Nathaniel Hawthorne, "Endicott and the Red Cross," in *Twice-Told Tales*, David McKay, 1889.

cities are thoroughly interwoven in time and will remain compounded until they are divided at the final judgement."[7] If in the gravest matters it is impossible to distinguish the two cities from one another—with even the institutional Church, in Augustine's model, compounded of both cities—how can we so lightly mock, topple, or cancel our own family members, fellow countrymen, and past?

The charitable route is the arduous route, but the best. It will be cleared for us by the old virtues. In the case of Thanksgiving and the historical celebrations of the autumn season, I find now that the virtue of piety is fitting. I look with wonder and gratitude on the hopes, initiatives, labors, and sacrifices of all my brawling and varied ancestors. I ponder whether I can live up to their dreams. I am humbled by their energy and achievement. I am chastened and anxious when I look upon their flaws, which history preserves for me as their warning—for I recognize their flaws in myself.

In 1939, when Pius XII wrote in celebration of the established Catholic Church in the United States, he said:

> To one who turns the pages of your history and reflects upon the causes of what has been accomplished it is apparent that the triumphal progress of Divine religion has contributed in no small degree to the glory and prosperity which your country now enjoys. It is indeed true that religion has its laws and institutions for eternal happiness but it is also undeniable that it dowers life here below with so many benefits that it could do no more even if the principal reason for its

---

7 Augustine, *City of God*, 1.35.

> existence were to make men happy during the brief span of their earthly life. It is a pleasure for Us to recall the well-remembered story.[8]

He praised "the American people, by nature inclined to grandiose undertakings and to liberality,"[9] called them to be thankful for the origins and their blessings, and asked them to reflect upon the consequence of refusing to recognize and thank God for His paternal love:

> The refusal to recognize the Divine Majesty, the neglect of the moral law, the origin of which is from Heaven, or that regrettable inconstancy which makes its victims waver between the lawful and the forbidden, between justice and iniquity. Thence arise immoderate and blind egoists, that thirst for pleasure, the vice of drunkenness, immodest and costly styles in dress, the prevalence of crime even among minors, the lust for power, neglect of the poor, base craving for ill-gotten wealth, the flight from the land, levity in entering into marriage, divorce, the break-up of the family, the cooling of mutual affection between parents and children, birth control, the enfeeblement of the race, the weakening of respect for authority, or obsequiousness, or rebellion, neglect of duty towards one's country and towards mankind.[10]

---

[8] Pius XII, *Sertum Laetitiae*, https://www.vatican.va/content/pius-xii/en/encyclicals/documents/hf_p-xii_enc_01111939_sertum-laetitiae.html, §2.

[9] Pius XII, *Sertum Laetitiae*, §42.

[10] Pius XII, *Sertum Laetitiae*, §19.

Perhaps, if we return to a calm, pious, intentional celebration of our heritage, symbolized by Thanksgiving, we can renew our families and country. The day should not be a cause of sorrow but of praise for God's blessings on the country that emerged from the meeting of many tortuous paths within our family lines. The day is richer than drumsticks and drink and a paid day off. Let those things remain, but let them become prompts for our recollection and our gratitude. For another has paid for the feast.

Works Cited

Augustine, *City of God.*

Bradford, William. *Of Plymouth Plantation.*

Hawthorne, Nathaniel. "Endicott and the Red Cross." In *Twice-Told Tales.* Philadelphia: David McKay, 1889.

———. "The Maypole of Merry Mount." In *Twice-Told Tales.* Philadelphia: David McKay, 1889.

Morton, Thomas. *The New English Canaan.* Society, 1883.

Pius XII. *Sertum Laetitiae.* https://www.vatican.va/content/pius-xii/en/encyclicals/documents/hf_p-xii_enc_01111939_sertum-laetitiae.html.

Allan C. Carlson, PhD

Allan C. Carlson holds his PhD in Modern European History from Ohio University. He has taught at Hillsdale College and the Pontifical John Paul II Institute for Studies on Marriage and Family at the Catholic University of America. He was a 1988 appointee by President Ronald Reagan to The National Commission on Children. His books include *From Cottage to Work Station: The Family's Search for Social Harmony in the Industrial Age* (Ignatius Press), *The New Agrarian Mind* (Routledge), *The Natural Family Where It Belongs: New Agrarian Essays* (Taylor and Francis), *Land and Liberty: The Best Essays of FREE AMERICA* (The Wethersfield Institute for Catholic Thought), and *In the Family Way: Agrarian Dreams and Dilemmas* (forthcoming from Front Porch Republic Books). His media appearances include ABC, CBS, PBS, CNN, BBC, MSNBC, CBC, EWTN, Maria Vision TV, and Catholic Answers. He is married to Betsy, and they have four children and eleven grandchildren. They reside on a farm in Northern Illinois.

CHAPTER 2

BACK TO THE LAND: THE AMERICAN AGRARIAN CAUSE REVIEWED

Allan C. Carlson

The first stirring of modern agrarianism in North America came from the pen and organizing energy of Liberty Hyde Bailey. Born and educated in Michigan, he became the Professor of Practical and Experimental Horticulture at Cornell University in New York in 1888. Economic stress in rural America caused by low commodity prices, mounting debt, and foreclosures led him to emphasize the moral, social, and cultural importance of the small family farm. He argued that agriculture of this kind produced strong and large families, which supplied the cities "with fresh blood, clean bodies, and clear brains that can endure the strain of modern urban life."[1] In addition, daily contact with the earth produced persons "original" in thought and "independent of group control," which transformed farmers into "the

[1] Liberty Hyde Bailey, *Report of the Country Life Commission* (U.S. Government Printing Office, 1909), 20.

fundamental fact" of true democracy. In 1908, President Theodore Roosevelt appointed Bailey to be the chairman of a National Commission on Country Life.

Bailey's spiritual emphasis came from a combination of liberal Protestantism and enthusiastic Freemasonry (he was a frequent contributor to the Masonic "idea" journal *The Outlook*). This approach found its consummate expression in his 1915 book, *The Holy Earth.* He also launched the American Country Life Association to encourage the "rebuilding of a new agriculture and a new rural life."[2]

Alas, Bailey's campaign began to run out of steam in the early 1920s. The collapse of agricultural prices following the end of World War I and another wave of lost farms left him pessimistic over the prospects for building a "new" rural civilization. The situation also revealed the frailty of the spiritual foundation to his agrarianism. Bailey's intellectualized, modern pantheism proved unable to inspire and mobilize real farmers facing financial stress. Attendance at Country Life meetings dwindled.

During these same years, though, an alternative agrarianism emerged in an unlikely place: among American Roman Catholics! This was surprising because the Church in this era was overwhelmingly urban in focus and composition. Nonetheless, Catholic leaders rallied around the idea of a "Green Rising," or alternatively a "Green Revolution," that

---

2 Liberty Hyde Bailey, *The Holy Earth* (Ithaca: New York State College of Agriculture, 1980 [1915]), 87; L. H. Bailey, *What Is Democracy?* (Ithaca: The Comstock Publishing Co., 1918), 95–96; and William L. Bowers, *The Country Life Movement in America, 1900-1920* (Port Washington: Kennikat Press, 1974).

would encourage and defend a rural landscape dominated by small family farms. Representative were Edwin O'Hara, who launched the campaign during the 1920s, and John C. Rawe, who gave it deep intellectual substance during the 1930s and early 1940s.

Born 1881 in Fillmore County, Minnesota, Edwin Vincent O'Hara grew up on a fairly prosperous 320-acre family farm.[3] In 1898, he began study at the College of St. Thomas in Saint Paul. This school was the project of Bishop John Ireland. As a progressive on matters of economics, Bishop Ireland frequently referenced Pope Leo XIII's 1891 Encyclical, *Rerum Novarum*. While addressing the crisis of urban-industrial life, this document actually affirmed key agrarian principles: all wealth ultimately derives from the land; through both "the activity of his mind and the strength of his body," a man "makes his own that portion of nature's field which he cultivates"; and "the law should favor the ownership" of productive land and induce "as many as possible of the people to be owners" of large gardens or farms.[4] O'Hara also studied with a young professor of social ethics, John A. Ryan. The latter's doctoral dissertation, entitled *A Living Wage*, demanded that all practical matters of economic life and policy give primary attention to the health and security of the natural family.

---

3 A thorough biography of Edwin O'Hara was actually written by the current archbishop of New York: Timothy Michael Dolan, *"Some Seed Fell on Good Ground": The Life of Edwin V. O'Hara* (Washington, DC: The Catholic University of America Press, 1992).

4 Leo XIII, *Rerum Novarum*, no. 9, 46.

Ordained to the priesthood in 1905, O'Hara took up duties in a rural parish of the Diocese of Portland, Oregon. A dozen years later, as the United States entered the Great War in Europe, he became a chaplain with the U.S. Army in France. This experience also exposed him to new currents in Continental social thought. Notably, he began to read the work of Hilaire Belloc and G. K. Chesterton. Inspired by *Rerum Novarum*, they called for a decentralized economy built on the widespread ownership of homes, gardens, and farmland, a recovery of artisanship, and renewed village life. As a positive alternative to both communism and capitalism, they labelled their system distributism.[5]

In practice, such a task required radical steps, even a revolution. Relative to agriculture, Chesterton favored the term "Green Rising," which he saw occurring throughout central and eastern Europe in the wake of the Great War's end in 1918. From Finland in the north to Bulgaria in the south to Czecho-Slovakia in the west, farmer-controlled political parties were gaining political power. Chesterton called this "a vast victory for the peasants, and, therefore, a vast defeat for both the communists and the capitalists."[6] The Green Rising, he said, should be seen as "a huge historical hinge and turning point, like the conversion of Constantine or

---

[5] G. K. Chesterton, *What's Wrong with the World* (1910), in *The Collected Works of G. K. Chesterton*, ed, George J. Marlin, Richard P. Rabatin, and John L. Swn, vol. 4 (San Francisco: Ignatius Press, 1987); and Hilaire Belloc, *The Servile State* (Indianapolis: Liberty Classics, 1977 [1912]).

[6] G. K. Chesterton, introduction to Helen Douglas-Irvine, *The Making of Rural Europe* (London: George Allen and Unwin, 1923), 7–8.

the French Revolution."[7] While sometimes involving violence and military mobilization, the "main interest" of the Green Rising was "economic and ethical." As Chesterton concluded, "in a sort of awful silence" the peasantries were fighting "one vast and voiceless pitched battle with bolshevism and its twin brother, which is big business," and the farmers were winning.[8]

Father O'Hara embraced the term "Green Rising" and resolved to bring a peaceful Roman Catholic version of this development to America. The first sign of this interest came on his return to the United States in December 1918. He met with leaders of the Catholic Education Association to discuss the poor conditions of the rural Catholic churches. These officials urged him to study the problem and prepare a formal report, which he did in 1920. In it, Fr. O'Hara focused on families and children. "The primary product of the farm," he wrote, "is not wheat or potatoes or cattle, it is people." Crafting a phrase that he would often repeat, the farm was "the natural habitat of the family." Why? Rural living embraced "home ideals and attitudes," avoided "social competition" in consumption, favored more and earlier marriages, cemented the functional partnership of husband and wife, and welcomed children as economic assets. Industrial society, in contrast, worked against the family, favoring divorce, desertion, temporary unions, weak marriages, and the avoidance of

---

7 Chesterton, introduction to Helen Douglas-Irvine, *The Making of Rural Europe*, 7–8.

8 Chesterton, introduction to Helen Douglas-Irvine, *The Making of Rural Europe*, 7–8.

children. The key lesson was simple: "on the farm alone . . . the economic forces work for the unity of the home."[9]

The challenge facing the Church was that only 18 percent of American Roman Catholics resided on farms, compared to nearly half of American Protestants. At the same time, 90 percent of Church parish buildings and schools were in the cities. Given urban sterility and rural institutional neglect, the Church faced a dismal future. This was ironic, O'Hara emphasized, because "the Catholic Church is the strongest and most cohesive social force known to history" and "the divinely appointed guardian of the Christian home."[10] Moreover, there were solid examples of a vital Catholic agrarianism to be found in Europe. He concluded that "the future will be with the Church that ministers to the rural population."[11] His parish-centered recommendations included the training of more priests for rural service and an upgrade in their status, the building of more rural parochial schools, the encouragement of young, rural Catholic men and women to stay in farming, and the launch of new projects to make farm living more socially, culturally, and religiously attractive.

At the national level, O'Hara resolved to create Catholic rural organizations that would be functionally autonomous. His former professor at St. Thomas College, John Ryan, was now the Director of Social Action for the National Catholic Welfare Conference, a project of the Bishops' Conference and based in Washington, D.C. He agreed to create a Rural

---

9 Edwin O'Hara, *The Church and the Country Community* (New York: Macmillan, 1927), 7–34.

10 O'Hara, *The Church and the Country Community*, 21.

11 O'Hara, *The Church and the Country Community*, 9.

Life Bureau "to study the rural Catholic problem, to suggest remedies, and to enlist the active cooperation forces necessary to apply these remedies."[12] Father O'Hara became its part-time director. While still a rural pastor in Oregon, he also launched in 1922 a publication at his own expense, *St. Isadore's Plow.* Named for a patron saint of farmers, the monthly embraced the enthusiasm of the "Green Rising" while focusing on the practical problems and tasks facing rural priests.

The next year, Fr. O'Hara organized the "First National Catholic Rural Life Conference" in St. Louis. Held in conjunction with the annual meeting of the declining American Country Life Association, seventy-one full registrants and over a hundred observers attended the Catholic sessions. Participants voted to create a permanent National Catholic Rural Life Conference that would promote "the spiritual, social, and economic welfare of the rural population." Father O'Hara became its executive director.

Under his guidance, the NCRLC also linked parish life to the grand objectives of the "Green Rising." Regarding the former, O'Hara resolved to counter the "deplorable" catechetical education that most rural children received. He designed a curriculum for and promoted Religious Vacation Schools that would enroll all Catholic children in a rural parish, ages six to fourteen, to attend daily morning sessions for four summer weeks. Special attention would be given to the spiritual aspects of agriculture. By 1930, over one thousand of these schools were in operation. Regarding the latter,

---

[12] Quoted in David S Bovée, *The Church and the Land*, The National Catholic Rural Life Conference and American Society, 1923–2007, (Catholic University of America Press, 2010), 39.

Fr. O'Hara organized the 1924 National Conference in Milwaukee around the "Green Rising" theme. In announcing the conference in *St. Isadore's Plow*, for example, he wrote: "The world-wide agrarian revolution since the Great War connoted by the 'Green Rising' is undoubtedly having its counter-part in our own country." He then cut to the core issue: "It is radically a question of provision for family life. American farms are not so important for the production of foodstuffs as they are for the rearing of children."[13]

In 1930, Fr. O'Hara gained appointment as bishop of Great Falls, Montana. His new responsibilities required resignations from his posts at the Rural Life Bureau and the NCRLC. This change also coincided with the emergence of the Great Depression. As economic paralysis spread, faith in the American gospel of prosperity and confidence in the capitalist system waned. In addition, the early 1930s witnessed a reversal of the century-old, city-ward trend in migration. The larger number was now returning to the country. Many of these migrants aspired to be self-sufficient. The time was ripe for creative, radical thinking about the role of farming within the American culture and economy. The Italian-American priest Luigi Ligutti emerged in the 1930s to take on the more pastoral and parish-centered agrarian work of Fr. O'Hara. The philosophical and political aspects of the "Green Rising" in America would be taken up by the Jesuit priest John C. Rawe.

Rawe was born in 1900, near Carrollton, in central Illinois, the oldest of eight children. He grew up and worked

---

[13] Edwin V. O'Hara, "Why Attend the Conference?" *St. Isadore's Plow* 2, May 1924, 1.

on the family farm, taking on the tasks of large animal care. Graduating from the Carrollton public high school in 1918, he enrolled at St. Louis University, run by the Society of Jesus. In four years' time, he earned both a bachelor's and a master's degree in law. He also decided to enter the Jesuit order.

It was a time when the Society of Jesus was in full flower, growing in numbers and influence. Indeed, during the 1930s, the count of Americans in the order would surpass that of Spain, becoming the largest single national group. Jesuit training was rigorous, combining spiritual, philosophical, and military disciplines. As historian Peter McDonough writes, "the model was one of a muscular Christianity and imperturbable masculinity." As one novice of the era wrote, these were young men "grounded in the spirit of St. Ignatius—men of generous heart and powerful physical constitution equipped, themselves, to vanquish Satan and to snatch from the jaws of Hell souls who were made for Heaven and Happiness."[14]

Not coincidentally, the Jesuit seminaries in the Midwest were set in rural locations, such as the ones John Rawe attended in Florissant, Missouri, and St. Mary's, Kansas. These religious refuges, far removed from the corruptions of urban-industrial life, were well suited to nourish agrarian and distributist sentiments. As a husky farm boy with a good mind, John Rawe fit right in. The social encyclicals of recent popes also fed this American "Green Rising." *Rerum Novarum*, with its agrarian postulates, held special importance. Its message was amplified by *Quadragesimo Anno*,

[14] Peter McDonough, *Men Astutely Trained: A History of the Jesuits in the American Century* (New York: The Free Press, 1992), 144–59.

issued by Pope Pius XI in 1931. With the sweeping subtitle "On Reconstruction of the Social Order," the document called for new ways to secure "harmonious cooperation of the industries and professions,"[15] including those in the countryside. Specifics included affirmations of rural producer and consumer cooperatives, operated on democratic principles, as ways to reconcile family-scale farming with the larger economy.

From 1932 to 1936, John Rawe studied at St. Mary's Seminary in Kansas. He joined what has been described as a "zealous seminar of rural life advocates," so encouraging his vocational focus on agrarian restoration within a Christian framework. Members of this seminar helped to write "An Integrated Program of Social Order," published in 1935 by The Queen's Work forum in St. Louis. It was notable for its radical language, its specific policy platform, and its direct grounding in the papal encyclicals. This program labeled the Roman Catholic Church as the first and only supernatural organization. It called on Christian "comrades" everywhere to repudiate war, class conflict, all forms of human exploitation, and "unbridled competition." In ringing agrarian style, it proclaimed that the family was "a natural society" and also the primary unit of civil or public life, with "a right to soil and fireside." It was the duty of governments "to facilitate and further all that tends to stabilize a family [centered] economy." Taxation should be used to break up excessive concentrations of land and wealth. Farmers must be assured of "proper land distribution and land finance, making possible widespread

[15] Pius XI, *Quadragesimo Anno,* no. 81.

ownership of productive soil." They should also be guaranteed control over their "economic salvation, through marketing, purchasing, and credit organizations." Land speculation and industrialized farming should be banned.[16]

Ordained as a priest in 1935, Rawe also became active in the National Catholic Rural Life Conference. In a lengthy essay for *The American Review*, he praised the farming communes of the Catholic Workers' movement in the northeastern states, associated with Dorothy Day and Peter Maurin. He acknowledged the inspiration and concrete proposals provided by Hilaire Belloc and G. K. Chesterton in seeking to restore systems of small holdings. And he welcomed the work of the twelve "cultured Southerners" who produced in 1930 the volume *I'll Take My Stand: The South and the Agrarian Tradition.* He called the book a "trenchant" guide "to a saner, far happier, more correct way of living."[17]

Father Rawe quickly became active in such broader agrarian circles. In 1935/36, the American distributist historian Herbert Agar and the Southern poet Allen Tate compiled an agrarian manifesto entitled *Who Owns America? A New Declaration of Independence.* Father Rawe wrote the informal "Catholic essay" for the compilation. It focused on the flawed legal status of corporate business charters.[18] Rawe was one of three

---

[16] A Committee on Social Order of the Jesuit Provinces of the United States and Canada, *An Integrated Program of Social Order* (St. Louis, MO: The Queen's Work, 1943 [1935]), 8–9, 13, 17–18.

[17] John C. Rawe, "Agrarianism: The Basis for a Better Life," *The American Review* 6, December 1935, 180–81.

[18] John C. Rawe, "Agriculture and the Property State," in Herbert Agar and Allen Tate, *Who Owns America? A New Declaration of Independence* (Wilmington, DE: ISI Books, 1999 [1936]), 53–72.

Jesuits invited to attend a June 1936 meeting in Nashville, Tennessee, to promote "closer ties between the American and the English Distributists." The group chose him to serve as the recording secretary for the event. In this capacity, he drafted the "Report of the Platform Committee" which opposed "the denial of economic freedom" found in fascism, communism, *and* finance capitalism. The statement held "that the sacrifice of agriculture for the development of manufactures must be ended and recognition given to the primacy of agriculture in establishing a secure and desirable culture."[19]

Rawe was the common agent in the writing of two important agrarian manifestoes. In 1939, the NCRLC resolved to publish a *Manifesto on Rural Life.* The official authors were Aloisius Muench, the bishop of Fargo, North Dakota, and Vincent J. Ryan, soon to become the bishop of Bismarck. The real or "ghost" author was John Rawe.[20] A year later, he co-authored with Luigi Ligutti the so-called *Summa* of Catholic agrarianism: *Rural Roads to Security: America's Third Struggle for Freedom.* It was certainly the most explicit and thorough presentation of interwar Catholic thinking on these matters. My own review of the drafting of the manuscript clearly shows that while the more pastoral and practical sections of the book were drafted by Fr. Ligutti, the ideologically charged sections were the product of Fr. Rawe.[21]

---

[19] Published as: John C. Rawe, "The Agrarian Concept of Property," *The Modern Schoolman* 14, November 1936.

[20] Reported in: "Obituary: Reverend John C. Rawe, SJ," *The Province Newsletter [Missouri Province]* 16, October 1947, 106.

[21] *Manifesto on Rural Life* (St. Paul, MN: National Catholic Rural Life Conference, 1939); and Luigi Ligutti and John C. Rawe, *Rural Roads to Security: America's Third Struggle for Freedom* (Milwaukee, WI: Bruce, 1940).

In this robust advocacy for engagement in the American "Green Rising," Fr. Rawe focused on seven driving themes, all distinctive in certain ways to him. To begin with, he was an unabashed American. Among early twentieth-century Jesuits in the United States, the reputation of Europe's medieval era was high: the thirteenth had been the greatest of centuries. When turning to examples of well-ordered agrarian life, prior Jesuit writers also referred almost exclusively to European models, such as the Jobbist movement in Belgium or *Action Populaire* in France. Father Rawe, in contrast, stayed firmly in American history and precedents. As he wrote: "There is a wise, democratic Jeffersonian political economy in family-owned subsistence farming."[22] Rawe praised nineteenth-century American innovations such as the Homestead Act of 1862, which strongly encouraged settlement on the land by agricultural families, in contrast to earlier forms of public land sale which had favored speculators. He affirmed in particular the 160-acre model that took root in the Middle West, one specifically designed for "the support of the family." He repeatedly summoned "the great wisdom" of the American Founders "who made provision for a widely diffused freehold ownership" of land as the basis for their Republic.[23]

Second, Fr. Rawe called openly and frequently for a "Green Revolution"—his amplification of "Green

---

[22] Ligutti and Rawe, *Rural Roads to Security*, 308.

[23] Especially: John C. Rawe, "Life, Liberty, and the Pursuit of Happiness in Agriculture," address to the October 1936 session of the National Catholic Rural Life Conference, Fargo, North Dakota; in Series 8/1, Box 2, National Catholic Rural Life Archives, Marquette University, Milwaukee, WI. And John C. Rawe, "Agriculture—An Airplane Survey," *The Catholic Rural Life Bulletin* 3, February 1940.

Rising"—albeit one "far removed from the red rags of communist tyranny and the wriggling swastikas of frenzied [Nazi] dictatorships."[24] This revolution would be "Green" for it would take place on land rich in plant life and owned by "patient, productive, profitable, democratic, [and] free" farm families, seeking a "constitutional restoration of private property and personal rights."[25] In *Rural Roads to Security*, Rawe and Ligutti termed this revolution as America's "third struggle for liberty." The first had come in 1776 in reaction to British oppression which "threatened the human rights and happiness" of the American colonists. However, "liberty for all, Black and White," required a second war, this time in the 1860's—the Civil War. American liberties then fell prey to an alien "liberalistic system which Europe had fostered"—note the European origin here—that delivered "mammoth-scale industry, commercialized farms, human lives ground down by marvelous machines, efficiency substituted for liberty, money codes displacing justice, with God and his spirit forgotten."[26] A new, or third, American campaign for liberty must now occur, demanding "family unit operation and fee-simple, family-basis ownership of land based on religious principles."[27]

Third, in pursuing this restoration of an agrarian order, Fr. Rawe was stridently anti-urban, a theme hard for many to accept, then or now. Simply put, the city life that he observed was dehumanizing and sterile and especially hostile to

---

[24] Rawe, "Life, Liberty, and the Pursuit of Happiness in Agriculture," 18.
[25] Rawe, "Life, Liberty, and the Pursuit of Happiness in Agriculture," 18.
[26] Ligutti and Rawe, *Rural Roads to Security*, 9.
[27] Ligutti and Rawe, *Rural Roads to Security*, 3, 9–10.

Christian marriage and the birth of children. The true "roots of democracy," he argued, were to be found "in the country districts and in the rural cultures of America" that were grounded in vital families. In contrast, cities were "mere concentrated, collectivized aggregations of helpless, dependent individuals, a dying population." He described cities on the American East Coast as comprised of "congested housing, the families living in brick caves and canyons of steel and stone." Rawe despaired over "the gigantic size of the belching factories," the millions of persons wholly dependent on "low-wage incomes from subdivided, dehumanized, unskilled, monotonous" factory jobs, and the absence of children among deliberately sterile or "one child" couples.[28]

Fourth, Fr. Rawe also built a strong legal and historical case against the prevailing American corporate order. Initially trained in law, he focused on federal court decisions that had transformed commercial corporations into "artificial persons" bearing rights found in the U.S. Constitution. He deplored, in particular, the twisting of the Fourteenth Amendment from an instrument to guarantee "the liberation of the black man" into an opportunity "for the economic enslavement of both the white man and the black man." Court decisions striking down state laws seeking to restrain or dissolve corporate monopolies had, in his judgment, made joint stock corporations "a radically new danger in the history of mankind." Family and state, Rawe held, were "natural societies" while the Church was a "supernatural" one. In

[28] John C. Rawe, "Rural Life Conference Plans a Sound Democracy," *America* 64, 2 November 1943, 94; and John C. Rawe, "The Home on the land," *The Catholic Rural Life Bulletin* 2, February 1939, 24–25.

contrast, corporations were artificial and utilitarian, entitled to no more legal claims than those provided within specific state-granted charters. With the "dictatorial power and unrestrained greed" of commercial corporations now enjoying court-mandated protections, the only alternative was for the U.S. Congress and president to proceed against them as "internal enemies." As a key step in this "new cause of liberty," Rawe endorsed a proposed constitutional amendment that would end the treatment of corporations as "citizens."[29]

Fifth, as another positive remedy, Fr. Rawe held that the U.S. Constitution "implied the right and imposed the duty on government" to secure "distributism in private property" for real, human citizens. Families, not individuals, should be restored as "the basic economic unit." A form of progressive taxation should be used to break up great estates with absentee owners. The corporate ownership of farmland should be banned. The reason for such land reform was clear: "Rich acres and productive plants are safe only in the hands of a small owner . . . a family man, who can respect and cooperate with the laws of nature, make provision for crop rotation, prevent erosion, and give paternal care to the plants and animals that feed and shelter him and his loved ones."[30] Refugees from the cities would find a home on three-to-five acres to be an admirable site for part-time farming, allowing for a

---

[29] John C. Rawe, "Corporations and Human Liberty: A Study in Exploitation. I. Real and Artificial Persons," *The American Review* 4, January 1935, 255–71; and John C. Rawe, "Corporations and Human Liberty: A Study in Exploitation. II. Regaining the Rights of the Individual," *The American Review* 4, February 1935, 472–89.

[30] John C. Rawe, "Homesteading Solves the Problem of Farm Decline," *America* 60, 3 December 1938, 200.

high degree of self-sufficiency in food. The deeper goal was a rebirth of the American spirit grounded in a rich natural culture. As Fr. Rawe explained in a fine summary of the goals of the "Green Rising:" "The Agrarian wants a balanced life for all, lived out in a definite social tradition, a life in which religion, the arts, good manners, conversation, hospitality, sympathy, [and] family life" can thrive within "an equitable economy founded on the right relation of man to nature."[31]

Sixth, regarding families, Fr. Rawe emphasized their need to be refunctionalized to do things again. The urban-industrial family had weakened, as task after task was turned over to the commercial order or to the state. The results included fewer marriages, a plummeting birth rate, and frequent divorce. Rawe was insistent: "We must have a rising birth rate. We must have a new vitality in Christian home life and home culture." The "only way" to accomplish this, he argued, "is to provide for some family-centered production . . . where the child can soon become an economic asset instead of remaining an economic liability." Put another way, the children should be put to work at tasks appropriate to their ages. To help secure this end, Rawe said that every new housing development should be a "productive home" program, with housing resting on small acreages. Government-backed mortgages should require that new houses include workrooms and kitchens suitable for food preservation. Rawe held that recent technical innovations—the rural electrical grid, the small electric motor, the portable internal combustion engine—made such decentralization desirable, efficient,

[31] Rawe, "Agrarianism," 182.

and possible. In such homes, he concluded, families would find themselves surrounded by "independence, security, economic liberty, *and work-liberty*."[32]

Seventh, and finally, Fr. Rawe embraced biodynamic agriculture. This was the brainchild of the German polymath Rudolf Steiner. He held that a farm was healthy "only as it becomes an organism in itself," where the farmer stands "in living interaction" with larger ecological and spiritual realities.[33] Rawe tactfully dismissed those aspects of Steiner's approach that rested on a non-Christian spiritualism. However, he praised the biodynamic emphasis on organic procedures, composting, and soil health. He also celebrated the close attention to small but important things that biodynamic farmers brought to their work. For example, Rawe reported that the earthworm was a welcome visitor to a biodynamic farm, for this creature "is a connoisseur of the better soils."[34]

During the academic terms of 1938 and 1939, Fr. Rawe served on the faculties of St. Louis and Creighton Universities (the latter in Omaha), teaching philosophy, rural sociology, and economics.[35] He was then dispatched to New York City, where he became a founding member of the Institute of Social Order. This new organization, long in the planning, was "to encourage unification and coordination *of all*

---

[32] Rawe, "The Home on the Land," 25; Rawe, "Homesteading Solves the Problem of Rural Decline," 201. Emphasis in original.

[33] Rudolph Steiner, Agriculture: *Spiritual-Scientific Foundations for Agricultural Renewal* (Rudolf Steiner Press, 2024).

[34] John C. Rawe, "Biological Technology on the Land," *The Catholic Rural Life Bulletin* 2, August 1939, 21–22.

[35] Developments in John Rawe's life and work between 1938 and 1947, as reported here, come from the John C. Rawe files found in The Jesuit Archives and Research Center in St. Louis, Missouri.

the Jesuit forces . . . behind the movement to create a Christian Social Order" in the United States. Put another way, this national center for Catholic Social Action would be a "think tank" on how to implement the spirit and proposals found in *Rerum Novarum* and *Quadragesimo Anno.* Rawe became the ISO expert on Rural Life in America.

Unfortunately, he served the project for only six months. His experience there actually revealed the challenges facing Midwestern Catholic agrarianism within an overwhelmingly urban Catholic Church. For example, Fr. Rawe drafted passages for an ISO Teaching Curriculum, which included his usual criticisms of urban life: "Show some of the artificiality of city living, the crowded apartments, the artificial recreation, the absence of real family life"; and "Show the effect of apartment living and city life on the family, the falling birthrate, the ever growing selfishness even of Catholic families, standardization of everything from food to thought." However, inserted then in parentheses by his superior were deflating words: "This does not mean an attack on all city life," but only a rejection of extreme "urbanism."[36] Father Rawe's radical agrarian sentiments simply seemed out-of-place in a Manhattan-based institute, and he soon returned to Omaha.

John Rawe's last years bear a tragic symbolism, as failed projects and the onset of serious illness paralleled the disruptions of rural life brought on by the American entry into World War II. Back in Nebraska, a fine opportunity seemed to open when a Creighton University trustee donated the use

---

[36] John Rawe, "Institute of Social Order. Service Bulletin: Catholic Social Teaching through the Regular Curriculum," September 1940, box 3.0051, New York Province, Jesuit Archives-St. Louis.

of a 220-acre farm to create the Creighton University Rural Life Institute, with Fr. Rawe as director. This institute would provide a twelve-month course for a dozen young men seeking to become Catholic farmers. The curriculum was close to the director's heart, including sessions on "The Rural Family and the Way of Life on the Land," "The Family: Social and Economic Unit on the Farm," and "Production on the Farm for the Family," alongside the more practical subjects. Alas, the Japanese attack on Pearl Harbor occurred just as the institute was being launched. In less than a year, all of the initial students had been drafted into the military. Meanwhile, soaring food prices led the original owner to reclaim the farm for commercial production.

In 1943, Rawe's father provincial assigned him to serve as director of Farm and Rural Life at the Jesuit's Indian Mission in St. Stephens, Wyoming. His task was to guide Native American boys in the operation of the mission's 800-acre farm. Impressively, Fr. Rawe soon managed to produce a surplus of crops and animals for sale. However, a brutally cold winter took its toll. Fr. Rawe contacted severe blood poisoning and nearly died.

After a painful and never quite complete recovery, an influential fellow Jesuit arranged for Fr. Rawe to become the manager of rural life training for African-American boys at the Cardinal Gibbon's Institute, in St. Mary's County, Maryland. Rawe had already drafted the larger part of a new agrarian book, and his father superior assured him that his new duties would be light, allowing him ample time to finish the volume and do other writing. Alas, the assignment was a failure. In early 1946, Fr. Rawe reported that he had no working farm equipment, or help. Only eight students had enrolled in the program, and he was "teaching farming to boys who don't want it." He added: "I have not done any writing for the second book . . . since I have been here." In August 1947, Rawe's health collapsed, and he was hospitalized with anemia, a bad heart, and failing kidneys. He died on September 7 at the age of forty-six. His unfinished agrarian manuscript passed through several hands, with the trail disappearing at St. Mary's College.

How should John C. Rawe's career be assessed? In some obvious respects, his "Green Rising" failed. The Reconstructed Social Order of which he dreamed—factories decommissioned and cities shrunk, replaced by productive homesteads and family farms; commercial corporations stripped of unintended Constitutional rights; families broadly refunctionalized—these did not emerge. America after 1945 went in other directions: a vast industrial boom; densely packed suburban developments resting on hyper-consumerism; weak companionate marriages; a rapid consolidation of agriculture that saw a majority of farm families leave the land; and an expansion of the Constitutional rights of the great commercial corporations.

And yet, there are better ways to understand Fr. Rawe's legacy. Historian Peter McDonough notes that "Rawe wanted to restore a true Americanism" in and on the land, unlike other Catholic writers of the time who praised "a foreign model exhumed from an era" before Columbus. He adds: "Rawe's forte was the making of home[-centered] poetry out of a way of life."[37] Notre Dame historians Christopher Hamlin and John McGreevy find in Rawe's "Midwestern Catholicism" a distinct understanding of nature. Where others saw beauty and value in wild and scenic places, Fr. Rawe focused on "organic processes and temporal cycles." For him, nature was not sacred. However, "work in nature was sacramental." This aesthetic focused on "sky and soil, watching small parts of nature change through the seasons."[38] These were signs of the creative way in which John Rawe reconciled Christianity with the agrarian spirit in America.

In addition, Fr. Rawe grasped how political democracy absolutely depended on economic democracy, meaning the ownership of homes, farmland, woods, and tools by as many responsible families as possible. He stressed that strong marriages and the welcoming of children—that is, stable and large families—commonly required the cultivation of real tasks and real production within the home. And he clearly identified the dangers posed to family life and human flourishing by the institutions of a nearly lawless finance capitalism.

Today, Americans face a collapsing marriage system, a plummeting birthrate, the decay of a property-owning middle class, violent and ungovernable cities, a crisis of political democracy, and a legion of "woke" banks and corporations assaulting family, home, and Christian truth. Perhaps Fr. John Rawe's real legacy will lie in a rediscovery of his work by young, twenty-first-century Roman Catholics in America looking for a model of green agrarian living that boldly answers these challenges and is fully compatible with their faith.

---

[37] McDonough, *Men Astutely Trained*, 94.

[38] Christopher Hamlin and John T. McGreevy, "The Greening of America, Catholic Style, 1930-1950," *Environmental History* 11, July 2006, 484.

Works Cited

A Committee on Social Order of the Jesuit Provinces of the United States and Canada. *An Integrated Program of Social Order.* St. Louis, MO: The Queen's Work, 1943.

Baley, Liberty Hyde. *Report of the Country Life Commission.* U.S. Government Printing Office, 1909.

———. *The Holy Earth.* Ithaca: New York State College of Agriculture, 1980.

———. *What Is Democracy?* Ithaca: The Comstock Publishing Co., 1918.

Belloc, Hilaire. *The Servile State.* Indianapolis: Liberty Classics, 1977.

Bowers, William L. *The Country Life Movement in America, 1900-1920.* Port Washington: Kennikat Press, 1974.

Chesterton, Gilbert Keith. Introduction to Helen Douglas-Irvine. *The Making of Rural Europe.* London: George Allen and Unwin, 1923.

———. *What's Wrong with the World.* In *The Collected Works of G. K. Chesterton*, vol. 4, edited by George J. Marlin, Richard P. Rabatin, and John L. Swn. San Francisco: Ignatius Press, 1987.

Hamlin, Christopher and John T. McGreevy. "The Greening of America, Catholic Style, 1930-1950." *Environmental History* 11, July 2006.

Leo XIII, *Rerum Novarum*, https://www.vatican.va/content/leo-xiii/en/encyclicals/documents/hf_l-xiii_enc_15051891_rerum-novarum.html.

Ligutti, Luigi and John C. Rawe. *Rural Roads to Security: America's Third Struggle for Freedom.* Milwaukee, WI: Bruce, 1940.

McDonough, Peter. *Men Astutely Trained: A History of the Jesuits in the American Century.* New York: The Free Press, 1992.

"Obituary: Reverend John C. Rawe, SJ." *The Province Newsletter [Missouri Province]* 16, October 1947.

O'Hara, Edwin V. *The Church and the Country Community.* New York: Macmillan, 1927.

———. "Why Attend the Conference?" *St. Isadore's Plow 2,* May 1924.

Pius XI. *Quadragesimo Anno.* https://www.vatican.va/content/pius-xi/en/encyclicals/documents/hf_p-xi_enc_19310515_quadragesimo-anno.html.

Rawe, John C. "Agriculture—An Airplane Survey." *The Catholic Rural Life Bulletin* 3, February 1940.

———. "Agriculture and the Property State." In Herbert Agar and Allen Tate. *Who Owns America? A New Declaration of Independence.* Wilmington, DE: ISI Books, 1999.

———. "Agrarianism: The Basis for a Better Life." *The American Review* 6, December 1935.

———. "Biological Technology on the Land." *The Catholic Rural Life Bulletin* 2, August 1939.

———. "Corporations and Human Liberty: A Study in Exploitation. I. Real and Artificial Persons." *The American Review* 4, January 1935.

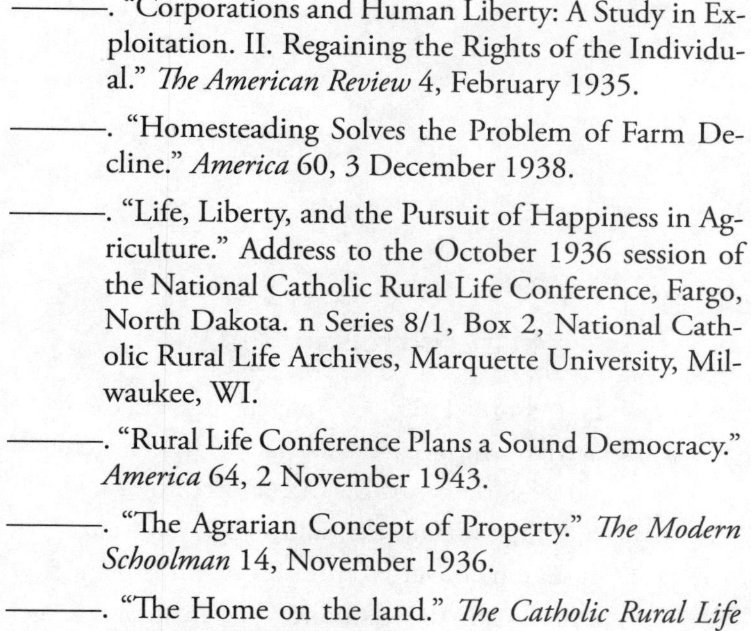

———. "Corporations and Human Liberty: A Study in Exploitation. II. Regaining the Rights of the Individual." *The American Review* 4, February 1935.

———. "Homesteading Solves the Problem of Farm Decline." *America* 60, 3 December 1938.

———. "Life, Liberty, and the Pursuit of Happiness in Agriculture." Address to the October 1936 session of the National Catholic Rural Life Conference, Fargo, North Dakota. n Series 8/1, Box 2, National Catholic Rural Life Archives, Marquette University, Milwaukee, WI.

———. "Rural Life Conference Plans a Sound Democracy." *America* 64, 2 November 1943.

———. "The Agrarian Concept of Property." *The Modern Schoolman* 14, November 1936.

———. "The Home on the land." *The Catholic Rural Life Bulletin* 2, February 1939.

Alan Harrelson, PhD

Alan Harrelson, PhD, completed his doctoral work at Mississippi State University. His research focuses on Southern intellectual and cultural history, with emphasis on the South's agrarian tradition. Harrelson converted from Protestantism and was confirmed in the Catholic Church in 2023. A native South Carolinian, Harrelson now lives on 200 acres in Kentucky with his wife and children. Although he taught history for several years, Harrelson is best known for his writings and video content on history, faith, and culture, which are published through his brand, The Pipe Cottage.

CHAPTER 3

SOUTHERN AGRARIANISM AND THE CATHOLIC CHURCH

Alan Harrelson

Have you ever wondered why modern life is so terrible? If so, the answer to that question is really quite simple. Most people living today come from nowhere, do not care to be from anywhere, and would not know how to be from somewhere if they tried. It's a landless, godless, silly generation that we currently inhabit. Speaking from a strictly "agrarian" point of view, a term that we must later define, the twenty-first century is perhaps the most strange, the most weird and disconcerting era of human history. Some things may be said in jest, but I think this particular point is the quintessence of tragedy, the likes of which the ancient writers could not have fathomed. Technology has all but destroyed our ability to speak, to write, to develop community, to contribute to the lives of others, to pray, to think, to simply be still and spend time with our God. Mindless, useless, technological entertainment now drives, motivates, and dictates values, morals, dreams, and expectations.

What is a Southern tradition of agrarianism? What's Southern about it? And why does it matter to use a regional adjective in the first place? Obviously, the South has no monopoly on good agricultural literature. Good literature is almost always going to tell us about the limits of our human condition and reflect the realities of life in a certain time and place. The South has a unique history and place within the confines of American society, and as such, the Southern past, including an experience of defeat, loss, and the search for continuity in a world of change, gives the South an instructive perspective from which to produce a lasting literary canon. Indeed, the three great contributions of the South to the world are its music, its literature, and the magnolia tree.

The Southern tradition is principally about agrarianism, a mode of life based on agriculture and landownership and thought to be superior to industrial, progress-centered societies and the subsequent deracination that often ensues. Agrarianism came into being during the modern era as a result of an industrial revolution that began in Europe almost simultaneously with European settlement and colonization of North America. One can find detractors of industrial ways of life on both sides of the Atlantic from at least the late eighteenth century to the present day. However, from the colonial period forward, the South alone among American regions has offered an impressively consistent and insightful series of literary warnings about the dangers of following a gospel of wealth and progress. Given this long history of defiance toward what is now mainstream American consumer culture, we may rightly recognize a Southern tradition of agrarianism and seek to learn from it.

A key example from the Antebellum Period should suffice to point out the deep-rooted tradition of agrarian thought in the South. Most readers are probably familiar with Thomas Jefferson's vision of the American future as a republic of self-sufficient farmers. But Jefferson wrote very little about it. John Taylor of Caroline County, Virginia, however, wrote much about this particular Jeffersonian vision. In his *Arator*, published in 1818, Taylor saw "agriculture as the guardian of liberty, as well as the mother of wealth."[1] Writing during a time of serious soil depletion and bad farming practices caused by tobacco and cotton monoculture, Taylor argued that "it is the office of agriculture, as an art, not to impoverish, but to fertilize the soil, and make it more useful than in its natural state."[2] This type of agricultural writing, as M. E. Bradford tells us, tends to "mix practical agricultural advise and moral reflection."[3] To be sure, the South has long produced some of America's greatest advocates of land conservation and what is now called "regenerative" farming. But more than that, agrarian thought in the South almost always teaches the value of not only soil conservation and proper land use but also agricultural work in the development of human character.

The term "Southern agrarianism" was coined during the late 1920s by a group of literary artists and scholars affiliated

1 John Taylor, *Arator: Being a Series of Agricultural Essays, Practical and Political, in Sixty-four Numbers* (LibertyClassics, 1977), 53.

2 Taylor, *Arator*, 68.

3 Taylor, *Arator*, 37.

to various degrees with Vanderbilt University. The Fugitive-Agrarians, as they were often called, fashioned a literary and intellectual movement intended to explain and defend the South's traditional farm culture in the midst of a growing industrial and corporate society. Their principal achievement, a collection of essays entitled *I'll Take My Stand*, was published in the fall of 1930 and received mixed reviews. The book sold approximately two thousand copies during the original publication but, quite amazingly, has remained in print ever since. Although written primarily for a Southern, regional audience, the book drew attention from readers around the Western world, including Hilaire Belloc and G. K. Chesterton. The Fugitive-Agrarians, not unlike the distributists before them, offered a well-articulated message about the dangers of a life removed from the soil and the natural world. Southern writers often resonated with this message in subsequent decades as farming and rural life continued to be far less common. Indeed, the message remains at least interesting, and sometimes compelling, to a growing number of readers today. But why?

Let me begin to answer that question with a description of where I composed these few scribblings. At the time of this writing, I was sitting in a hotel off the interstate in northern Kentucky as I made a two-day journey from my farm to Steubenville, Ohio, to give a talk on G. K. Chesterton and the time-honored art of pipe smoking. Outside my third-story window, I saw a legion of fast-paced automobiles rushing along I-75 in the foreground, the multitudinous smokestacks of industrial America on the horizon, a few airplanes carrying people away from the earth, and a sea of large retail stores, each promising consumer satisfaction with every new material purchase. Interestingly enough, a giant US flag towered above the nearby department store as a sort of symbol of all I surveyed, as if to say, "Welcome to twenty-first-century America."

This scene could be repeated in nearly every densely populated community in the US. Here, amidst the smokestacks and shopping centers, the busyness of the six-lane highway, the rush hour traffic, this is where our national economic and cultural standards now stem from. I look at this scene outside my hotel window and conclude we are now a society in a hurry to go nowhere. The automobiles carry husbands and wives away from their families to work for hours outside the home. The truck drivers will spend the night miles from their wife, children, and hearth. The local chain restaurants will offer nothing local, a plate of meat, vegetables, and breads shipped here from some distant, nameless farm and food processing facility. And even though the consumer culture gives most people a brief sense of joy and material contentment, at least until the next big thing arrives on the market, many Americans recognize a deep sense of dissatisfaction and emptiness, a longing for something more permanent and weathered. The Southern agrarian tradition admonishes us not to embrace trivial sources of contentment, such as temporary consumer satisfaction. Its history shows us how to go to war with our own complacency and to pursue truth, to search for meaning.

Within this context of buying, spending, and rootless living, the old warnings of Southern agrarianism whisper in our ears to say, "I told you so." John Crowe Ransom, one of the leading voices of the Southern agrarian movement, argued that the advent of modern salesmanship is a dangerous and powerful development. It's the basis of the consumer culture. If a businessman can persuade or convince another person, or persons, to buy a product or buy into an idea, even an idea about a product, then the businessman has achieved profit from a type of manipulation. The consumer culture cannot teach that the best interests of the consumer are paramount. If that were the case, businesses would create lasting products rather than gadgets and machines that are meant to break down and eventually require additional purchases in order to replace. Ransom knew that the great downfall of capitalism is human greed. Indeed, greed and self-interest is what helps make industrial capitalism work. And it is precisely this expression of greed and self-interest that the Fugitive-Agrarians took a stand against nearly a century ago.

The problems outlined by the Vanderbilt writers in the early twentieth century are far worse now, and their voices beckon to be heard. And at least a few people might be willing to listen. The agrarians outlined three core problems with an industrial society. First, industrial societies foster consumption as the most important result of human work and production. One works to buy machines that save time, time that is in turn used for nothing, for an aimless life. As Ransom asserted, "Modern man has lost his sense of vocation."[4] This has certainly become a major problem in American

---

[4] John Crowe Ransom, "A Statement of Principles," introduction to *I'll Take My Stand* (Louisiana State University Press, 1977), xlii.

culture. Children are taught to expect entertainment from technology, from screens primarily. When those options are unavailable or taken away for a short time, boredom ensues (an intensely modern issue that is not really an issue at all). Russell Kirk called this a lack of moral imagination. Children, and sometimes adults, must learn to appreciate the beauty and wonder of the natural world. One must cultivate the imagination through reading, conversation with learned and wise people, and such things as a simple walk through an ancient forest. To devote the bulk of our time to earning money for the sake of consumer purchases does not allow for this imagination to develop.

The second, and arguably the most important, criticism levied by the agrarians was that industrial society does not promote a flourishing religion. Industrialism approaches nature as that which is to be controlled and harnessed for the sake of wealth and progress. It is not seen as creation, and we as humans are not taught to recognize our own limitations. Indeed, over the past near century since the agrarians published their primary work, mainstream American culture has continued to promulgate the notion that one can be whatever they want to be, the sky is the limit, there are no boundaries if only the dream is big enough. This is not true, and it has never been true. It does not matter how bad someone wants to be Michael Jordan and shoot hoops for a living, it is not possible for one to simply become the best at random tasks through sheer willpower and determination. It is human nature to seek power, influence, and wealth. Industrial societies are built on such insatiable desires. It is terribly difficult for a religious culture, which requires humility and servitude, to thrive in the context of an economy that teaches material gain as the ultimate reality.

Finally, the agrarians believed an industrial society is incapable of cultivating human creativity, art, and good manners. To build a proper farm requires creativity. Industrial, consumer-oriented economies focus on personal gain, individual achievement at the expense of almost anything else, especially a moral creativity. There is a fine line between what corporations will do to gain a dollar and what is illegal business practice. Morality has little to do with the way most businesses within a market-oriented economy "do business." The pursuit of power, wealth, and influence supersedes the pursuit of genuine leisure, manners, and civility. Essentially, the Southern agrarian message was and has always been in favor of rural and agricultural life as the best and perhaps only human context through which a good-mannered and civilized community of people can thrive and reproduce itself in a meaningful way. The agrarians made the interesting point that a good farmer and landowner has to be a good artist, a reflection of the Original Artist who created the earth to begin with. Laying out a working homestead, deciding where the best fields are for certain crops, making sure one's home is safe, comfortable, and beautiful requires the work and talent of an artist. The agrarian philosophy about agriculture reflects the position of ancient writer Cato the Elder who wrote that among the greatest accolades offered to man is that he had become a good farmer.[5] And to be a good farmer means to recognize, as Wendell Berry put it,

[5] Marcus Cato, *De Agri Cultura [On Agriculture]*, line 2.

"the gift of good land,"[6] and, if I might add, the poetry and rhythm found in the simple change of seasons.

It might be necessary to point out that Southern agrarianism is not the same as modern, leftist environmentalist thought. To see the natural world, the soil, the landscape as part of a created order is far different than seeing nature as a thing to be cherished to the point of worship, which, for all intents and purposes, is a result of the intensely secular attitude of modern environmentalism. To be sure, secular environmentalists now influence major policies in American government, and they do so largely because the idea of protecting the environment *from humanity* offers a sense of moral superiority beyond the true morality of religion, which these people want nothing to do with. Truth is a Person who withheld ultimate power to perform a sacrificial task. Modern Man, as the Fugitive-Agrarian writer Andrew Lytle called it, craves and seeks power and money above all things.

In my mind at least, if Southern agrarian ideas were finally joined to the teachings about creation offered by the Catholic Church, a better way to encourage proper thinking about agricultural and rural life in our time could not be imagined. Fugitive-Agrarian Allen Tate made a similar point in his contribution to *I'll Take My Stand*. In "Remarks on the Southern Religion," Tate made the argument that the largely aristocratic South failed in its attempt to preserve a traditional, land-based way of life because it lacked a medieval religion—namely, the Catholic Church. Tate saw

---

6 See Wendell Berry, *The Gift of Good Land: Further Essays Cultural and Agricultural*.

Protestantism as a materialistic faith, unable to adapt to what some scholars referred to as the South's essentially pre-modern and pre-capitalist genius. In Tate's mind, the South lost the Civil War in part because it was not primarily Catholic. Whether or not history would bear this out is doubtful, as it is mere speculation. And while Tate was not yet a religious man when he wrote his essay in 1930, he eventually did join the Catholic Church in 1951 after an extended intellectual journey. He believed that the Catholic Church was the best hope to restore a traditional rural culture both regionally and nationally. The point still holds merit for our time.

For the message of the Southern agrarians to have a continued practical effect on the way we approach rural work and rural life, we must rethink what it means to pursue such avenues of living in today's culture and economy. The issues today are no longer the problems that spurned agrarian writers of the South to action during the early to mid-twentieth century. We live in a post-industrial society. Most of the industrial businesses that the Vanderbilt agrarians feared are themselves now fringe sources of local and national income. The United States is now a service-based economy with ample opportunities for people to earn a living in myriad ways, with more sources and combinations of income than has ever existed in human history. This is largely the result of increased technology and internet capabilities. G. K. Chesterton once made the argument that if a society truly wanted a return to a past form of society, it is entirely possible to turn back the clock and return to that society. The question, according to Chesterton, is never if it's possible but if it's truly desirable. Few if any people today wish to return to a life without electricity, running water, tractors, diapers, recent medical science, automobiles, and the many conveniences of current society. And for those who would wish that we could turn back the clock, it is doubtful many of those people could actually survive in a pre-modern world, if for no other reason than the skillsets *and mindsets* necessary for such a life are now largely lost to us.

So what do we do? What's the solution for those who want a more simple way of life, for those who want more responsibility for providing the little everyday necessities of food, joy, hearth, and home? Allen Tate said in the late 1920s that the South, still reeling from the Civil War and trying to make sense of that conflict, was at a crossroads and needed to decide which elements of the past to carry forward and which ones to leave behind. We are now at another crossroads moment, but it's not simply a Southern moment. It's probably not simply an American moment. Societies and cultures around the world are trying to find a way back to a more simple way of life that allows closer proximity to the natural order of things. In short, many people instinctively know that something is wrong or at least missing in their lives.

Many of the cultural, religious, and philosophical underpinnings that the Southern agrarians used to explain/defend traditional rural life in the 1930s remain relevant now, but the response has to be altered. The Southern agrarians' practical advice for readers of the early twentieth century was to stay on the land and continue to live simple, mostly unmechanized lives. A major goal was to help convince the rural South to remain so. As a result of WWI, many young people were deciding to leave the land to pursue professions and careers that could offer more discretionary income and technological conveniences. But the situation of rural America has changed drastically since the 1930s. Indeed, most people who now decide to live a more simple, agricultural lifestyle are at least two generations removed from people in their own families who once farmed for a living. Not only does this mean that many of the old skillsets are lost to us, but it means that one must be willing to make some serious sacrifices if a land-based lifestyle is to now be achieved either by individuals or families.

The Southern agrarians, and most notably Wendell Berry in more recent decades, argued that the best way to preserve a rural society is to stay put. The agrarians thought Southern rural families should remain on the land, hopefully ancestral family land. Berry has since argued much the same, based on the correct belief that rootedness and sense of place are of supreme importance. None of this is wrong, but it's not enough in itself as a way to suggest a path forward for those who want a land-based lifestyle today.

A cardinal point that I think more agrarian writers should consider is how necessary it is for hopeful farmers and homesteaders to be willing to relocate, even if that means moving a considerable distance to find a community of like-minded rural Americans, and quite frankly, a *rural* community of any real sort. And let us not forget that resettlement played a major role in the development of rural America's history to begin with. Contrary to what many of us were taught in grade school, most of this country was not settled by folks seeking religious liberty. Most people came here, and continued to do so through the nineteenth century, because they wanted land, the basis of any true and meaningful financial and family freedom. What is now called the American South was settled over the course of several hundred years by families seeking greater opportunities for land ownership. Until fairly recently in American history, self-sufficiency and independence were based on land ownership, not stock investments, diverse financial portfolios, or job security.

Some may think this is an insignificant point, but I think people who are tradition-minded are also the same people who seek to learn from historical and/or current agrarian ideas, and relocating does not come easy. It's difficult to leave extended family and friends for the sake of one's dreams of an agricultural lifestyle. Relocation is not necessary for everyone, but I think for most, it has to be an option. Indeed, it may be the only option. The United States' population is overwhelmingly urban, and many "rural" communities are becoming little more than victims of urban sprawl. This is especially the case in the most popular areas of the South. The simple fact is most Southerners, and Americans overall, now live either in urban areas or places very near urban areas. Land prices and the general price of living in those areas are much higher compared to more intensely rural places that do not offer the same conveniences or typical economic opportunities.

Emphasis on typical. Critics of the Southern agrarians frequently point to the fact that most of them had little real farm experience and made a living from the academy rather than the soil. But we must remember that, with perhaps the exception of Donald Davidson and Andrew Lytle, the Southern agrarian movement was a relatively small period within the context of individual literary and teaching careers. Perhaps one of the more important, practical lessons of the Southern agrarians stems from the various ways they had to capitalize on their individual talents in order to make a living. Agrarian writers and thinkers of that era did not have the ability to work remotely as we do now. Even though these were among the most significant writers of rural America during their time, they did what was necessary to put food on the table and a shelter over their heads. If they had the ability to live and work remotely from a piece of rural acreage, I am satisfied most of them would have seized the opportunity. In other words, prior to the advent of the internet and the technologies we now enjoy, even the most articulate and dedicated advocates of agriculture had to live and work anywhere they could earn a decent living, usually close to urban centers. Such restraints were once typical. Not so today.

While the Southern agrarians were principally concerned with preserving the South's rural/agrarian identity and its historical/regional consciousness, their writings help us better understand how to be from somewhere. Their collective work brings to mind Wendell Berry's quote, "What I stand for is what I stand on."[7] *I'll Take My Stand* remains in print today in part because of this cardinal principle of place that Berry so pointedly reiterates.

We must do a better job of connecting the mindset necessary for agrarianism to thrive with the practical lifestyle objectives that such a mindset should be designed to facilitate. The Southern agrarians were writing at the beginning

---

[7] See Wendell Berry, *What I Stand for Is What I Stand On* (Penguin Classics, 2021).

of the rise of our current system of industrial agriculture. They were prescient enough to realize the pitfalls of this system. But they could not have foreseen the full spectrum of problems caused by this system in the twenty-first century. Today we live in a country of massive obesity and health problems caused by diets that result from industrial agribusiness. While the Southern agrarians can help us understand the philosophy and cultural implications of an agricultural lifestyle, their writings alone are not enough to convince us to prioritize home food production, which, at the end of the day, should be a major goal of anyone calling themselves agrarian. Armchair agrarianism is almost useless. Agrarian ideas should produce practical results. In this regard, we need less talk and more action.

The Southern agrarians were hopeful that their fellow Southerners would take courageous action against industrialism. Their "Statement of Principles" ended with a charge, "For, in conclusion, this much is clear: If a community, or a section, or a race, or an age is groaning under industrialism, and well aware that it is an evil dispensation, it must find the way to throw it off."[8] The charge ends with a warning that was a key point for the whole project, "To think that this cannot be done is pusillanimous. And if the whole community, section, race, or age thinks it cannot be done, then it has simply lost its political genius and doomed itself to impotence."[9] Few, if any, took the charge seriously. Looking

---

8 Ransom, "A Statement of Principles," introduction to *I'll Take My Stand*, xlviii.

9 Ransom, "A Statement of Principles," introduction to *I'll Take My Stand*, xlviii.

at the movement from the vantage point of 1980, Andrew Lytle wrote, "So the Agrarians failed. We failed at least to make any practical impact upon the amoeba-like growth of the machine and its technology . . . none is prepared for the violent revolution which changes the nature of the familiar."[10]

But just because something once failed does not mean it is unworthy of reconsideration. Chesterton made the point well, "The task of modern idealists is made much too easy for them by the fact that they are always taught that if a thing has been defeated it has been disproved. Logically, the case is quite clearly the other way. The lost causes are exactly those which might have saved the world."[11] If we could imagine Chesterton speaking encouragement to Mr. Lytle in 1980, we could rightly imagine him repeating his own line that "the great ideals of the past failed not by being outlived (which must mean over-lived,) but by not being lived enough."[12] If Chesterton was right, and I think he was, then the vision cast by the Southern agrarians continues to have unrealized value. But it would be incorrect to simply say such a vision was that of a regional agrarianism. As Davidson and Lytle eventually came to see, as well as Richard Weaver and M. E. Bradford in their respective explanations of Southern agrarianism in later decades, the lost cause in question was not the Confederacy, nor was it the Southern agrarian movement: the cause was nothing less than the

---

[10] Andrew Nelson Lytle, *From Eden to Babylon: The Social and Political Essays of Andrew Nelson Lytle* (Regnery Gateway, 1990), 185.

[11] Gilbert Keith Chesterton, *What's Wrong with the World* (Cassell, 1910), 36.

[12] Chesterton, *What's Wrong with the World*, 39.

preservation of a historical and principally religious interpretation of what a truly civilized society should be. Each writer and thinker involved in this Southern agrarian effort in the years succeeding the publication of *I'll Take My Stand* knew almost instinctively that the South was in a particularly unique position to help make sense of a society actively moving away from its rural base to the much different basis of urban thought and work.

After studying Southern intellectual and cultural history for twenty years now, and if there is some small contribution I am now able to make on the topic of agrarian thought in the South (both past and present), I would argue that if the historical principles of Southern agrarianism are worthy of both rediscovery and reconsideration, then those principles would be best articulated and possibly realized through Catholicism. I do not think Protestant Christianity is the ship capable of carrying us back across the sea of mistakes instituted by modern man. This includes the serious mistake of looking at nature, God's creation, as something only to be conquered into submission for whatever consumer and/or materialist purposes we demand from it. One of the chief points of modern economics, and a point mentioned in any high school or college-level Protestant textbook I've seen, is that land is capital. Few, if any, students, even among our Christian schools and universities, are taught that land is far more than that.

The Southern agrarian tradition, as espoused by the Fugitive poets, is based on a religious worldview and does not make sense without it. Indeed, the focus on religion is a hallmark of Southern agrarianism that separates it in a real way from other approaches to rural life and understandings of nature. While Southern agrarianism held a few things in common with the earlier intellectual movements of American romanticism and New England transcendentalism, most notably reservations about the Industrial Revolution and its impact on the natural world, the dissimilarities outweigh any similarities. (No Southern farmstead had a "Walden's Pond.")

North Carolina native Richard Weaver, a Southern agrarian writer in his own right, explained these dissimilarities in his essay "The Older Religiousness in the South." Weaver argued that the South's Christianity was, from the beginning, intensely orthodox, suggesting "there was much in its religious attitude to recall the period before the Reformation."[13] Weaver pitted North against South by showing how "New Englanders cultivated metaphysics and sharp speculation." The South, on the other hand, remained solidly "inimical to the spirit of rationalism." Weaver believed the South was the greatest expositor of American Thomism. He argued that the South's religion reflected Aquinas's idea that it is crucial to have "some form of knowledge which will stand above the welter of earthly change and bear witness that God is superior to accident." For Weaver, and for the Fugitive poets before him, people in the South looked at nearly every aspect of human existence through the lens of orthodox Christianity, including how best to look at nature and how to steward a piece of land. This is quite different from a literary or intellectual tradition that approaches

---

[13] Richard M. Weaver, "The Older Religiousness in the South," Sewanee Review 51 (1943): 237–49.

nature from a worldview where religion is either subsidiary or non-existent.

I have three reasons to think Southern agrarianism needs the Catholic Church. First, Catholicism offers a necessary formality. A great loss of the last one hundred years of American history is the decline of formality in most all aspects of life, from academics, to relationships, to language, and to dress. Formality offers direction, a sense of respect, cohesion, and a unique meaning to what is being accomplished and to the pursuit of a desired goal. The Church is and should be focused on eternal matters, but the Church also serves as a massive storehouse of standards and expectations that give real form to questions of how to behave, how to treat God and our fellow man, and how to approach nature as the created order.

Secondly, the Church had been taking a stand against modern philosophies and views about humanity and the natural world long before a Southern agrarian movement came into being. At best, Southern agrarian thought articulated for an American audience those same issues of deracination and secular humanism that the Church had been defending itself against since at least the Reformation. The South was, and to some degree remains, a most anti-modern society within the most modern of nations: Catholicism is a most pre-modern and, quite frequently and quite rightly, an anti-modern religion. One must remember that the Fugitive poets were fairly young scholars during the late 1920s when their movement began. They had in fact tuned in to a much older intellectual and philosophical conflict between an orthodox Christian view of humanity and that of nominalism and existentialism, for example. But as the Fugitive poets grew older, their subsequent writings often placed Southern agrarianism within its proper context, as a serious American defense of this nation as heir to a great Western tradition.

To elaborate further on this point, we can learn much from the perspective of Eugene Genovese, among the greatest historians of the South and a devout Catholic to boot. In his 1994 publication *The Southern Tradition*, Genovese suggested that "Catholic spokesmen, like southern-conservative spokesmen, do not attack markets per se. They recognize that markets, especially in earlier times, have served as meeting places for face-to-face exchange of goods and had a civilizing function."[14] After quoting Pope Leo XIII and Pope John Paul II on this very topic, Genovese concluded that both Catholics and Southern agrarians "protest against the transformation of the market, especially with the rise of a world market, into an impersonal arena in which human relations themselves are treated as commodities."[15] A global market continues to dominate our money system at the expense of local, home-based economies. The commodification of human relationships plagues us still.

The third reason is that mainstream American Protestantism cannot stand against the alienation that currently plagues our rootless culture. Recall the old expression about being too heavenly minded to be any earthly good. Protestantism in the American South has become a multi-million

---

[14] Eugene D. Genovese, *The Southern Tradition: The Achievement and Limitations of an American Conservatism* (Harvard University Press, 1994), 15.

[15] Genovese, *The Southern Tradition*, 15.

dollar megachurch industry that seeks quantity of people "saved" over the quality of discipleship offered. This is not universally true, but it is the principal trajectory of American Protestant denominations. Pastors often make decisions based on corporate business models: ministry must serve a large customer base in order to make the largest profit. A spirit of entrepreneurial competitiveness has become a central focus of too many Protestant communities in the South. Things that should not matter tend to matter entirely too much (how large the congregation is, how big the buildings are, how more advanced a youth ministry is compared to the church next door, the list goes on and on). By its very nature, Protestantism denies the authority of ancient tradition and is often incapable and/or unwilling to learn from it, which, in turn, makes it the perfect American religion. It is intensely presentist and futuristic. This is not to say that Protestants are not our brothers and sisters in Christ, nor is it to say that such people are not bringing others to the Kingdom. The point is, Protestantism does not have sufficient depth of tradition and historical experience to adequately meet the cultural and intellectual challenges of our increasingly secular, money-driven, and progressive American society. Donald Davidson thought the agrarian South to be the final stronghold of Western civilization in America. And Flannery O'Connor was right when she said the day might come when the spiritual traditions of the South are best preserved within the Catholic Church. We are at that moment, and probably have been for some time.

Anyone who wants to live a rural lifestyle now needs to do it because there is a real desire to do so. It cannot be done for the sole purpose of making money. The small farm can return. But it will take a change in mindset. Agrarianism can promote a philosophy, be thought and written about infinitely, articulated by the finest literary artists, but it's still about farming, the production of wholesome food within the context of a wholesome life. Let us not be armchair agrarians. The purpose of good ideas is to produce good action that results in good existence. A better American culture, one that makes a return to the land, will never happen as long as we merely think and write about farming without doing it.

My first and most powerful dream as a boy was to be a farmer. (Getting a PhD was not a dream, just a goal.) When I look back at my tradition, I see Cato the Elder, Virgil, Jefferson, the Southern agrarians, my South Carolina tobacco-farming grandparents. The most accomplished, educated, and astute thinkers have always known that agriculture is a most serious topic worthy of the mightiest pen. But let us not simply write. Let us put our hands to the plow.

Richard Weaver, mentioned previously in this essay, and arguably the greatest student of the Southern agrarians, presciently noticed in the early 1940s that the agrarian South was in danger of vanishing. In his 1943 dissertation *The Southern Tradition at Bay*, Weaver said that "the agrarian South, close to the soil and disciplined in expectation, has never behaved as the spoiled child. . . . It accepts the unchangeable and hopes that it is providential. This acceptance of nature, with an awareness of the persistence of tragedy, is the first element of spirituality, and a first lesson of the bewildered modern who, amid the wreckage of systems, confesses inability to understand the world."[16] Weaver looked at the South as it was eighty years after the fall of the Confederacy and concluded it still possessed "the mind of a religious agrarian order in struggle against the forces of modernism."[17] But much has changed in the eighty years since Weaver penned these words. And maybe South Carolina poet Archibald Rutledge was just as prescient when he wrote approximately the same moment as Weaver that, somehow, there are quite a few people in the South who have become insufficiently Southern.

Historian Jack Temple Kirby argued in *Rural Worlds Lost* that the South witnessed a "seismic shift" away from agrarian life between 1920 and 1960.[18] He rightly pointed out that this shift away from a predominantly agricultural and rural society happened to the South much later than other Western cultures. My own doctoral research dealt with this issue in great detail, but I do not have the occasion to explain the historical narrative of the rural South's twentieth-century decline for our current purposes. Here's the main point: The memory and sympathy for old times remains strong in the South, and its story is well-suited to help encourage current and future men and women of fortitude who do not accept the false standards of secular humanism and the deracination inherent to American modernism. If America is to once again believe in the time-honored merits of a "religious

---

[16] Richard M. Weaver, *The Southern Tradition at Bay: A History of Postbellum Thought* (Skyhorse Publishing, 2021), xvii–xviii.

[17] Weaver, *The Southern Tradition at Bay*, xxviii.

[18] See Jack Temple Kirby, *Rural Worlds Lost: The American South, 1920-1960* (LSU Press, 1987).

agrarian order," then it will need both the South and the Catholic Church to do it.

Works Cited

Chesterton, Gilbert Keith. *What's Wrong with the World.* Cassell, 1910.

Genovese, Eugene D. *The Southern Tradition: The Achievement and Limitations of an American Conservatism.* Harvard University Press, 1994.

Kirby, Jack Temple. *Rural Worlds Lost: The American South, 1920-1960.* LSU Press, 1987.

Marcus Cato, *De Agri Cultura [On Agriculture].*

Taylor, John. *Arator: Being a Series of Agricultural Essays, Practical and Political, in Sixty-four Numbers.* Liberty Classics, 1977.

Ransom, John Crowe. "A Statement of Principles." Introduction to *I'll Take My Stand.* Louisiana State University Press, 1977.

Taylor, John. *Arator: Being a Series of Agricultural Essays, Practical and Political, in Sixty-four Numbers.* Liberty Classics, 1977.

Weaver, Richard M. "The Older Religiousness in the South." *Sewanee Review* 51 (1943): 237–49.

———. *The Southern Tradition at Bay: A History of Postbellum Thought.* Skyhorse Publishing, 2021.

Colin Miller, PhD

Colin Miller, PhD, is a Catholic Worker and the Director of the Center for Catholic Social Thought in St. Paul, Minnesota. He received his doctorate in theology from Duke University in 2010 under Stanley Hauerwas, having previously studied at Yale and the University of Minnesota. He has taught at various universities, usually as an adjunct, and most recently at DeSales University in Pennsylvania. He stays active academically by occasionally publishing in journals such as *Church Life Journal, Communio*, and *New Polity*, and he is recently the author of *We Are Only Saved Together: Living the Revolutionary Vision of Dorothy Day and the Catholic Worker Movement* (Ave Maria Press). A former Episcopal priest, Colin converted to Catholicism in 2016 under the influence of John Henry Newman, Dorothy Day, Peter Maurin, and life in a Catholic Worker house. He has been on staff at Church of the Assumption since 2019, and lives with his wife and five children in Minneapolis at the Maurin House (maurinhouse.com).

CHAPTER 4

THE AGRARIAN HEART OF THE CATHOLIC WORKER MOVEMENT

Colin Miller

The Catholic Worker Movement, founded by Dorothy Day and Peter Maurin in New York City in 1933, is best known for its houses of hospitality and its often heroic practice of the works of mercy. The movement consists of (1) houses of hospitality for sheltering, feeding, and clothing the poor (and in general sharing life with them); (2) "clarification of thought" on the social issues of the day, aided by group discussion and newspapers/pamphleteering; and (3) farming communes or a back-to-the-land movement to cut at the problems of industrial society at their root.

This program is meant to provide a uniquely Catholic alternative way of life to the American industrial-techno-capitalist status quo, while allowing for the participation of all sorts of people of goodwill, Catholic or not. As such, the movement has always attracted a wide range of enthusiasts, from secular left-wing activists looking for a space to put their convictions into action, to orthodox Catholics (like Maurin and Day) trying to live out the Sermon on the Mount and realize the life of the first Christians. This diversity can sometimes lead to a rift between those Catholic Workers looking primarily for a political counter-culture and those who identify more strongly as Catholics.

Yet what many on both sides of the movement, as well as many looking in from outside, have often not sufficiently appreciated is that it is an *agrarian* vision that animates *all* of Maurin's program, including its evaluation of modern life, and its proposals for the future. The land is the heart of the Catholic Worker, in the sense that it is the source from which its trenchant critiques flow and the ultimate destination towards which it is always propelling us. Maurin does not just tell us what is wrong but why it is wrong and where we should be going, and he knows all this because he knows the difference agriculture makes. The Worker is thus fundamentally a back-to-the land movement built on the conviction that the industrial capitalist order is fundamentally opposed to human flourishing as well as to the practice of the Faith.

But it's not just that industrial society is opposed in a general way to "Christian civilization," whatever that might mean. More urgently, it often subtly makes living the gospel extremely difficult for each one of us every day. In a thousand practical ways, it frustrates the pursuit of sanctity, fragments community life, and marginalizes the Church. Faced with this reality, Maurin's genius was to devise a plan of attack that did not require that Christians *first* re-take the world from the top-down by winning the culture wars, or by going back to the middle-ages but, on the model of the early Christians, by simply starting to live the gospel here and now—to, as he said, "build a new society within the shell of the old."[1] The Catholic Worker's core contribution to American agrarianism is a unique fusion of farming and deep Catholic commitment in a plan of practical action that, finally, does not just tell us where we should be going but how to get there as well. The purpose of this essay is to lay out the essential and distinctive features of this unique vision.

I have been referring to *Maurin's* program. This is in no way to detract from the inestimable significance of Dorothy Day, or any other important personalities, in the history and development of the Catholic Worker. It is, rather, simply to acknowledge what Day herself often underlined: that it was Maurin who was the real founder of the Catholic Worker. And Day was right, at least in terms of theological vision and intellectual grounding. It was Maurin who gave Day her theological education and "a Catholic view of history,"[2] it was he who had read deeply in social and cultural theory and whose three-point program would become the backbone of the movement. None of this vision, to be sure, would have ever gotten off the ground practically speaking, and no one would have ever heard of Maurin, if it weren't for Day's organizational and journalistic gifts; she quickly and understandably became the face of the movement, and is rightly considered its co-founder. But Dorothy's pre-Catholic

---

1 Peter Maurin, "The C.P. and the C.M.", accessed June 7, 2024, available at catholicworker.org/easy-essays-html/#the-cp-and-cm.

2 Dorothy Day, *All the Way to Heaven: The Selected Letters of Dorothy Day*, ed. Robert Ellsberg (New York: Image Books, 2010), 66.

radicalism would have never been Catholicized in the first place—we would have never had Dorothy Day either—if it weren't for Peter Maurin.

This is doubly true when it comes to the Worker's agrarian heart. Few have seen the social *and* spiritual problems of his day (or ours) as clearly as Maurin did, but this is only because he rightly traced them to their root in the recent breakup of the land-and-craft economy that had been the only other economy the world had ever known. Maurin's peasant upbringing in France, subsequently sharpened by voracious reading in both secular and Catholic cultural criticism, provided him this unique perspective. For this reason, this essay will be mostly Maurin-centric. But this provides us with a unique vantage. For if an agrarian vision and critique is at the center of the movement, and if no one since has surpassed Maurin's articulation of it, then what follows has some claim to be the core of the core of the Catholic Worker—its heart. And, of course, the only reason any of this is interesting is because it is still so profoundly relevant and inspiring for us today.

And the farms themselves are, indeed, a present, living reality, if not nearly as widespread as Maurin would have hoped. The Catholic Worker website lists twenty-five current farms across the US and three overseas.[3] Like the movement in general, these show a wide diversity both in outlook and in terms of physical plant, from a single family on a half-acre producing almost all of their own food, to larger plots

[3] "Catholic Worker Farms," The Catholic Worker, accessed May 23, 2024, https://catholicworker.org/catholic-worker-farms/?paged=1.

run by singles. Many are long-time establishments run by veterans of the movement, but new and youthful energy is not far to seek, nor a variety of different projects and means of support.

So, for example, the recently founded John Paul II Catholic Worker farm in Kansas City, Missouri, is run by a twenty-something married couple, recently both converts to Catholicism from the radical left. The latter includes with it the "Peter Maurin Academy for Regenerative Studies," a vibrant operation focusing on online courses and discussions about Catholic Worker philosophy and tradition. Elsewhere, the Lake City Catholic Worker, in southwest Minnesota, run by a middle-aged married couple, includes a large house for guests built entirely from sustainable and recycled materials, perennial agriculture, and the "John the Baptist Beverage Company," which supports the farm by selling kombucha. And the agrarian spirit often finds itself a place even in the movement's urban houses of hospitality, such as my own, with backyards put as far as possible to productive use ("urban homestead" is probably claiming too much), sometimes with a flock of chickens, large gardens, permaculture, compost, or woodsheds.

As Dorothy Day wrote, in getting people back to the land, "Peter saw the solution to all the ills of the world: unemployment, delinquency, destitute old age, man's rootlessness, lack of room for growing families, and hunger."[4] What follows will be just a brief account of why he thought this was

---

4 Dorothy Day, "Communitarian Farms," in *Loaves and Fishes* (Maryknoll, NY: Orbis Books, 1963), 44.

the case. We'll look, first, at three important sources for the Worker's critique of industrialism: Karl Marx, Artur Penty, and Emmanuel Mounier. Next, we'll highlight the ways the movement adopted the agrarian impulse in the Church's teaching, especially in its propagation of *Rerum Novarum* and *Quadragesimo Anno*. Finally, we'll look in more detail at Maurin's own vision for the Catholic "green revolution."

The Critique of Industrialism

Maurin contended with socialists, communists, Marxists, capitalists, and individualists, as he variously names the positions that he wishes to distinguish from his own. He did this in an idiosyncratic genre he called the "Easy Essay." These were short, poem-like statements of basic positions in socio-cultural and political philosophy designed to distill complex matters for the man in the street. In these, he sometimes offered his own creative criticism of the world that industrial capitalism had created, but more often, he simply takes over a variety of critiques of industrialism already widely available at the time. With these, he was largely sympathetic, and his writing often assumes the reader is familiar and sympathetic with them too. Often, he'll reference a number of positions by one name each, for the sake of locating the Catholic Worker's own anti-industrial program within those accounts.

Karl Marx is certainly an important one of these positions. But Marx is doubly important in that he is perhaps the most widespread single backdrop for the context of the social thought and practice into which Maurin and the Catholic Worker spoke. Everyone knew Marx, at least by caricature, and many in great detail. If you were critical of the present order, then Marx was a source that could help you, even if you didn't endorse his more general philosophy or his prospective program. If you wanted to preserve the status quo, you had to frame your case against him. If you were just one of the rabble, you at least had some notion of what he stood for and against. Maurin himself was certainly well acquainted with Marx.[5]

What is not always recognized, however, is that Marx had a considerable appreciation for agrarianism. His radical critique of the injustices and deformations of capitalism are at the same time largely critiques of industrialism. He is from this perspective not unlike his contemporary Pope Leo XIII (to whom we shall come), lodging a massive complaint about what he saw happening to the world around him. To be sure, industrialization is at the heart of Marx's hopes for the dawning of communism that would bend the machine to its own ends. But he has more than a little nostalgia for and sometimes explicit endorsement of the feudal system he at other times castigates. At times he expressly (and rightly) recognizes the unity of capitalism and industrialism, so that it is notoriously unclear how he thinks they could be uncoupled in the future.[6] This means that in practice, Marx is as little a friend to industrialism as he is to capitalism and

---

[5] He had read at least *Capital* and the *Communist Manifesto.* See Peter Maurin, *The Forgotten Radical: Easy Essays from the Catholic Worker*, ed. Lincoln Rice (New York: Fordham University Press), 48–52. This volume is now the most complete collection of Maurin's essays and other materials. Unless otherwise indicated, citations of Maurin's work below are taken from it.

[6] Karl Marx, *The Communist Manifesto,* in *The Marx-Engels Reader*, ed. Robert C. Tucket (New York: W.W. Norton & Co., 1978), 341.

he is as withering against the one as the other. Some of his account of industrialism is particularly relevant to what would become the Catholic Workers' emphases, especially on the topic of labor.

Marx saw better than perhaps anyone else the dignity of labor and the, we might say, anthropological changes it undergoes in the transition to an industrial economy of commodity production. Under industrialism, he points out, workers no longer produce things that they have personal relations and attachments to and that they use and consume in their own everyday lives. They now produce commodities, which are entirely abstract and interchangeable because they are defined solely by exchange value. Put differently, the thoroughly abstract substance called "money" is the ontology of commodities and homologizes the once-important differences between hand-crafts, and so between workers as well.[7] More simply, when work is done in a factory, all work becomes practically the same—able to be done by anyone. The very nature of labor therefore changes. Work is not constituted, as in agrarian societies, by a personal relation to the objects one produces, lives from, surrounds oneself with, and consumes; one no longer lives in a world that she crafted. Workers are interchangeable, and commodities can be produced by anyone who is plugged into the same station at the factory.

Labor then, Marx rightly sees, for the first time in history becomes an abstract concept. [8] What was once a personal, loving, if grueling, *particular task*, almost always constituted

---

7 Marx, *The Communist Manifesto,* in *The Marx-Engels Reader*, 178.

8 Marx, *Wage Labor and Capital*, in *The Marx-Engels Reader*, 201–2.

by (and constituting) a particular place, time, material, custom, level of society, and place in the gender line, becomes generalized, and so a concept like "labor power" becomes thinkable. This is what the industrial laborer has to offer on the market, it is all he has, and it is a commodity like any other. He sells his labor power, and the object of his labor power (what he has made) is then taken away from him to be sold.[9] He is thus alienated from his labor and also from the personal nature of life that in previous times always reflected his own creative ordering. As a result of specialization gone crazy (which is the same dynamic as the homogenizing power that creates abstract work), the unique personal skill of the worker becomes worthless.[10]

It is hard to overestimate the historical significance of this, as well as the implications for each individual. For, Marx shows, in a more general way, the industrial worker is also alienated from his *whole life*. As opposed to the peasant, the farmer, or the artisan, whose creative work *is* his life and vocation, under industrialism the exercise of labor power, labor, is the worker's own life-activity, the manifestation of his own life. And this *life-activity* he sells to another person in order to secure the necessary *means of subsistence*. Thus his activity is for him only a means to enable him to exist. He works in order to live. He does not even reckon labor as part of his life, it is rather a sacrifice of his life. It is a commodity which he has made over to another.[11]

---

[9] Marx, *Wage Labor and Capital*, in *The Marx-Engels Reader*, 169.

[10] Marx, *Wage Labor and Capital*, in *The Marx-Engels Reader*, 187–88.

[11] Marx, *Wage Labor and Capital*, in *The Marx-Engels Reader*, 170–71, italics original.

Industrialism is a degradation of humanity previously unknown, for it is the transformation of what humans spend most of their time doing, working, into an impersonal, meaningless act that he finds compensated for with nothing but wages, which are not even themselves a partaking of the proceeds of his work, but are part of an already existing commodity with which the capitalist buys labor power as a commodity.

A slavery of a new kind results. On the one hand, because selling his labor power is now his only means to even exist, the worker cannot abandon the capitalist without renouncing his existence; he is therefore a slave to him. On the other hand, humans have become things (Marx calls it "reification"—"thing-ification")—just another part of the factory machinery, as well as mere commodities themselves—and where a human being is a thing, it too becomes property, and so humans become slaves in this way as well.[12] Leo XIII may have simply been echoing Marx then, when he said industrialism was in many cases "little better than slavery itself."[13]

Moreover, Marx points out, the homogenization of work—the creation of labor as an abstract category—is also an assault on gender differences. As Ivan Illich would later put it, picking up on this theme from Marx, gender in traditional, agrarian societies was constituted by a certain overlapping, asymmetric, complementarity: some tasks, tools, places, and times were assigned to men, and others to women. This meant that most of the world was a "gendered"

---

[12] Marx, *Wage Labor and Capital*, in *The Marx-Engels Reader*, 239.

[13] Leo XIII, *Rerum Novarum*, no. 3.

reality, with gender differences attaching to things, language, and even knowledge itself. But once factory work—and its modern analogues—make any work accessible to any human being, the gendered world is replaced by neutered *roles* that can be played by anyone.

Inasmuch as such gender-and-work grounded a whole way of life, industrial capitalism's abstraction of labor destroyed a way of life millennia old. But it is also, Marx noted, simply intolerant of tradition in general, in favor of the constantly novel. The demand for ever-new products is the motor that drives production, and so no sooner can any tradition re-establish itself than it becomes the prey of ever new ways of doing things. For industrialism is not merely a new way of producing goods, but of producing constantly new forms of life. In this way, at the hands of the machine, "venerable tradition is swept away," and "all that is solid melts into thin air, and all that is holy is profaned."[14] The international result has been a cultural war of industrial change, and commodities are the artillery.[15]

The implications for the life of local communities (which, prior to industrialism, were really the only forms of community—industrialism created mass society) are implied in all of this: no society could sustain the breakup of their traditions, religious practices, and modes of production, which always formed one vital whole, without collapsing and becoming something completely different. In so remaking human community, industrialism changed, in a way, what

[14] Marx, *The Communist Manifesto,* in *The Marx-Engels Reader*, 338.

[15] Marx, *The Communist Manifesto,* in *The Marx-Engels Reader*, 339.

it is to be human. And Marx points out that this is at least in part because of the fragmentation that occurs as citizens come increasingly to relate to each other solely in the act of exchange of abstract commodities. Direct relations between people in real flesh-and-blood gives way to a society held together by the market, where relationships are relations between products.[16] As such, the bonds of society (if they can be called bonds) become naked self-interest,[17] and even family relations are re-thought in terms of money.[18] Human action itself comes to be seen as the action of our products, the iron economic laws which rule us rather than us ruling them.[19] Marx would not have been surprised at the atomization we experience today.

In all these ways, industrialism set the background of oppression that the Catholic Worker sought to address. But the movement also took an important philosophical point from Marx that Maurin often underlined: the inseparability of our spiritual lives from their material basis. Marx had of course come close to saying that religion, morality, the flow of history, philosophy, and even conscious thought itself were *nothing but* the disguised results of the purely material social relations of the means of production. This is obviously a position no Catholic could hold. Yet in it, Maurin saw an important truth related to the sacramental nature of all reality: human beings are morally, spiritually, psychologically, and somatically shaped to a great extent by

16 Marx, *Wage Labor and Capital*, in *The Marx-Engels Reader*, 217.
17 Marx, *The Communist Manifesto,* in *The Marx-Engels Reader*, 334.
18 Marx, *The Communist Manifesto,* in *The Marx-Engels Reader*, 334.
19 Marx, *The Communist Manifesto,* in *The Marx-Engels Reader*, 219.

our contingent historical and material surroundings, including the kind of activity we find ourselves engaged in every day. Human beings are, Maurin might say, always in large part products of their social context.[20] Being a Christian is not therefore just about individual acts of piety and interior exercises but, especially under industrialism, consists in the project of remaking our material surroundings, including our community, as a necessary part of remaking our souls. We can't do one without the other, and this is why Maurin called the attempt to separate the material from the spiritual, as so many Catholics at the time were in the habit of doing, the biggest error of modern times. It was this recognition that increasingly led him towards the land.

I have labored at this length on Marx because his contribution to the discontent with industrialism that inspired agrarian movements like the Catholic Worker is often not sufficiently appreciated. Of course his own positive materialist philosophy as well as his political vision has rightly been criticized by the Church as incompatible with central Christian tenants, and of course his work ended up being socially and institutionally embodied in regimes of unspeakable horror. Yet the horror and suffering caused by the regime he was criticizing has on a global scale not been incomparable. There is no doubt that in Catholic circles, his work (and probably his person) have been unnecessarily villainized, and there is no reason we cannot learn from his significant insights.

Arthur Penty (1875–1937) was an English architect and consort of the better-known English distributists such

---

20 Maurin, "CM," 351.

as Chesterton and Belloc. I include him here as a significant and representative influence on Maurin's thought for the opposite reason I included Marx: Marx influenced the movement if in no other way than simply by being "in the cultural air." Chesterton and Belloc were also relatively well known, at least among Catholics. Penty, on the other hand, is an intellect of the first rate known to very few, but whose influence on the movement through Maurin was deep, especially in the area of agrarian distributists.

Penty wrote prolifically, but we know two of his works were especially important for Maurin. *A Guildsman's Interpretation of History* (1920) is a long, ingenious subversive re-writing of Marx's *Capital* from a Catholic "medievalist" and distributist perspective at times (intentionally?) reminiscent of Augustine's own re-writing of Roman history in *The City of God.* Against Marx's contention that capitalism is a relatively late phenomenon, roughly subsequent to feudalism and penultimate only to history's socialist/communist goal, Penty casts the whole of the pre-Christian classical world as capitalist, and its attendant development of a money economy as responsible for its incessant wars and social discord. It was only the coming of Christianity and its communitarian economic practices, showcased in the opening chapters of the Acts of the Apostles, that redirected humanity back towards its primordial unity: "it sought, as it were, by a strong appeal to what was centripetal in his nature, to counteract the natural centrifugal tendencies in man."[21] Indeed for Penty,

---

[21] Arthur Penty, *A Guildsman's Interpretation of History* (London: George Allen and Unwin, 1920), 36.

Christianity always was simply meant to *be* this totalizing economic and social impulse.[22] While the radicality of the apostolic age eventually waned, the communitarian impulse lived on in many usually-unrecognized forms such as monasticism, medieval village life, feudalism, and eventually in the creation of the guilds. Only with the coming of industrialism in the wake of the Reformation was such a communal economy, and especially the guilds, slowly uprooted and the path paved for a neo-pagan return to the old capitalism that ruled before the coming of Christ.

The guilds, Penty assumes you know, were a sort of non-socialist way of socially controlling the economy. Each particular craft, art, or profession in each particular locale formed a body (a guild) that set prices, quality standards, limited production, oversaw training, procured the raw materials, and regulated the local market (in the sense of a literal *place* of commerce). Apprenticeship in a craft involved a standardized process overseen by the masters, and those who did not abide by the guild standards were excluded from the market, and so simply could not make a living. Guilds were regulated and animated (at various removes, of course) by the various (and sometimes variant) moral and economic teachings of the Church, which made one's work of one piece with moral and religious life, and thus bound the small, local community together in the pursuit of a tangible set of tangled common goods. In this way, property was privately owned but socially controlled. Guilds were thus one important part of the distributist practice of a wide and equitable distribution

[22] Penty, *A Guildsman's Interpretation of History*, 34–46.

of the ownership of the means of production and a political map marked by decentralized nodes of genuinely local authority of government, jurisdiction, and administration.

Following Penty, guilds were paramount in the land-based economic vision of the Catholic Worker. A certain division of labor, trade, and mutual supply will be an essential part of any economy of even the most independent homesteaders, and if such trade is not to be a mere turning back the clock to an earlier stage in the development of liberalism, it will have to be the local community that regulates the means of production according to its sense of the common good. This was what Maurin called a *functional* economy, wherein a common vision of a local form of life set the terms for production rather than the market determining a form of life. Such functional economies, in Maurin's vision, following Penty, would inevitably be craft- and trade-based, with production centering first in households and agriculture, and then regionally and in urban life in support of this agrarian economy.

In *Post-Industrialism* (1922), Penty argued at length why such a land- and craft-based economy was the only alternative to the industrial status quo, and why a mere reform of industrialism would not suffice. Penty's architectural training had made him keenly aware of the way that our material environments shape and determine the moral and spiritual possibilities of our lives. Moreover, material objects and indeed the development of new technologies have a certain logic of their own that tends to become the logic of their human users (as Jacques Ellul would later argue), rather than being "mere" instruments under their control.

Thus for Penty, the central problem of modern times was not capitalism per se but "the relation of men to machines."[23] This is what Marx and the socialists had overlooked when they opposed capitalism with a merely economic centralization.[24] Marx was right that the logic of the machine under capitalism would only lead to social disintegration but wrong to think it could be redirected into industrial socialism.[25] So Penty suggests that the logic of the development of the machine *just is* the logic of capitalism: finance follows the evolution of technology.[26] This, in turn, predictably calls forth socialism (at least as an ideal) as a way of trying to get a handle on the social disintegration brought on by the free market and the machine.

Penty describes this disintegration with a clarity that is still impressive and relevant today. The logic of industry, that bigger and more is always better, must, he thinks, lead to chronic over-production that can only find its satisfaction in ever-new foreign markets. This, in turn, could only lead to a militarism necessary to ensure those markets. As such, Penty sees that one major motor that drives industry, as we subsequently experienced during the course of the twentieth century, is the development of weapons used to ensure its own continuance. War and industry thus serve each other, as was obvious to Penty in the wake of the First World War:

23 Arthur Penty, *Post Industrialism* (London: George Allen & Unwin ltd, 1922), 41.

24 Penty, *Post Industrialism*, 34.

25 Penty, *Post Industrialism*, 32.

26 Penty, *Post Industrialism*, 36.

both form one single "cult of mechanism."[27] Or, as Maurin later put it: when "people began to produce for profits they became wealth-producing maniacs. When people became wealth-producing maniacs they produced too much wealth. When people found out that they had produced too much wealth they went on an orgy of wealth-destruction and destroyed ten million lives besides."[28]

Thus for Penty industry signaled the coming of a permanent and perpetual revolution; not one, as many claimed, that would foster a new civilization, but one that constantly overturns it: "What follows in the wake of the machine is chaos and confusion."[29] Art, in the broad sense of creative human work—philosophy, architecture, music, handicrafts, carpentry, husbandry, food preparation—is degraded, since the assembly line cannot reproduce human craftsmanship, but only a dull mechanical shadow of it. Such creative work—true culture—"cannot exist apart from life"; art must be a part of everyday life, so that work, culture, and moral formation are coextensive.[30]

For Penty, replacement of the daily work of art by the machine, as Marx had claimed, changes the nature of work.[31] It also destroys the unity of life, for we no longer find the pleasures of life *in* our work, and so we have to reach for "mechanical amusements."[32] Moreover, trying to

---

[27] Penty, *Post Industrialism*, 36–38.

[28] Peter Maurin, "Mechanized Labor," accessed June 10, 2024, https://catholicworker.org/easy-essays-html/#mechanized-labor.

[29] Penty, *Post Industrialism*, 39–40.

[30] Penty, *Post Industrialism*, 46.

[31] Penty, *Post Industrialism*, 47.

[32] Penty, *Post Industrialism*, 46.

compensate for the factory's moral and intellectual torpor, we invented something called "education," which Penty thus reveals as another industrial product. In other words:

> The links which bound culture and life are broken, and they cannot be repaired so long as man remains a slave of the machine. And so all art and culture disappear from life, for it cannot be kept alive by the [educated] few. All must share it or none. If any art is to revive, it must be an art that is the common possession of the whole people, and such an art cannot be grafted onto a machine society. On the contrary, the arts (if we may so call them) that a machine population can share, are the arts of the cinemas and the gramophone, and the only culture is the culture of mechanism, whether it be motor-cars or aeroplanes . . . they are the arts of plutocracy.[33]

Far more than any materialist philosophy, then, for Penty the machine is the real cause of the modern rejection of Christianity.[34] It has degraded morals and, he helps us see, separated religion from a whole way of life it used to unite and animate. "Religion" is no longer, as Maurin would put it, the "cult" that is inseparable from "culture" and "cultivation"—as inseparable in practice as the three terms are linguistically. Rather, under industrialism, "religion" becomes what it is today: a private realm of arbitrary individual beliefs or sentiments, which, being confined to itself, leaves

33 Penty, *Post Industrialism*, 47.
34 Penty, *Post Industrialism*, 48.

most of life without meaning or inherent order. As such, the machine has created an inhuman world, robbing everyone of a baseline sense of wellbeing so that man becomes "a bed of live nerves ever stretched to high tension."[35] Marx was wrong, thinks Penty, that the means of production have always dominated and determined human nature, but he was right that they do so today.[36]

The final major contributor to the Catholic Worker's critique of industrialism we shall examine is Emmanuel Mounier (1905–1950), the leader of the French personalist movement and founder of the journal *Esprit*. A Catholic himself, Mounier was perhaps the greatest single contemporary influence on Maurin outside of official Catholic social teaching. Along with the latter, Mounier's "personalism" contributed much of the positive vision animating the Worker's program, to complement the more negative critiques like those of Marx and Penty (which, to be sure, always stand on a positive, though often implicit, vision of their own). Maurin recommended especially Mounier's *Personalist Manifesto* and his (still untranslated) article on the "Personalist Revolution." And though Maurin in practice adopted many different labels for his thought, including especially his advocacy of Mounier's "communitarianism," Maurin once said that the two most important ones were "Catholic" and "personalist."

The *Personalist Manifesto* is clearly intended to articulate a social and political alternative to both Marx's *Communist*

---

35 Penty, *Post Industrialism*, 49.

36 Penty, *Post Industrialism*, 49–50.

Manifesto and the regnant industrial capitalism. He penned further articles in this same vein on the "Communitarian Revolution" and the "Personalist and Communitarian Revolution." The leading idea in all this is that modern society in both its capitalist and socialist guises produces a mass of passive automatons devoid of that personal initiative, creativity, self-organization, and self-direction that characterize human flourishing.

The reign of the machine is a prime culprit here, especially insofar as it institutionalized the separation of spirit from matter so that a Cartesian "dead" matter replaced the "living" matter of the guilds, where work was mixed with prayer and "people never thought of [matter] except in its living relation to man."[37] The factory or the cubical has thus stripped the human person of his inherently creative teleological impulse and made of him yet another appendage of the means of production.

This mechanization of the person is driven by the ascendency of the bourgeois virtues of comfort, power, security, ease, and the elimination of suffering at all costs. "For [the bourgeois] there is only prosperity, health, common sense, balance, sweetness of life, comfort."[38] Such a character, for Mounier, is in fact a direct descendent of the true Christian ideal of sanctity, though now become progressively corrupted by chivalry, Protestantism, and capitalism. Thus, though culture was at one time rooted directly in the gospel, achieving today's bourgeois ideals requires the suppression of all

[37] Emmanuel Mounier, *A Personalist Manifesto* (New York: Longmans, 1938), 21.

[38] Mounier, *A Personalist Manifesto*, 18.

spirituality.[39] Over time, we have "come to the tyranny of the merely mechanical: by reducing man to an abstract individuality without vocation, without responsibility, without resistance, bourgeois individualism became the responsible harbinger of the reign of gold, that is, of the anonymous society that is impersonal in its exercise of power."[40] From this society we have all inherited first bourgeois humanity, then bourgeois morality, and now, worst of all, bourgeois Christianity.

As opposed to this anxious, surfeited, risk-averse machine society, for Mounier the development of true personhood requires a process of detachment and internal dispossession, facilitating objective contact with nature and communion with others.[41] There is not a little salutary Romanticism here, which the Catholic Worker often echoes, including a fundamental "affirmation of mystery"[42] in life and work. Unlike the technocratic bourgeois who never transcends the merely material, the personalist and communitarian's work is precisely that which facilitates the infusion of the divine into the mundane: "It is above themselves and outside themselves that artists and thinkers and savants must go to recognize the spiritual reality—pictorial, musical, etc.—that they put into their works. There is only one possible means of communication between this reality and man, and that is personal mediation. Every work, every culture that aims at

39 Mounier, *A Personalist Manifesto*, 16–17.
40 Mounier, *A Personalist Manifesto*, 26.
41 Mounier, *A Personalist Manifesto*, 75–81.
42 Mounier, *A Personalist Manifesto*, 81.

less than this reality must ever remain a minor work or a minor culture."[43]

Thus, for Mounier, in spite of what some commentators have said, today's mass industrial conformism is the farthest thing from the triumph of Nietzsche's strong individual superman: "If we want to study community decay today, it is not a Nietzschean world that we confront, but rather a faceless society. . . . Each person gradually abandons himself to the anonymity of the world of the masses. The modern world is this collective collapse, this massive depersonalization."[44] Community in Mounier's day, as our own, had become mere collective homogeneity, a false community of mechanical "connectedness" aided by the speed of transportation and the "togetherness" of "Managed Information Agencies" (or what we would call "information technology").[45] The very idea of "communion" is corrupted, for there are no longer any others who are different than myself to commune with:

> Commune with each other? There are no more, no more *others.* There is no more neighbor, only duplicates. Dull couples, where each rubs shoulders with the partner in a vulgar and distracted consent to standardized habits . . . grouped by circumstances or functions, not by events or choices. A bland amalgamation of the readers of the daily tabloids, and all these

[43] Mounier, *A Personalist Manifesto*, 158.

[44] Mounier, "Révolution Communautaire," *Esprit* 3, no. 28, January 1935, 549, author's translation. The phrase I have rendered "world of the masses" is *monde de l'on*, more literally "the world of the one."

[45] Mounier, "Révolution Communautaire," 551.

> precipitates mixed in a big city, suspended, unstable: a drop of chance has agglomerated them, a drop of chance will dissipate them. This is the desolation of the man without interior dimensions, incapable of real encounters. . . . The world of the masses is below the threshold marked by the first traces of community.[46]

What is most needed today, for Mounier, in direct opposition to industrial society's lethargic conformism, is personalist leaders who will take the initiative in creating new forms of communitarian society. This is a theme that Maurin often echoed: "The communitarian movement stands for personalist leadership. . . . A Leader is a fellow who refuses to be crazy the way everybody else is crazy and tries to be crazy in his own crazy way."[47] Rather than waiting for governments or institutions to tell them what to do, to manage their lives for them, people must organize themselves. Again Maurin: "If the best kind of government is self-government, then the best kind of organization is self-organization. When the organizers try to organize the unorganized, then the organizers don't organize themselves. And when the organizers don't organize themselves, nobody organizes himself, and when nobody organizes himself, nothing is organized."[48]

---

[46] Mounier, "Révolution Communautaire," 551, AT. "Daily tabloids" renders "Paris Soir," a popular Paris newspaper.

[47] Maurin, "The C.P. and the C.M.", accessed May 24, 2024, catholicworker.org/easy-essays-html/#looking-for-leadership and "Self-Organization," accessed May 24, 2024, available at http://www.easyessays.org/self-organization/.

[48] Maurin, "Self-Organization."

We'll return to this personalist theme, and the deep connections Maurin saw between it and agrarianism, in our final section.

The Agrarian Foreground of *Rerum Novarum* and *Quadragesimo Anno*

Surely the strongest encouragement for the Catholic Worker's land movement, however, came from that agrarian Catholic vision that was given fresh legs in the social encyclicals *Rerum Novarum* (1891) and *Quadragesimo Anno* (1931). The general import of these documents is well known, so here I will merely underline what is often missed, or at least downplayed, in these encyclicals, but that Maurin rightly saw as their center: a return to a society based on farming and crafts.

Perhaps the most obvious theme in *Rerum Novarum* is advocacy for widely distributed "private" property. This, it is often pointed out, is an alternative to both capitalism and communism, both in terms of property ownership and juridical structure.[49] For years this "third way" has been known as "distributism" and has more recently happily been rebranded by the much more intuitive "localism."[50] What is not always appreciated about this localism is that property

[49] For the best exhibition of what decentralized government looks like, see Andrew Williard Jones, *Before Church and State: A Study of Social Order in the Sacramental Kingdom of St. Louis IX* (Steubenville: Emmaus Academic, 2017).

[50] See Dale Ahlquist and Michael Warren Davis, eds., *Localism: Coming Home to Catholic Social Teaching* (Manchester, NH: Sophia Institute Press, 2024).

ownership and juridical decentralization are only desirable as part of a general return of a large part of society to the land from the factories and to the country from the cities. For the *purpose* of property, Leo XIII makes abundantly clear, is to return to that state of relative economic independence and self-sufficiency that was from time immemorial enjoyed by the vast majority of people in history: the peasants. Without denying peasants' manifold hardships, Leo recognized that it was the movement away from the land that degraded labor, stifled creativity, made the worker entirely dependent upon either the capitalist or the state, and so reduced him to a "condition little better than slavery itself" (§3). The conclusion, Maurin saw very clearly, was to go back to the land.

Property, therefore, for Leo, means, broadly speaking, the "permanent instruments of production" to which man is entitled as a rational being (§6): land, animals, dwellings, tools, furnishings, and all those things that are necessary for the maintenance of the substance of his own body and that of his progeny "from the earth and its fruits" (§7). One's children, for instance, should be able to keep themselves "decently from want and misery amid the uncertainties of this mortal life. In no other way can a father effect this except by the ownership of productive property, which he can transmit to his children by inheritance" (§13). Such property thus becomes "properly" one's own because one puts, as it were, the impress of his personality on it (§8).

It was obvious to Maurin that in light of the social and economic turmoil of the Great Depression, it was the land and only the land that could provide this security on a society-wide basis. Catholic Worker farms, therefore, were designed to immediately put into practice the pope's teaching in an immediately practical way, by allowing the destitute to go directly back to the land. To aid this process, Maurin underlined Leo's exhortation to employers to pay their workers not only a family wage but an additional amount that can be put away. For the laborer to earn enough to build up savings was thus not only a matter of just remuneration in the abstract but part of a strategy allowing industrial workers to move toward "obtaining a share in the land" (§47, cf. §5).

Rerum Novarum had thus quietly affirmed small farms and a craft-based society as *the* Catholic social vision. It had only mentioned the guilds briefly (§49), as the economic infrastructure necessary to make this sustainable. Elaborating the place of the guilds was a central task, therefore, taken up by Pius XI in *Quadragesimo Anno* in 1931. Pius first repeats and affirms the program of *Rerum Novarum* and then proceeds to elaborate upon it. He notes that since Leo's time, things had gotten even worse, since "through the evil of what we have termed 'individualism' [i.e., capitalism] . . . following upon the overthrow and near extinction of that rich social life which was once highly developed through associations of various kinds, there remain virtually only individuals and the state" (§78). Such statist-individualism was made possible only by the destruction of workman's associations.

By "associations," he makes abundantly clear at various points, he means economic organization on the model of the guilds (see §29–33). He also calls them (confusingly for English-speaking Americans) "industries or professions" (§83) and makes it clear that the agrarian vision of Leo required this kind of non-socialist social control of the means of production. Otherwise, the result of a return to the land would simply be a turning of the clock back to a slightly earlier time in the development of industrial capitalism. A renewed land-based population would then simply fall prey to the machine all over again. To avoid this regression, guild-like associations would once again have to be developed in which communities could protect themselves.

On the other hand, by reaffirming Leo's emphasis on productive property and the land (§61), Pius implied that modern "unions," while required as stop-gaps by the exigencies of the time (as also affirmed by Leo), could only do so much, and at worst were only an underwriting of the industrial status quo. Maurin constantly affirmed this and was correspondingly cool on the question of unions.[51] Without the guilds, there could be no permanent land movement; without a return to the land, the guilds were just welfare capitalism. A comprehensive Catholic alternative takes both. Pius does not say this in so many words, but it's the logic of his position, and (more importantly for our purposes) exactly the one that Peter Maurin propagated.

Distinctives of the Catholic Worker Land Movement

Much of the above was adopted in one way or another by the Catholic Worker. Its unique interaction with Marx, Penty, Mounier, and the encyclicals has already indicated a lot about the characteristic shape and temperament of the movement. Anyone who is familiar with its history will recognize in these thinkers and their works a substantial

[51] Maurin, "Commercializers of Labor," 33.

amount of the Worker's patrimony. It remains to spell out its own distinctive traits in a bit more detail by reference to Maurin himself and the farms he inspired.

In 1949, the Worker collected and published many of Maurin's Easy Essays in a single volume, called *Catholic Radicalism: Phrased Essays for the Green Revolution.*[52] The title says a lot. First, it captures the vision that the Church *herself*, especially when properly placed on its agrarian moorings, is a truly radical alternative to other social and political options. Maurin would often emphasize that this land-radicalism was the only radicalism truly deserving of the name, since to be radical is to be *rooted.* He accordingly dismissed Catholics who styled themselves as conservative, seeing so little in the present order worth conserving. Thus, in place of the communist Red Revolution stood the Catholic "Green Revolution." This referred not, of course, to the industrialization of agriculture, but the very opposite: the return to a society that was green in the sense of being based on small landholdings. And there was another sense in which Maurin's revolution was green as well: he saw a compelling model for it among the medieval *Irish*: "The only way to prevent a Red Revolution is to promote a Green Revolution . . . to make them look up to Green Ireland of the seventh century."[53]

At the most general level, the Catholic Worker land movement was a response, as Maurin saw, to "the separation of the spiritual from the material [that] is at the base of the

---

[52] New York: Catholic Worker Books, 1949.

[53] Peter Maurin, "America and Russia," in *The Forgotten Radical Peter Maurin: Easy Essays from the Catholic Worker*. (Fordham University Press, 2020), 127.

modern chaos."[54] By failing to recognize that Christianity could only be practiced as an embodied, historical, communal reality, Christians have created a spiritualized religion of mere individualistic piety, having only an indirect relation to the rest of life. This, at the same time, cuts most of life loose to follow its own course, sometimes as the purported realm of the merely "natural." In this "great modern error of separating the spiritual from the material," the Church is complicit in making "the secular," as a realm of society separate from the Church.[55] For Maurin, the separation of the Church and society from the land was the greatest single instance of this. "Modern society" is thus "a materialist society because modern Christians have failed to translate the spiritual into the material."[56] The machine has accordingly displaced the land-and-craft society, generating successively capitalism, Marxism for the failures of capitalism, and fascism for the failures of Marxism.[57] But, Maurin saw, if "we had a Land and Crafts Society we would not have Capitalism. If we did not have Capitalism we would not have Marxism. And if we did not have Marxism, we would not have fascism. So to foster a Land and Crafts Society is to oppose Capitalism, Marxism, and Fascism."[58]

In place of this, the Worker's call "Back to Christ—Back to the Land!" was a summons to return to a "functional

[54] Peter Maurin, "A Modern Plague," in *Forgotten Radical*, 39.

[55] Maurin, "Another Open Letter to Fr. Lord M. Ag.," in *Forgotten Radical*, 56.

[56] Maurin, "The Hope of the People," in *Forgotten Radical*, 183.

[57] Maurin, "Revolutions," in *Forgotten Radical*, 352–53.

[58] Maurin, "Land and Crafts," in *Forgotten Radical*, 318.

society" from an "acquisitive society."[59] "The new order brought about by right decisions will be functional not acquisitive, personalist not socialist, communitarian not collectivist, organismic not mechanistic."[60] Maurin in particular rightly doubted that there could be a humane industrial capitalism: there could exist no halfway house that might be a compromise between the status quo and the agrarian vision. He quoted Lenin approvingly that "the World cannot be half agricultural and half industrial,"[61] for the latter will always prey on the former, as a Chinese friend of Maurin related: "What would Western industrialism do to us? Our people would become robots. Our cultural traditions would be destroyed."[62]

Maurin's ideal of the functional society was one in which the guilds (or their modern equivalent) would once again have to play a central role. A functional society meant a society where the economy was a function of a common vision of the good life, rather than allowing an unfettered economy to set the terms in which people live. Markets, in other words, serve life, rather than visa-versa. And this, Maurin had learned from Penty, was what the guilds had ensured: guilds and capitalism were incompatible, and it was capitalism itself that had recognized this and intentionally broken up the guilds. In a long Easy Essay, Maurin traced the basic stops of this economic fall narrative, drawn from Penty,

---

59 Maurin, "A Radical Change," in *Forgotten Radical*, 106–7; "The Age of Order," in *Forgotten* Radical, 410.

60 Maurin, "The Age of Order," in *Forgotten Radical*, 410.

61 Maurin, "Industrialization," in *Forgotten Radical*, 170.

62 Maurin, "From a Chinese," in *Forgotten Radical*, 174.

from the guild system of the high Middle Ages to the rise of the middle men, the bankers, manufacturers, economists (Adam Smith), to world war, and world economic depression.[63] If the land movement was to work in the long run, there would have to be such non-socialist social control of the economy. In the meantime, Maurin wanted to create little pockets of functional communities where that future could be lived right now. This is what his land movement was purposed to do.

The Catholic Worker variously called their land communities "Communitarian Farms," "Agronomic Universities," "Parish Subsistence Camps," "Farming Communes," or "Farming Colonies," depending on which aspect of it they wished to highlight. It got a start, practically speaking, when the New York community found and purchased one acre on Staten Island, which included an eight-bedroom house and large garden that provided enough vegetables for the inhabitants and many for the New York hospitality house. A short time later, they moved the operation to a larger piece of land in Easton, Pennsylvania, which they called Maryfarm. Within a few years, Day reports that Catholic Worker farms had been born in Minnesota, Michigan, Ohio, Massachusetts, Vermont, another one in Pennsylvania, and in Newburgh, New York.[64]

While certainly emphasizing the properly agricultural component, the farms were also meant to be new centers of distinctively Christian community on the model of the

---

63 Maurin, "The Light of History," in *Forgotten Radical*, 147–52.

64 Dorothy Day, "Communitarian Farms," in *Loaves and Fishes*, 55.

early Church and the medieval communes. They were to exemplify and be training grounds in what Maurin called *communitarianism*—the Church as a lived *social* reality, an alternative society, where Christians could once again have "all things in common" (Acts 2:44). As such, they were to be more than places to grow vegetables and raise animals, but included some communal property, voluntary poverty, shared work, study and discussion, life with the poor, and the daily practice of the works of mercy.[65] "To Dictatorial Pagan Communism," said Maurin, "I am opposing Utopian Christian Communism."[66] For, as "St. Ambrose says, 'The Church presents the most perfect form of admirable communism and social life.'"[67]

The gospel, for Maurin, just *is* the solution to the world's problems, including its "economic" problems because Christianity is a social form that has to be enacted. Its practices such as common prayer, voluntary poverty, fasting, almsgiving, turning the other cheek, or sheltering the homeless are not mere "religious" pieties for private individuals but "the basis of a Christian Society."[68] The Sermon on the Mount was for Maurin a social manifesto meant for everyone, the original Catholic social teaching revealing the way to be truly human. "Christianity has not been tried because people thought it was impractical. And men have tried everything

[65] Maurin, "Reconstructing the Social Order," in *Forgotten Radical,* 52, passim.

[66] Maurin, "To Our Readers," in *Forgotten Radical,* 62.

[67] Maurin, "The Communism of the Catholic Worker," in *Forgotten Radical,* 156.

[68] Maurin, "Christ the King," in *Forgotten Radical,* 104.

except Christianity,"[69] but the "Sermon on the Mount will be called practical when people make up their mind to practice it."[70]

The Catholic Worker, said Maurin, "is taking monasticism out of the monasteries. The Counsels of the Gospel are for everybody, not only for the monks."[71] "Catholic communes are not a new thing. . . . The Communist ideal is the Common Good ideal—the ideal of Blessed Thomas More, the ideal of St. Thomas Aquinas, the ideal of the Irish Scholars, the ideal of the first Christians. . . . We don't need new doctrine, we need an old technique."[72] "Catholic people . . . must return to the Catholic extremism of the early Christians."[73] Or, as Day put it: "One must give up one's life to save it. Voluntary poverty is essential. To live poor, to start poor, to make beginnings even with the meager means at hand, this is to get the 'green revolution' under way."[74]

Practically speaking, however, life on the farms could take any number of different forms. Like everything in the Catholic Worker, nothing was to be dictated from the top down but adapted gradually and organically as the circumstances required. But Maurin did have some suggestions. Each family, he thought, should have its own house, and he was not a fan of community kitchens. That each family should have some space to itself was necessary to keep the authority

[69] Maurin, "Christianity Untried," accessed June 3, 2024, https://catholicworker.org/easy-essays-html/#christianity-untried.

[70] Maurin, "Logical and Practical," in *Forgotten Radical*, 384.

[71] Maurin, "Franciscans and Jesuits," in *Forgotten Radical*, 210.

[72] Maurin, "Fighting Communism," in *Forgotten Radical*, 115.

[73] Maurin, "Catholic Extremism," in *Forgotten Radical*, 386.

[74] Day, "Communitarian Farms," 48.

structure within the family clear to the children. Still, each family should have one or more single people living with them, which enriches the nuclear family and prevents loneliness in both directions. In terms of property ownership, this meant that Maurin advocated:

> The combination of the two kinds, private ownership and communal ownership. I always make a case for communal ownership which is the ideal. Here in America people homesteaded but they became victims of their isolation and their children left the farms and went to the cities. They forgot the village idea which was in Europe but went off by themselves. It was really the spirit of individualism which came from the Reformation and Catholics unfortunately followed it, forgetting the community, the liturgical idea.[75]

The community and liturgical idea was Maurin's way of emphasizing the Green Revolution's Catholic identity. Indeed, he sometimes named them "*Parish* Subsistence Camps" to underline that his program had nothing to do with the rugged romanticism of the libertarian frontiersman but was simply aimed at helping the Church to be the Church. Accordingly, Maurin often drew up suggested *horariums* (the daily schedules followed in monasteries) and posted them for viewing during common meals. There was to be an equal balance, he thought, between prayer, work, study/discussion, and sufficient time for leisure and family life.

---

[75] Maurin, "Four Interviews with Peter Maurin," in *Forgotten Radical*, 495.

Still, at the end of the day, each community would have to make its own path. "Trouble is," Maurin said, "people want blueprints. I don't want to give blueprints. Let them struggle with it."[76] Some would have to be devoted to farming, some to crafts, some to childcare, and others to any of the numberless tasks such a life requires, but that would have to be figured out along the way. "The practical ways of getting [to a functional society] are left to the initiative of individuals who have learned what to do with liberty and who always keep in mind the importance of pure means."[77] "One thousand families [on a commune] wouldn't be too many, if they had the right idea. St. Dunstan College on Prince Edward Island is doing the right thing; fostering a movement to bring craftsmen back to the villages."[78] Indeed, part of the point was that the farm was a training in personalism, that each person had to take the initiative, be creative, *act*, in contrast to the passivity encouraged by hyper-institutionalization. Rather than waiting for an agency to do it, Maurin wanted people to learn to organize themselves.

The Catholic Worker thus puts substantial flesh on the sometimes-abstract personalism that we saw in Emmanuel Mounier. And Mounier is indebted to Maurin's program, as it was actually (often heroically, and sometimes harrowingly) lived in the hospitality houses and the farms, for providing perhaps the finest example of what the *Personalist Manifesto*

---

[76] Maurin, "Four Interviews with Peter Maurin," in *Forgotten Radical*, 492–503.

[77] "Peter Maurin's Radio Interview, 1937," in *Forgotten Radical*, 507.

[78] Maurin, "Four Interviews with Peter Maurin," in *Forgotten Radical*, 494.

looks like in practice. Like Mounier, for the Catholic Worker, the personalism that opposes industrialism's regime of the impersonal constitutes an entire political philosophy. At the most obvious level, this means that for the Worker, no society without a healthy relationship to the land will be personalist and thus humane, just, and healthy: agriculture is always an essential part of personalist politics, precisely because personalism is one aspect of life on the land.

We've already seen one way this is the case, as farmers and artisans are able to surround themselves with their own creative work. Maurin also emphasized the further point that on the land, people can learn to work and think for themselves. A machine society takes much of the decision making out of life, and thus the virtue of prudence—knowing what to do in particular situations—is degraded for lack of development. People are not only passive today but wouldn't know what to do if they did want to act. A land-and-craft economy is thus a personalist economy because it rehabilitates our capacity for true freedom.

Maurin thus found an alternative political program embedded in the nature of agrarianism itself. And up to a certain point, Maurin no doubt simply shares this program with the distributist tradition, which has long recognized that a commitment to an agrarian society also means a preference for certain forms of limited and decentralized governmentality. Accordingly, Maurin cited favorably the Jeffersonian ideal of a nation of small farmers and as little government as possible; he also valorized the distributist and (as we have seen) guild-based economies of the middle ages.[79] Yet Maurin gives this philosophy his own distinctive twist and adopts neither the libertarian individualism sometimes associated with Jefferson nor the medieval integralism (or monarchism) which is increasingly popular today among conservative Catholics. Nor, however, was he a liberal, rightly seeing the principled separation of Church and state as one more form of separation of the material from the spiritual.[80]

Rather, Maurin's political twist involved the Catholic Worker in a sort of non-coercive or even pacifist integralism. The gist of this position is that Christianity is indeed meant for the whole world (as the integralist holds). It *should* be the religion of all society and must work itself down into the farthest reaches of everyday life. But—and here's Maurin's twist—it must do this without ever abandoning the non-violent supernatural ethic of the Sermon on the Mount. Taking over from Jacques Maritain, the notion of "pure means," the "weapons" necessary for the Green Revolution, Maurin thought, were the simple but radical practices of the gospel: voluntary poverty, hospitality, the liturgy, common life, care for the poor, preaching, sanctity, and all of this as part of a personalist ethic embedded in the land. These were the ways that the first Christians took over the world and that resulted in the best of the Middle Ages, and Maurin saw no reason they couldn't do it again in a grassroots sort of way.

The Catholic Worker's political platform therefore is an *agrarian* platform, but it is not one that is much concerned to be involved in what we usually think of as the political

---

[79] Maurin, "Jeffersonian Democracy," in *Forgotten Radical*, 274.

[80] Maurin, "Church and State," in *Forgotten Radical*, 37–38.

realm. Its interest is rather to start right now to "build a new society within the shell of the old," *by living it*, rather than angling to reconstitute society from the top down. The latter, for Maurin, is a violation of the principles of personalism. Rather than forcing others to do the good, Maurin emphasized that real change happens by being who you want the other person to be and that all real change was necessarily voluntary and organic. From this basis in personal initiative, in hospitality houses and on the farms, a new order really could begin to emerge. Thus, as Maurin put it: "We don't want to take over the control of political and economic life. We want to reconstruct the social order through Catholic Action exercised in Catholic Institutions."[81]

Finally, Maurin's principled pacifism is itself deeply connected with his agrarianism. At the level of formal military participation, even just-war Christians, he thought, would "see and know the injustice of practically all wars in our modern pagan world," and hoped that such Christians in our country would "form a mighty league of conscientious non-combatants."[82] Yet resisting militarism today requires more than simply refusing to take up arms, for the militarism of modern society is inscribed in the heart of industrialism itself, which must always be anxious to defend and expand both its markets and its supply: "The search for markets and raw materials is at the base of modern imperialism. And modern imperialism is at the base of modern

---

[81] Maurin, "For Catholic Action," in *Forgotten Radical*, 51, 90, passim.

[82] Maurin, "Disarmament of the Heart," in *Forgotten Radical*, 277. See also, "Soldiers and Scholars," 279.

wars."[83] For instance, Maurin helps us see that a society that requires oil in order to eat, move, or talk, as does our industrial agriculture, automobiles, and telephones, will have to be a deeply violent society, as our way of life is only assured by having bigger guns. Thus the Green Revolution seeks the (re)establishment of a more peaceable people by the only means practically possible, an increased local self-sufficiency.

Maurin sometimes called the type of agrarian order he imagined "pluralist":

> The Pluralist state is one where Humanists try to be human, Jews try to be Jews, Protestants try to be Christians, and Catholics try to be Catholics. . . . The Cooperative Movement, the Guildist Movement, the Agrarian Movement, the Communitarian Movement, find themselves at home in the pluralist state. The pluralist state does not try to solve the social problem by passing laws or creating bureaus, but by removing from the Statute Book all the laws that hinder the activities of the social movements based on personal responsibility.[84]

Yet such agrarian pluralism obviously has little to do with what is sometimes called pluralism today in the liberal West. It should be seen, rather, as an affirmation of, and aspiration to, true difference, made possible by being rooted in the soil of a particular place that is not any other place. Today, pluralism names something like a policy of allowing entirely

[83] Maurin, "Adam Smith," in *Forgotten Radical*, 358.

[84] Maurin, "The Pluralist State," and "Allied Techniques," in *Forgotten Radical*, 224–26.

predictable prosaic expressions of private self-determination within a reality of the strictest technocratic conformity. Such pluralism is industrial pluralism because it is simply the Taylorist conformism of the factory come to totalize all of society. Maurin's agrarian pluralism, by contrast, allows real difference because it does not divinize it. As agrarians have long rightly seen the reinstitution of productive property as necessary for democracy in its proper sense, so too genuine varieties of human culture can only grow and be appreciated when they are literally rooted in the local soil.

***

Modern society drives relentlessly toward what Marx called the "thing-ification" (reification) of everything—from labor to products to people themselves. Today this is so more than ever, with people's every trackable move, desire, and (sometimes it seems) thought, calculated, squeezed, and sold. Our cars keep track of us while we move, our phones what we say and think, Alexa our habits at home, our banks a rolling list of what we have and desire to have. We pay for these latest industrial toys, but by using them, we make ourselves into their products, and we are sold to the highest bidder. All aspects of life are increasingly a matter of producing *ourselves* as commodities. We are still cogs in an assembly line, a mere extension of the machine, only now the workday never ends. No longer do we grudgingly submit our bodies; we willingly submit our souls. We are progressively folding ourselves into one great factory where every bit of us, including what we think are our "own" desires, are fitted for maximum efficiency. Most of us spend most of our waking hours in jobs that at least indirectly support this way of life. We are approaching the total capitalization of human society and of the human being. We are all becoming more like a machine, and it is a war machine.

Catholics must resist this regime with all our might. Our daily pursuit of sanctity demands it. Yet a renewed land-and-craft economy remains the only alternative. This is because, as Maurin helps us see, the only livable world is a personal world, and only a real relation to the land at every level can make life personal. So we have a choice. Either we will begin to foster that real relation in our own lives or we will slowly become the violent atomized cyborgs personal experience and recent history is more and more revealing us to be. This is especially true for those of us who will continue to live in cities.

Agrarianism thus appears not as one "social issue" among others, a soap box for liberals, or a retreat for traditionalists. It appears, rather—even for urbanites—as a necessary part of the practice of the Faith itself. What we need, in other words, is an agrarian Church. None have helped us imagine what this can look like better than the Catholic Worker.

Works Cited

"Catholic Worker Farms." The Catholic Worker. Accessed May 23, 2024. https://catholicworker.org/catholic-worker-farms/?paged=1.

Day, Dorothy. *All the Way to Heaven: The Selected Letters of Dorothy Day*. Edited by Robert Ellsberg. New York: Image Books, 2010.

———. "Communitarian Farms." In *Loaves and Fishes.* Maryknoll, NY: Orbis Books, 1963.

Leo XIII. *Rerum Novarum.* https://www.vatican.va/content/leo-xiii/en/encyclicals/documents/hf_l-xiii_enc_15051891_rerum-novarum.html.

Marx, Karl. *The Communist Manifesto.* In *The Marx-Engels Reader*. Edited by Robert C. Tucket. New York: W.W. Norton & Co., 1978.

———. *Capital.* In *The Marx-Engels Reader*. Edited by Robert C. Tucket. New York: W.W. Norton & Co., 1978.

———. *Wage Labor and Capital.* In The Marx-Engels Reader. Edited by Robert C. Tucket. New York: W.W. Norton & Co., 1978.

Maurin, Peter. *Catholic Radicalism: Phrased Essays for the Green Revolution*. New York: Catholic Worker Books, 1949.

———. "Christianity Untried." Accessed June 3, 2024. https://catholicworker.org/easy-essays-html/#christianity-untried.

———. "Mechanized Labor." Accessed June 10, 2024. https://catholicworker.org/easy-essays-html/#mechanized-labor.

———. "Self-Organization." Accessed May 24, 2024. http://www.easyessays.org/self-organization/.

———. "The C.P. and the C.M." Accessed June 7, 2024. catholicworker.org/easy-essays-html/#the-cp-and-cm.

———. *The Forgotten Radical Peter Maurin: Easy Essays from the Catholic Worker*. Fordham University Press, 2020.

Mounier, Emmanuel. *A Personalist Manifesto.* New York: Longmans, 1938.

———. "Révolution Communautaire." *Esprit* 3, no. 28, January 1935.

Penty, Arthur. *A Guildsman's Interpretation of History.* London: George Allen and Unwin, 1920.

———. *Post Industrialism.* London: George Allen & Unwin, 1922.

Fr. Francis Bethel, OSB

Fr. Francis Bethel, OSB made his vows as a Benedictine monk in 1977 and was ordained a priest in 1983. In 1999, he was among the founders of the Benedictine monastery of Our Lady of Clear Creek in Hulbert, Oklahoma. Author of *John Senior and the Restoration of Realism*, Fr. Bethel currently serves as Master of Studies at Clear Creek Abbey and teaches Dogmatic Theology.

CHAPTER 5

JOHN SENIOR AND THE REDISCOVERY OF REALITY IN MODERN AMERICA[1]

Fr. Francis Bethel, OSB

In 1999, thirteen Benedictine monks from France arrived at the backlands of Oklahoma to establish a monastery along a remote streamlet, Clear Creek. While they issued from the venerable abbey of Notre Dame de Fontgombault,[2] one could say that the beginnings of their foundation lay,

---

[1] This chapter consists of excerpts, with slight editorial adjustments, from the book *John Senior and the Restoration of Realism*, by Fr. Francis Bethel, OSB (Merrimack, NH: Thomas More Press, 2017). Used with permission.

[2] The Benedictine abbey of Our Lady at Fontgombault was founded in 1091. After flourishing in the Middle Ages, it suffered decline in the eighteenth century and was closed even before the onslaught of the French Revolution. Monastic life was reestablished there in 1948 by the abbey of Saint Peter of Solesmes. Fontgombault subsequently made four foundations: Randol (1971), Triors (1984), Donezan (1994) in France and Clear Creek (1999) in the United States. All are now abbeys in their own right. In 2013, Fontgombault also took over the monastery of St. Paul of Wisques.

in fact, in the United States, not so far from Clear Creek, shaped by Providence in the halls of the University of Kansas and set in motion when two of its students knocked at Fontgombault's doors twenty-seven years before. In many ways, the monks' foundation was the final outcome of a quest that had begun in the 1970s, when some of the same men, immersed in the anti-culture of the day, entered the university's Integrated Humanities Program (IHP). Designed and conducted by Professors Dennis Quinn, Frank Nelick, and John Senior, the program was built upon a most revolutionary tenet: reality is real. And the means for communicating this fact was quite simply Western culture—prose and poetry, music, architecture, and art—bolstered by the book of nature.

At the time they enrolled in the Integrated Humanities Program, most were typical students of the 1970s, their vision molded by the deconstructionist trends of the day, believing Western ideals and institutions to be outmoded and empty conventions. They knew not where to turn except to what the moment had to offer. Scarcely any realized the immensity of what awaited them; yet very early in the coursework, something awoke in their slumbering souls. Led on by their professors, they discovered, to their surprise, that the old Western tradition was full of treasures, a deep goldmine to be explored. They came to recognize that there are true, good, and beautiful realities which give meaning to life—that indeed there are things greater than self which are worth living for. For a multitude of students, the IHP class was a turning point in their lives. They acquired convictions that continue to guide and stimulate them in their decisions even today.

There are some rather spectacular statistics pointing to the religious effect of this program taught in the context of a secular university. An unofficial count numbers some two hundred among its students who entered the Catholic Church, as well as dozens who returned to the Catholic faith they had abandoned. Among IHP graduates, as of 2012, there is an archbishop, a bishop, an abbot, a prior, and a prioress; two have been religious superiors, another the rector of a seminary; three have been novice masters; one served the US Congregation of Catholic Bishops for ten years. The secular world has also profited. Former students include a judge, lawyers, school principals, teachers, and medical doctors; one alumnus was the head of a US presidential council. Flourishing schools have been inspired by the program; many groups have tried to imitate it. And of course many large, healthy families have sprung up from it.

How did the IHP bring about the extraordinary and unexpected intellectual and spiritual flowering of young lives? Quinn, Nelick, and Senior were in agreement regarding the basic needs of education, given the prevailing crisis in learning and culture. In particular, they recognized that relativism was at the root of the students' disorientation. Most of their generation had fallen into the prevailing philosophy of the times: the conviction that there is no permanent, universal truth. Each so-called "truth," they assumed, was subjective, restricted to one's own choices.

Given this state of affairs, the three professors knew that the first thing needed was a "conversion" to truth as such, to *reality* itself. Nothing constructive in education could be accomplished until students would accept the fact that there is a difference between truth and error. In fact, the entire IHP project can be summarized as a nurturing of realism, taking this latter term not in the sense of a particular philosophical system or school, but simply as the conviction that there is an absolute truth, that the exterior world can be known in itself, and that the mind depends on the senses to know it.

To understand the IHP adventure, one must delve into John Senior's thought and what led him to help start such an institution. He alone of the three professors elaborated in some detail the theory of this prephilosophical, pre-scientific education.

While this work is not biographical in the strict sense of that term but rather a study of John Senior's thought, it will nevertheless have a biographical character, as his deep convictions and doctrine grew out of his personal intellectual and spiritual journey: from a Marxist materialism that denied spiritual realities, through an Oriental spiritualism that strove for the spiritual stars by discarding man's roots in sensible realities, to realism and ultimately to the Catholic Church. The phrase "Made for the Stars but Rooted in the Soil" represents the pivotal philosophical point of that pilgrimage as well as the crux of all of Senior's thought. He realized by his own experience that the human plant, in order to tend to the stars, must be nourished in the soil of this world. His turnabout and then his work with students deeply impressed on him that we must ground all intellectual and affective life on the experiential and imaginative level. This concrete way of nourishing realism underlay everything he taught and the way he taught it. It is the key to entering into a deep understanding of his doctrine.

Flight to the West

One day in 1936, a boy in his early teens, tired of the mechanized and comfortable life of Long Island, put together a few things and the little money he had saved, sneaked away from home, and hopped onto a Greyhound bus going west, telling the driver to take him as far as his money would allow. A couple of days later, he was wandering down a road in South Dakota while a storm was brewing. A truck pulled up and the driver pointed in the distance, shouting: "Kid, there's a tornado brewin'. Get in!" Thus began John Senior's first season as a cowboy.

Senior always said he had had a great youth, referring especially to his days in a rugged life out west. The cowboy ideal, with its nobility, chivalry, and healthy comradeship, caught his fancy as a boy and never left him. This man, steeped in European culture, would always be proud of nineteenth-century "free, frank, friendly" America. His adventure in the Dakotas is emblematic of Senior's life. Already as a boy he fled from whatever he found artificial in search of reality.

Perhaps John's flight west was undertaken in part to ease the family's financial burden [during the Depression], something not uncommon in those days. But mostly, John was dismayed at seeing Long Island lose its farms and open spaces because of the economic slump and steady urbanization. His hometown even changed its name from Christian

Hook to Oceanside in order to attract development. A life close to nature was fading away. He touched on that experience in "A Second Childhood's Garden":

> When I awoke on attic cot
> I looked across a Camelot
> of red and green, steep-slanted roofs
> and heard the milkman's horse's hoofs;
> . . .
> And now the fields conglomerate
> into suburban real estate;
> where the landscape, days and nights,
> is cacophonies of lights;
> . . .
> When the wind no longer whispers
> there will be no Lauds or Vespers;
> when there isn't any dawn,
> chanticleer will not go on.[3]

Thus it was that, at the age of thirteen, the impulsive youngster sought the cowboy life that he had dreamed so much about. In his words:

> Having had from childhood an urge for good times lost, I satisfied it first with poetry and then with cowboy stories . . . and at thirteen ran away from home and the encroaching city which by the 1930's had metastasized suburban cells in our rural fields. But by that time fenced farms had pretty much destroyed the open range . . . so it was something of a miracle that as

[3] John Senior, *Pale Horse, Easy Rider* (Lawrence: Shakespeherian Rag Press, 1992), 38–39.

> late as 1936 I found a ranch in the Dakota Badlands where cowboys still rode horses on roundups.[4]

It was a Norwegian, Morgan Tinzer, who had picked up the young New Yorker as a tornado formed not far away. At his invitation, John stayed in Tinzer's summer house and for a time, assisted him in strip mining coal. He eventually wrote his parents—who were understandably frantic and had authorities looking for their son in several states—but did not tell them where he was. Tinzer finally contacted the Seniors and informed them of the boy's whereabouts. His father, Roy, hurriedly flew out to South Dakota, rented a car, and drove across a roadless prairie to retrieve his son. Upon John's return back home, his siblings would not speak to him, being all the angrier that he had not even been punished!

Fearing that their son might run off again, the Seniors consented to his going west every summer, provided he return home afterward to continue his schooling during the winter. Through various connections, they found a job for him with another Norwegian, Vic Christensen, on a ranch in the Red River Valley, near Grand Forks, North Dakota. This arrangement proved to be a perfect compromise. John could still live much as his cowboy heroes had, riding horses, drinking coffee at the campfire, and sleeping in the bunkhouse with the hands. "In those days it was the real thing," he said. "They had roundups and horses—none of the modern conveniences."[5] He went on cattle drives of more than

---

4 Senior, "The Restoration of Innocence: An Idea of a School" (mss 1994), 73.

5 Kempton Lindquist, "Professor Senior," *University Daily Kansan*, August 21, 1974, p. 2.

sixty miles that often lasted two or three weeks. Mr. and Mrs. Christensen had no children except an adopted son and readily accepted the young New Yorker as a member of the family, letting him lounge about the house and read in the library during his free time.

Senior later recounted some anecdotes from his days in the Dakotas. The hands used a trolley with a grapple hook powered by horses to carry big piles of loose hay into the barn. One day, John was given the task of guiding the hay by a rope. He accidentally pulled on the trip rope and the whole load fell right on the foreman. John heard a muffled voice screaming furiously from underneath the hay. The hand next to him cried out, "Get out of here, you little idiot. He's gonna kill you! Get lost for the rest of the day!" John did as he was told and only that evening crept back quietly to the bunkhouse. He concluded the story with: "I learned then that I'm no durn good with machinery!"

Another time he was charged with taking provisions to some workers about five miles away. He was proud to be given such a responsibility and was happily singing to himself as he went along driving the horses, listening to the birds and looking at the flowers. Unexpectedly, he heard a horse wildly galloping and a man yelling, "Can't you see what you're doin'?!" John looked back and had the spectacle of sacks of flour and cans of pork and beans strewn along the road behind him. He had forgotten to close the wagon's clapboard.

Of course, much of the experience was less poetic and romantic than John had dreamed—they did, after all, use trucks!—but he persevered year after year. These five or six summers at the ranch provided him with a rich experience of nature, animals, weather, men, and hard work. He once mused that Will James's book *Sand*, about a boy who practically fell out of a train in Montana and became a man among the cowboys, was the story of his own life.

Senior continued to be consumed by dreams of a rustic life where he could leisurely write poetry. One day, following his graduation [from Columbia], he and his wife [Priscilla] jumped into their Studebaker, hauling a trailer behind piled high with their belongings, and escaped to the wilderness. They purchased some cheap land in the mountains near Taos, New Mexico, obtained some goats, and began settling into their mountain shack. But the adventure was short-lived. As Senior told it, "The indians stole the goats. And the winter came along and we almost died. We had to run down from the mountain. Besides that, our first child was going to be born. I ran all the way back east again and got myself a job."[6]

Still trying to find a more romantic, rural life, he at one point investigated the possibility of moving to a Caribbean island, and for years retained the property in New Mexico, just in case. His preference for living in the country was fulfilled when he was fortunate enough to find an old farmhouse on a few acres of ground near Huntington, New York, close to his wife's family.

In 1954, Senior was awarded a scholarship from Columbia University to spend a year in Ireland and England doing research for his doctoral dissertation. He thoroughly enjoyed

---

[6] Lindquist, "Professor Senior," 2.

living in a small village in Ireland, but "what really brought me home was the awareness that even though I could achieve the life that I wanted over there, it would be wrong for me to do that. . . . You can go off and succeed by yourself, but you become some kind of nut."[7] From that year forward, he fully invested himself in teaching. He passed his comprehensive doctoral exams summa cum laude in 1955 and joined the English department at Cornell University.

Senior found a pleasant old country house in the tranquil Finger Lakes district of upstate New York, built a barn, and bought an old horse he named Sam Bass that he and his daughter often rode. A Cornell professor of the time tells the following story:

> John invited my wife and me to attend a race. The weather had been unusually dry, but I hadn't realized how much dust a group of horses could make, especially if lined up side by side on a dirt track. Almost as soon as the race commenced, the dust so billowed up that the spectators could see nothing of the horses and riders, only the sound of galloping hooves. Upon finishing the race, the riders and their mounts trotted away from the clouds of dust, the one who came in first dust-free, but each horse and rider that followed increasingly covered with it. Maybe ten horses competed; John and his horse came in last, and they were both so shrouded in dust they seemed like ghost-like

[7] Lindquist, "Professor Senior," 2.

> apparitions—like a modernday Don Quixote and his beloved but plodding Rocinante.[8]

While teaching and writing his dissertation—and riding horses—John maintained an interest in films. He was well acquainted with the principal actors and directors of the time and even produced some home movies himself. For a while he also found time to delve into making pottery and raising bees. Priscilla, meanwhile, earned a degree from Cornell and began raising Afghan hounds, in her turn, which were to be famous members of the Senior household for decades. She and her hounds would be successful at several dog shows.

In 1957, Senior completed his dissertation, receiving his PhD in comparative literature—that is, literature of various languages. Senior was by then a young, vibrant, and popular professor at one of the most prestigious universities in the country. Yet during those years, he was obviously searching for something more, something of a different order than academic success.

Discovering Reality

John Senior's quest for meaning in life led him first to an interest in the occult, which was the stuff of his published dissertation, *The Way Down and Out*. As such, the book is a deposit of Senior's thought before his conversion, or at least the expression of what he was then exploring. It provides us with a means of knowing what it was that Senior later reacted against, and thus can greatly contribute to an

---

8 James McConkley, letter to Francis Bethel, October 27, 2005.

appreciation of his definitive thought. The work helps us obtain a deeper understanding of "the way down" and, ultimately, of what is at the base of modern culture. Senior's shift from the "way down" to the "way up," from considering the world as a shadow to looking upon it as real, valuable, and truly pointing to God, its creator.

It was critical for all that followed in his life that in the mid-1950s, Senior should begin to focus on Eastern philosophy rather than the lesser Western brands of occult thought, having found in the former the "primordial philosophy" in its depth and purity. "Yoga," he wrote in this regard, "is the exact science of what is yet only a parlor game with us."[9] Two elements of this purer and deeper view would push Senior to realism, to the West, and ultimately to Christ. First, Eastern philosophy's denial of *being*, and therefore of rationality, ran counter to his intellect. Second, the absence of a personal relationship with God struck against his heart.

Senior was once asked how to advise a student who was venturing into Eastern religion. His suggestion was to push him deeper into the subject: "Have him read Coomaraswamy. That way he will get to the bottom of Hinduism and may be shocked out of it. That's what happened to me. I discovered that for Hinduism there is finally no difference between existence and nothing!" As he said elsewhere, "Oriental doctrine . . . brought me face to face with Nothing."[10] Shocked as he was in the 1950s to read such teachings,

---

[9] Senior, *The Death of Christian Culture* (New Rochelle, New York: Arlington House, 1978), 34.

[10] Senior, *The Remnants: The Final Essays of John Senior* (Forest Lake, MN: The Remnant Press, 2012), 128.

Senior could perhaps have continued his mental journey and accepted the East's bewildering goal as a mystery had he not read St. Thomas Aquinas. This philosopher enabled him to perceive the nihilism and mental destruction intrinsic in Hindu doctrine.

Coomaraswamy often quoted Western philosophers, notably St. Thomas Aquinas. Senior himself cited St. Thomas twice in *The Way Down and Out*, giving Coomaraswamy's writings as reference. One day in 1959, Senior began reading the *Summa Theologica* for himself. As he once told an interviewer: "[Coomaraswamy and Guénon's] poor reading of St. Thomas nevertheless led me to the *Summa Theologica*."[11] As previously noted, Senior identified his first two steps toward conversion as his readings first of Marx and then of Plato. The discovery of St. Thomas, he said, was the third and final step. His initial reading of St. Thomas broke the spell of Eastern thought as he discovered "the notion of truth. Thanks to reading St. Thomas, I understood what is meant by 'common sense' . . . To use the phrase of Hamlet's: 'to be' exists while 'not to be' does not exist."[12] This pithy and allusive statement linking truth, common sense, and existence calls for some reflection.

In spite of his deviations at the time, Senior had had a healthy experience of reality, cultivated by a poetic and literary formation that had given him a taste for concrete things. This made for a well-disposed soil for sowing realism when he finally ran into a vibrant and convincing presentation of

---

[11] Senior, *The Remnants*, 135.

[12] Senior, *The Remnants*, 135.

it. He recognized that there was no possibility of denying the fact that the dog in the backyard really is; that it was impossible to truly think that the dog is the tree or that he himself was both of them. Even if there is a mystery of communion among entities upon which one can focus, one cannot deny the reality of their differences; one cannot obliterate their separate existences. And nothing can be beyond existence.

For Christians, even more than for Aristotle, the self and the world are good, and meant to be cultivated. It is evident that Christians are often worldly, but Senior knew now that this is not because they hold things to be real: "Worldliness is to forget that things are creatures—not illusions, but creatures created by God for the purpose of getting us to Heaven."[13] Things and our desires for them are God's gifts to help us come to Him. By making idols out of things, worldliness—or sin—has twisted our relationships with them so that they no longer lead to God. The Christian "way down" is the discipline of human desires so that we use things in accordance with their and our true relation to God. The effort sometimes feels like a destruction of self, but, in fact, the Christian strives only to destroy his disordered attachments, to purify his knowledge and love. He does not want to annihilate the tree but prune it in order to concentrate its energy so that it may grow vigorously straight up and bear fruit.

Catholic realism, as it permeated the life of the faithful, was also a point of attraction for Senior. He discovered the realism of the intensely Catholic medieval art and literature.

[13] Letter to Francis Bethel, December 4, 1974. 67.

He had already experienced some Catholic culture in the 1950s while studying French in Quebec and again during his year in Ireland.

Now, as he actively investigated the Catholic Church, he encountered a thoroughly Catholic environment. Perhaps partially under the influence of Huysmans, the erstwhile Symbolist who frequented Benedictine monasteries, Senior made a retreat at Mount Savior Monastery, not far from his home near Ithaca. The liturgy, the Gregorian chant, and the artwork certainly moved him. However, in an interview, he referred to only one aspect of his retreat as having been decisive in his conversion: his reading of *The Rule of St. Benedict.* He explained the reason for this in one phrase: *Ora et labora*, "Pray and work," commonly considered to be the Benedictine motto. "Everything I have learned in literature and philosophy can be summed up by *ora et labora.*"[14] He expanded on this thought elsewhere: "Truth, St. Thomas says, is a relation of the mind and thing. Founded on work and prayer, [the monastic life] is proportioned to the dual nature of man in his mind and body. Both work and prayer are intellectual habits relating the mind to thing."[15] Senior had found a deep and healthy realism in Benedictine life, rooted in the soil and pointing to the stars. This insight helped him recognize the realistic wisdom of the Catholic Church. During the retreat, he bought a medal of St. Benedict which he always wore from that day forward.

---

[14] Senior, *The Remnants*, 139.

[15] Senior, *The Restoration of Christian Culture* (San Francisco: Ignatius Press, 1983), 165.

Teaching Reality

Senior's years in Wyoming were peaceful and happy ones. He at first lived in the university town of Laramie. Later, Senior bought a wide-open, tumbledown 750-acre ranch—a small tract for that prairie state. "It is sensationally beautiful here," he wrote, "physically, frightingly [*sic*] so."[16] He soon possessed a milk cow or two, some chickens and geese, and an old horse for his daughter to ride—his own horseback days were pretty much over. His wife continued to raise and show Afghan hounds. Economic prospect came from raising alfalfa for hay and leasing land for cattle grazing.

When he moved to the ranch, Senior was an energetic forty-year-old man. Up at the crack of dawn, he would check and feed the animals, break ice on the creek for them if necessary, milk the cow, drive the children into town for school and continue on to the university. In the late afternoon and on Saturdays, he would complete the necessary and often rugged chores on the ranch. Senior, quixotic intellectual that he was, could not of course keep up with professional ranchers. Like the knight of La Mancha, his knowledge came from books and, although he was physically hearty, he was not very handy. He would come home in the evening lamenting—and laughing—about his difficulties digging post holes in a straight line or repairing fences. When a neighbor cut off his irrigation, he had no idea how to appeal for his water rights, unfamiliar as he was with the "law of the land."

As noted previously, already as a child Senior suffered from that distance, even separation, from the natural world

---

[16] Senior, letter to Mark Van Doren, July 14, 1967.

characteristic of an artificial, industrialized society. Literature, much of which celebrated nature and some of which in modern times expressed great nostalgia for it, had made his perception of this separation still more acute. One could quote Wordsworth, that poetic chronicler of man's lost harmony with nature at the beginning of the industrial age:

> This Sea that bares her bosom to the moon;
> The winds that will be howling at all hours,
> And are up-gathered now like sleeping flowers;
> For this, for everything, we are out of tune.[17]

In Senior's own poetry, there rarely are verses that rejoice in the beauty of nature because, unfortunately, his experience at the time was rather of an artificial world; thus, he mainly expressed regrets. For example, here are a few stanzas from "The Appalachian Trail." Note the "prelapsarianly clean"—no stains in our artificial paradise!

> citizens of Earth, not Nations,
> up the blazing trail—but nervous,
> under safety regulations
> of the Park and (now) Health Service.
> . . .
> ecumenically super, prelapsarianly clean,
> self-composting
> toilet paper
> UPS from L.L. Bean.
> "Oh, for camps without the counselors,
> trails without the guides,

[17] William Wordsworth, "The World Is Too Much With Us."

birds without binoculars
and uninstructed brides!

. . .

If only we were virgins still
this great, green forest, you and I,
a wilderness, a boy, a girl
and no technology!"[18]

Coomaraswamy, Guénon, and other authors such as Ruskin and Father Vincent McNabb provided Senior with reasons to support his wistful desire for earlier times. They showed him why industrial society has in many ways degraded human life and how superficial the materialist scientific view of reality is. But Senior went further in precisely expressing that our artificial world turns us from the recognition of *being*.

We have no systematic development from Senior on the reason why deficiencies in the domain of learning result from modern technology, but he touched on the question here and there under various aspects. Our reflections can focus on the following passage from Senior's "History and the School":

> Cut off from direct experience of the book of nature by city, suburban and rural life (farms are "factories in the field"), we learn to love false images of God through the distortion of his works on television and the science fiction that passes for science in textbooks.[19]

[18] *Pale Horse, Easy Rider*, 49.

[19] Senior, "History and the School" (Mss., 1995), 13.

Christian tradition speaks of two books in which God teaches us about Himself: the Bible and the world He made. In some measure, the "book of nature" is the more fundamental of the two because the Bible itself uses images and ideas that come to us only through nature. In modern society, then, we are "cut off" from the world that God made to lead us to Himself.

We are dealing with our being immersed in an artificial world. Senior often strove to help his audiences become more aware of the degree to which this fact alienates us from nature. We have almost no direct contact with God's creation:

> Generations brought up in centrally heated and air-conditioned homes and schools, going from place to place encapsulated in culturally sealed-off buses, swim in heated, chlorinated pools devoid of current, swirl or tide, where even the build-up from one's own pushing of the water is suctioned off by vacuums so as not to spoil the pure experience of sport-for-sport's sake; they play summer games like shooting balls through hoops, but reinvented as "basketball" and on winter nights, dressed in short pants; they play football under air-conditioned geodesic domes in heavy jerseys and ski on artificial snow in July.[20]

We might illustrate the damage caused by this separation from the world of nature with another passage that directly concerns realism: "Poor little rich suburban children who

---

[20] Senior, *The Restoration of Christian Culture*, 136.

have all these delights, and living in constant fluorescent glare, have never seen the stars, which St. Thomas, following Aristotle and all the ancients, says are the first begetters of that primary experience of reality formulated as the first of all principles in metaphysics: that *something is.*"[21] Among the many experiences of nature that modern man is deprived of, Senior underlines here that of gazing at the stars. In their fundamental texts on the beginning of philosophy, Plato, Aristotle, and St. Thomas spoke of the order of the stars soaring over the entire sky as provoking wonder and launching the intellectual quest for the cause of all things, of the very universe.[22] These passages do not explicitly mention the awakening of consciousness to the fact that "something is," that the real is really real. Yet, Senior well understands what was present in their doctrine; ultimately, it was indeed the mystery of the stars' existence that launched the first philosophers in their quest.

The very fact that something exists is wonderful, and the stars, with all their seemingly gratuitous beauty, are a striking example of this. They spark the realization that there is mystery in the fact that something is, that the universe is, that there are untold riches in *being*.

The passage we are studying specifies that we are not only cut off from the book of nature but are confronted with "false images of God." The world God made bears His trace and leads to Him, but if we bend it out of shape, it is no longer a good path to God. The first of the two false images,

---

21 Senior, *The Restoration of Christian Culture*, 136.

22 See Plato, *Timaeus*, 47a; Aristotle, *Metaphysics,* 1.2.982b; and St. Thomas, *In Duodecim Libros Metaphysicorum Expositio*, I, lesson 3.

Senior explains, consists in a "certain distortion of [God's] works." Senior was especially thinking of television. In *The Restoration of Christian Culture*, he provides a striking example of such a distortion: "A sixty foot whale splashing across nineteen inches of your living-room while you sip your Coca Cola is not reality."[23]

Moreover, the whale hunt on television, like many electronic representations of things, has an "insidious irreality."[24] Senior writes about records and CDs: "Electronic reconstitutions of disintegrated sounds are not real sounds any more than reconstituted sterilized lactates are milk"[25]—but we easily take them for real. Indeed, television, CDs, iPods, and other devices aim at producing an illusion. They are not like a painting that signifies; they are intended to replace reality. They provide, as it were, a counterfeit experience. For Senior, our technological world "where the magician-intellect invents gigantic global systems of relativist science [and] develops virtual realities"[26] is similar to the modernist dream of confusing fantasy and reality. One understands that when children unplug from their iPod or put aside their video game, they have trouble distinguishing between real things and virtual reality. And, as Senior so aptly says in *The Restoration of Christian Culture*, "we learn to love these false images." We become attached—even addicted—to these virtual simulations, to this artificial sensationalism. Both the

---

[23] Senior, *The Restoration of Christian Culture*, 189.
[24] Senior, *The Restoration of Christian Culture*, 28.
[25] Senior, *The Restoration of Christian Culture*, 29.
[26] Senior, *The Remnants*, 138.

imagination and emotions are forcibly cut off from reality and applied to something else.

The second false image Senior mentions is the "science fiction" of textbooks. Another passage from "The Restoration of Innocence" helps us understand what he was referring to:

> When I was a child, the fifth grade teacher taught us that atoms were miniature solar systems—electrons like planets orbiting a nucleus like the sun. We drew atomic maps and memorized charts of weights, not having a single rock in front of us. We were taught to believe that atoms were real and rocks illusions. Brought up on mathematical models, we took them for reality.[27]

Whatever may be the value, speculative or practical, of such mathematical models, they reduce much of our knowledge of the world to quantitative description. Furthermore, here again one experiences an "insidious irreality." Modern man, accustomed to such models and impressed by science's success, takes them for reality—as the really real—and develops a prejudice against the value of sensible experience. His pseudoscientific imagination replaces God's creation with a false image. In the grip of an artificial substitute, he rejects the immediate, intuitive, sensible, and emotional experience of reality. He believes "that atoms are real and rocks illusions," that H_2O is more real than the cool, slightly muddy creek he swims in. Senior writes that students who believe that the world consists of hollow mathematical structures

[27] Senior, "Restoration of Innocence," 78.

have "minds lost in abstraction through the science of an 'empty universe,' to use the expression of Charles Konink."[28] We have here a strong "disrealization."

Thus, by both virtual simulation and mathematical schemas, the imagination and emotions are cut off from reality only to be connected to distortions. Modern man's very experience and imagination incline him toward a mental disconnection from reality. The world seems less real to him, and this predisposes him to modernism, to consider imagination—or rather fantasy—as real as, or even more real than, anything else.

One is not obliged to accept all the details of Senior's thought on the relationship between the modern apparatus and relativism, but it is certain that man today often has an imagination and emotions disconnected from reality, and that modern science and technology have much to do with that. Our devices make us distant from real things. Watching the whale hunt on television imparts next to nothing of the real adventure and danger, of the smells, of the feeling of the air, nor the skill, strength, endurance, and patience required. Also, pushing buttons on computers cannot connect one's mind, sense, emotion, and imagination to reality as can guiding a horse, hammering nails into boards, and maneuvering a sail on a ship. Driving through our neighborhood in a car does not familiarize us with the lay of the land, the trees and lawns, as walking does. Anyone can recognize that modern man needs to reconnect with the world God made so that healthy experience and imagination may

---

[28] Senior, *The Remnants*, 137.

nurture his intellectual and spiritual life. Such recognition suffices substantially for one to understand Senior's goal of restoring a healthy imagination. Nothing can replace experience: "No serious restitution of society or the Church can occur without a return to the first principles, yes, but before principles we must return to the ordinary reality which feeds the first principles."[29]

A Poetic Approach to the Great Books

A noteworthy reaction emerged, in the mid-twentieth century, to the modern stance that would promote early technical specialization in education. It was spearheaded by the founders of the Great Books program: Van Doren himself, Mortimer Adler, Robert Hutchins, and others.

Experience of the value of an education gained directly from the masters led them to recognize the need there was to rehabilitate undergraduate formation in general knowledge before professional, more specific training could be provided. These teachers turned to the Middle Ages and to the Greeks for light on how to do this. They decided to restore the liberal arts and sciences through great literature, such as Homer, Shakespeare, and Tolstoy, and through foundational scientific texts such as Euclid, Galileo, and Newton, with an initiation into philosophical reflection through, for example, Plato, Descartes, and Kant.

Senior appreciated the Great Books, effort from which he himself had greatly profited at Columbia University, but he acknowledged that it did not bear the hoped-for fruits. He

---

[29] Senior, *The Restoration of Christian Culture*, 138.

writes: "The 'Great Books' movement of the last generation has not failed as much as fizzled, not because of any defects in the books . . . but like good champagne in plastic bottles, they went flat"[30]—the recipients were not prepared for such rich fare. He more often used a different metaphor, comparing today's educational situation to the erosion of the 1930s when farmers had to sow common plants in order to nourish the barren land and render it capable of growing food crops. Similarly, teachers today have to enrich their students' memories and stimulate their delight in reality and their wonder at its mysteries through gymnastic and music before they can undertake more elevated studies like the liberal arts and philosophy. Learning is gradual, and first things must come first.

One tends to neglect the elementary level partly because deficiency in that domain is a rather recent thing. Training in gymnastic and music has often been taken for granted without too much detriment because in other times and places they were largely assured by ordinary activity, as one walked, rode horses, hunted, worked with hand tools, sang, and read together. Today, however, the remnants of gymnastic and music that subsist in home and school are so disordered that a special and deliberate effort must be made to restore them. The scant and warped experience of students and their consequently disconnected and even diseased imaginations were for Senior the most fundamental problem in education.

Gymnastic and music are all the more important in that they are not merely a preparation for the next stages, and

[30] Senior, "The Thousand Good Books, or, What Everyone Should Have Read," appendix added to The Roman Catholic Books reprinting of *The Death of Christian Culture*, 179.

ultimately for the scientific. Each educational level has its own inherent value. Mastering reasoning and expression while reflecting on great human questions in the liberal arts is worthwhile regardless of what one does afterward, even if one does not specialize in a science. Likewise, it is not necessary for everyone to study logic, abstract grammar, and high mathematics, yet everyone needs to cultivate, through gymnastic and music, the primordial engagement with reality. Gymnastic and music—the culture of senses and delight, of imagination and wonder—are a necessary basis for a man's full life.

Senior describes this first level of education as "a vigorous training of the body, the purpose of which [is] not just health and recreation but the acuity of sensing, as sight is sharpened and coordinated by archery."[31] It is "the art of right sensation."[32] The delight Senior speaks of as the goal for this first step is not the sensual. His entire environment compels him to gaze vaguely and listen idly; he is both overwhelmed with too much to see and hear, and deprived of anything genuinely interesting to look at or listen to. His senses are restless and distracted with background music everywhere and images flying by as he rushes about in a vehicle. Senior writes about television: "Watching it, we fail to exercise the eye, selecting and focusing detail."[33] And it is easy enough to realize that the industrial world of fluorescent lights and chlorinated pools attracts our attention and stirs our emotions far less than stars, ponds, candles, or fountains. An

---

31 Senior, *The Restoration of Christian Culture*, 135.

32 "Restoration of Innocence," 88.

33 Senior, *The Restoration of Christian Culture*, 27.

airplane is not as beautiful and graceful as a bird, nor can cars measure up to horses from the aesthetic point of view.

Gymnastic does not consist simply in a few exercises now and then. Our homes, schools, work sites, and places of recreation should provide an habitual contact with natural things. In that way, the senses are spontaneously sharpened and coordinated and can ripen into a lively sensible and emotional connection with reality. We know that Senior always lived in the country while teaching. He had noticed the profit that came to Mark Van Doren from growing up on a farm and, as a teacher, living and working part of the year in a rustic context.

Thus, regardless of age, every human being needs regular activity in contact with God's creation, but this is most important for a child so that he may be formed in a sound relationship to reality by receiving good things in his fresh soul. "Children," writes Senior, "need direct, everyday experience of fields, forests, streams, lakes, oceans, grass and ground."[34] The child needs to discover reality in its manifold and harmonious riches, to be introduced to it through delight.

As Senior understood, it is vital that both gymnastic and music be restored if we are to capture again the reverential, loving gaze to which reality's secrets are revealed. We all must learn to love the true, the good, and the beautiful; and music—built on healthy gymnastic, on *eros* and delight in existence—is the language and exercise of this love. Before going on to Senior's advice on practical applications

---

[34] Senior, *The Restoration of Christian Culture*, 27.

of gymnastic and music today, it would be profitable to elaborate a point of a more speculative nature on which he often touched—namely, the type of knowledge particularly involved at the musical or poetic level. This study will help us grasp in some depth the importance of gymnastic and music for the restoration of realism.

Restoring the Home and Village

Here we will consider Senior's recommendations on gymnastic and music in some of those "dull low places"—namely, the home, the neighborhood, and the workshop. He does not propose techniques for this but simply provides a few principles, aware that culture must develop naturally.

First of all, it is necessary to cultivate home life. It is in the home that one discovers love and joy, that one learns manners, discipline, responsibility, respect, generosity, and how to relate to others. More than half the battle of life is already won when someone comes from a good family milieu. And it is only through renewed families that a general restoration of culture can be possible. Senior writes: "If even a fraction of the next generation" should practice this home life, the restoration, if it comes, "will come because of them, far from the madding crowd, far from the protests, bull horns, klieg lights and cameras, in that quiet place at home by the fire which in the meantime, little as it is, is of immediate and lasting worth."[35]

Yet, today the home is often little more than a dreary place of transit where one sleeps and sometimes eats, devoid of

[35] Senior, *The Restoration of Christian Culture*, 74.

common life. To remedy this state of affairs, Senior provides some fundamental directions for the restoration of home life using gymnastic and music. Let us examine how gymnastic and music play a role in their formation.

Starting with gymnastic, it is around the home that we acquire basic habits of sensation; it is here that we receive the first good or bad impressions that form our soul. For Senior, it would be best to live, work, and play in a rural or semi-rural area so that sharpening the senses and tying them to reality would become part of daily life. In fact, he suggests northern Canada for those who dared to go far from the web of technology: "For young and more adventurous souls, there is the vast, still-virgin wilderness to the north waiting for saints."[36]

Though Senior scarcely elaborates on the theme of home gymnastic, it can be deduced that if one cannot live in a rural region, it would be desirable to have regular experiences in nature through camping trips, or visits with family and friends in the country. Even in town, some neighborhoods are closer to nature and more delightful than others. The home itself should be of natural materials, simple and attractive, with harmonious wood furnishings and handmade objects. It would be good to live among animals: domestic ones—cats, dogs, chickens, pigs, horses; and wild ones not far away—ducks, squirrels, rabbits, blue jays. Recreation should likewise be close to nature, and active rather than passive. Walking in the countryside or across parks, drawing, juggling, horseback riding, golfing, and hunting

[36] Senior, *The Restoration of Christian Culture*, 102.

are far superior to video games and watching television. Senior writes:

> My football game! the old man cries. . . . The armchair quarterback, puffing his gut on insipid American beer and potato chips, gapes like Nero at his gladiators hacking each other up, while his neglected children take up punk rock on their car-cassettes. If you really like football, get out on Saturdays and play it with the boys.[37]

By engaging gymnastic roots to grow from, wonderful music can be cultivated, forming a healthy imagination and deep emotions. Literature, poetry, songs, and conversation in the home are the normal basis for culture, for a thriving human and Christian life. Senior observes: "Parents are the primary educators and no school, no matter how advanced or clever the curriculum, can do anything more than develop as it were the film that has been taken in the home."[38] Systematic school education cannot replace music in the home: "Twelve years of formal instruction in reading and composition given in modern schools are ineffective substitutes for the habit of poetry and prose which can be acquired only by reading the best aloud night after night. . . . The best instruction in writing is good reading and good talk."[39] Lack of music in the family milieu has its consequences in the classroom, as Senior testifies from his own experience:

---

37 Senior, *The Restoration of Christian Culture*, 28.
38 Senior, "The Uses of Education,"· *Wyoming University News*, June 1967.
39 "Restoration of Innocence," 7.

> Why are students coming down from high schools and colleges . . . so appallingly deficient they cannot read a normal paragraph in Matthew Arnold, a popular writer of less than one hundred years ago? . . . If there were music, poetry and art at home, they would have learned despite bad teaching—teaching has always been mostly bad.[40]

Senior, then, urges leisurely reading, singing, and conversation together of an evening: "Read, preferably aloud, the good English books from Mother Goose to the works of Jane Austen. . . . And sing some songs from the golden treasury around the piano."[41] The prospect may seem idealized and romantic, but it is what Senior experienced as a boy growing up and accomplished in some measure as a father. Keeping everyone around the piano is more difficult today than in the 1920s when he was a child, and the city is more distracting than his Wyoming ranch. There are so many activities today that lure one to go out somewhere, so much communication with the world that plucks the attention outside; home life is interrupted in so many ways. Senior's advice is to begin with one evening a week using simple material at first, like "the songs of Stephen Foster, Robert Burns, the Irish and Italian airs."[42]

There are two prerequisites that Senior proposes for music in the home. The first of these does not come as a surprise, after all we have heard from him: "If you measure the hi-fi

---

[40] *Senior, The Death of Christian Culture*, 95–96.

[41] Senior, *The Restoration of Christian Culture*, 42.

[42] Senior, *The Restoration of Christian Culture*, 25.

against a piano, for example, you can see that families don't gather around the stereo and sing. Families don't draw their chairs up closer to the central heating duct. No one sings while attending to the automatic dishwasher."[43] Television and videos are so attractive and easy—we have supposedly the best entertainment in the world there in our living room at the push of a button—but, among the already mentioned negative consequences, these machines take away interaction among family members, and ultimately destroy family life. With such gadgets on, there is no reading, singing, or conversation. Senior concludes that we must put the modern conveniences aside, at least some of the time: "Smash the television set, turn out the lights, build a fire in the fireplace, move the family into the living room, put a pot on to boil some tea and toddy and have an experiment in merriment."[44]

Another condition for drawing the family back together and fostering music and love is that the heart of the home be habitually present there:

> If women stayed home . . . food would taste like meat and vegetables again because it would be cooked, not just defrosted; life would be wholesome, good and full of love again because she would be home; pianos would shake old music from the scores, children, parents and grandparents would sing together of an evening and tell stories by the fire. Someone would

---

[43] Senior, *The Restoration of Christian Culture*, 72.

[44] Senior, *The Restoration of Christian Culture*, 73.

> even be home to love and care for the crippled, sick and dying.[45]

The culture of the home—homemaking—is the foundation of all culture, and is the special role of the woman. Senior knows there is no family life without the woman to animate it, no authentic home without her to put love into it and make it a place where people like to be. Referring to the etymology of the Anglo-Saxon word "lady," he comments: "All those feminists who want to free women from the drudgery of making a home don't know what a home is. . . . The lady—maker of bread, the bread of life, even the bread of angels. [The] home, [the] living room, [is] a holy place."[46]

Senior was a chivalrous man, having great respect and love for women: "Men's perfections are mediated to themselves by women."[47] He appreciated the differences and complementariness between the two sexes: "Woman was created for man, she is his helpmate, made from his rib and finds her happiness only in serving him; and man is a beast until he fully becomes himself in loving her."[48] As such, society is deprived when women take on roles counter to their nature. About the news of a woman in the Armed Forces having been wounded, he wrote:

> The worst is not that the Soviets are firing laser beams at us, but that girls are out there fighting them. . . . What does this do to the imagination, the heart, the soul, of

[45] Senior, *The Restoration of Christian Culture*, 78.
[46] Senior, *The Restoration of Christian Culture*, 78.
[47] "Restoration of Innocence," 91.
[48] "Restoration of Innocence," 90.

> the next generation? What becomes of girls made by God in their nature to be their husband's helpmates and to bear and raise their children, whose influence, stronger than the moon's on the tide, attracts man's rougher self to all the gentle, tender, soft, sweet, loving moments that make love possible.[49]

He described an instance of this "influence, stronger than the moon's" in a letter to his professor, Mark Van Doren, pointing to Mrs. Van Doren's discreet presence and impact: "Her influence over so many lives, secret, working through things you have said and written and through the way she looks and talks and is, is incalculable."[50]

Senior grieves that our economy compels women to find jobs outside the home: "The worst fact in the present crisis is the creation of an economic system in which women must work to make ends meet. In the worst of the '30s depression the vast majority of women were housewives."[51] Explaining further: "It is against the natural law for women to engage in socially productive industry unless necessity demands it. According to the law of nature a woman's place is in the home because by nature she is nurse and nurturer of children."[52] Let us at least say, with the Church, that society should cultivate esteem for the beautiful role of the housewife and mother, which is intimately concerned with what really counts in life—forming human souls.

---

[49] Senior, *The Remnants*, 105.

[50] Letter to Mark Van Doren, April 16, 1970.

[51] Letter to his brother, Hereward, nd.

[52] Senior, *The Remnants*, 112.

A family cannot avoid influences from the outside, for good or for bad. In fact, it cannot be all it should if kept isolated, enclosed within itself; it needs other families for a full life. The natural milieu for it is a family of families. In the climate of our day, many have come to realize that there is a need to form local communities where intellectual, moral, and religious life can be sustained and cultivated, where friendships are made possible. Senior, with his colleagues Drs. Quinn and Nelick, taught a course on "The Village," painting a charming picture of what a healthy community could be. He insisted on the advantage of living on a human scale "where," he wrote, "we can walk at a normal human speed, shop in friendly stores where the butcher and the grocer know their customers, send our child off to school where the parents know the teacher and the teacher loves his subject and his students."[53] A community such as this—where people know each other, where the common interest is more manifest—will foster in each person a better sense of cooperation, of responsibility, of the common good. Only in such a community can there be sympathy and affection for individual members and the whole, and young and old relate regardless of age; only there can stability nurture local experience and memories, and imagination take hold. Small towns on this level still exist, and neighborhoods of this kind were a familiar thing in larger cities as late as in the 1960s.

To convey a sense of this normal and humane community life, Senior cites Oliver Goldsmith's poem "The Deserted Village," which laments the passing of the village of the

[53] Senior, *The Restoration of Christian Culture*, 63.

poet's youth in the early eighteenth century. Here are some lines describing its common musical life:

> Dear lovely bowers of innocence and ease,
> Seats of my youth, when every sport could please,
> . . .
> How often have I bless'd the coming day,
> When toil, remitting, lent its turn to play,
> And all the village train, from labour free,
> Let up their sports beneath the spreading tree;
> . . .
> These gentle hours that plenty bade to bloom,
> Those calm desires that ask'd but little room,
> Those healthful sports that grac'd the peaceful scene,
> These, far departing, seek a kinder shore,
> And rural mirth and manners are no more.[54]

There have been instances where some have drawn detailed plans to manufacture such a place, but in the end the outcome is an artificial utopia. Senior himself at one time dreamed of starting a village. As time went on, however, he recognized that a community needs to develop naturally. In *The Restoration of Christian Culture*, he simply indicates that some likeminded families could group together in the country, in a village or in a neighborhood, and little by little a community life would come to be: "The cornerstone will come back again, the barbershop and the convivial bar . . . and more important still, the tearoom will reopen."[55] And,

[54] Senior, *The Restoration of Christian Culture*, 67–69.

[55] Senior, *The Restoration of Christian Culture*, 75–76.

as in Goldsmith's lost village, families would come together for gymnastic and music, for play and conversation.

Humanizing Work and Returning to the Land

Work is a significant part of the environment in which we live and is therefore a factor of culture. "We become the work we do," Senior writes.[56] Of course, we have a duty to accomplish our work well, but first we must have good work to be accomplished, one that is, as Senior explains, "really necessary for the common good." He continues:

> A large amount of work in the bureaucratic state consists in what is called management but is really manipulation of labor, supplies and markets. . . . Managers take pride in facilitating and expediting, but how many useless products and needless services are multiplied just for the sake of being facilitated and expedited?[57]

In this instance, the goal, the object in view, is profit rather than what is useful, truly needed, and worthwhile.

We also need work that is morally and spiritually invigorating. Senior enumerates some occupations that do not provide support for faith because they are particularly ungymnastic—that is, removed from natural reality—and unmusical, having little or nothing that inspires or leads to personal, interior growth: "[Christians] who work in factories, banks, insurance companies, government agencies and

---

[56] Senior, *The Restoration of Christian Culture*, 222.
[57] Senior, *The Restoration of Christian Culture*, 83–84.

fast-food shops have to rely on faith alone."[58] Less hours, good wages, job security, and benefits do not adequately compensate for the better part of a day spent in inhuman, frustrating, meaningless work. There was a time when one could scarcely tear a man—the smith, the cobbler, the joiner, the farmer—away from his work, which he took pleasure in doing well and was for him more of a vocation than a "job."

Senior insists on the importance and value of working with one's hands: "Manual labor, accomplished at the hands of the artisan . . . constitutes a path toward spiritual perfection. Machines turn by themselves and give a result without effort from us; they lead the mind and the body to idleness and fantasy."[59] The "blows" require effort and discipline. Work is a "support for contemplation" because in it, the person encounters resistance to which he must adapt, and the mystery of anotherness that calls for an appropriate response. He applies his mind to reality—a type of wood, the soil, climate, plants—and thus discovers new facets of God's creation, acquiring a poetic, participating, sympathetic knowledge of the thing in hand. Such work tests, purifies, and enlightens thought and heart. As Douglas van Steere writes in *Work and Contemplation*: "[The mind of man] requires a certain manual expression to keep its balance. Robbed of this manual expression, the mind goes askew and we get the shallow, rootless quality of thought that has so largely marked our time."[60] While Senior eschewed machinery, it is

---

58 "History and the School," 1.

59 Senior, *The Remnants*, 138.

60 Douglas Van Steere, *Work and Contemplation* (New York: Harper and Brothers, 1957), 93.

true that hand-operated machines, at least, still retain much of the benefits just mentioned. However, in most cases, they do, to a degree, separate the worker from physical reality. This is especially true of factory work, with its dominating mechanical gear at which one can grind away while day-dreaming, mentally cut off from reality.

A return to the land is encouraged by Senior, who considers farming and ranching to be the normal type of work for most men. He envisions a model order in society, which indeed had some reality in the not too distant past: "sixty per cent farmers; twenty, craftsmen; ten, clerks; five, soldiers; and finally, the 'zero' status (not a class) of outlaws (beggars, criminals, cripples and clowns)."[61] While carpentry, gardening, and crafts put us into relationship with the physical world, agriculture involves a greater immersion into, and requires a more all-encompassing adaptation to, God's creation. Senior quotes a beautiful passage from Pius XII on the physical, moral, and spiritual benefit of regular agricultural work:

> It cannot be too often repeated how much the work of the land generates physical and moral health, for nothing does more to brace the system than this beneficent contact with nature which proceeds directly from the hand of the Creator. The land is not a betrayer, it is not subject to the fickleness, the false appearances, the artificial and unhealthy attractions of the grasping city. Its stability, its wide and regular course, the enduring

[61] "Restoration of Innocence," 91.

> majesty of the rhythm of the seasons are so many reflections of Divine attributes.[62]

It is possible to have natural work even in town. If one's job does not revolve around natural reality, there are always chores and maintenance to be done around the house. One can still have a regular second occupation, or at least a useful hobby, such as raising a few animals, gardening, or perhaps cutting hay or making wooden objects or pottery. Senior advises: "If you would dig up your front and back yard by hand and plant them full of flowers and vegetables, you would replenish the table, beautify your lives, lose weight, and gain physical and emotional strength and cheer sufficient to cancel the trip to the mountains and quit the absurd and unhealthy exhibitionism of jogging."[63]

We know that Senior usually had some type of manual hobby going on, and more than a hobby at the ranch in Wyoming. We can suppose that he was able to use this as a "support of contemplation." Father Taylor tells of a day when he went to see the professor and, not finding him at home, walked around to the back to see if he was in the barn. Sure enough, there he was milking the cow. When Senior saw him, he exclaimed, "Father, this is a holy place! Our Lord was born in a place like this!" Father Taylor closes the story: "*That* is John Senior."

In his directives, Senior has in mind primarily the individual and the individual's immediate circle. "The question here," he writes, "is not the reform of the social and economic

---

[62] Senior, *The Restoration of Christian Culture*, 221.

[63] Senior, *The Restoration of Christian Culture*, 100.

system however important that may be, but the particular moral choice each one of us must make in the meantime."[64] Still, he has comments at a more general level regarding a social ideal. He opines that "unless the determinate number [of people in a society] are land owning farmers, the virtues necessary to citizenship atrophy, and the vices destructive of the human race flourish."[65] A "determinate number" is a very useful notion elaborated by Belloc, signifying not necessarily the majority but a number that sets the tone of a society, provides its character. According to Senior, we need enough farmers working their own land to establish a whole, stable society that is well rooted in the soil, in harmony with God's creation. There, care for the land arises spontaneously, as well as a natural sympathy for neighbors and even the animals that share that space with us.

Otherwise, society tends to lose the foundations of civilization, built on adherence to natural law and basic human values, resulting in a greater tendency toward individualism and, thus, a quest for profit above all other considerations.

This of course would be a revolution in these our times of a distant, "remote control" economy that works with statistics instead of real things, run by financiers. Senior speaks of "voodoo economics," which, like magic, multiplies signs and appearances cut off from reality, "where money itself, cut free from the gold (or any) standard [is] no longer a means of exchange but of manipulating value."[66] For his ideal, he has in mind the still largely self-sufficient villages with

---

[64] Senior, *The Restoration of Christian Culture*, 84.

[65] "History and the School," 7.

[66] Senior, *The Restoration of Christian Culture*, 10.

surrounding farms of the latter part of the nineteenth century.[67] There we would find the model human-sized communities, where the worker was familiar with the supplier and the user of his product, and where each knew his place and that his role for the common good was well established. For Senior, after that period—which is when Modernism emerged—Western man left behind "the golden mean of ordinary life."[68]

Senior believes that Catholic teaching supports his views. He writes that "Catholic social teaching, against both socialism and capitalism proposes an essentially agrarian economy of family farms and the workshops needed to support them as the normal basis of society."[69] In his view, the popes' social encyclicals "teach essentially that . . . the political and social power of the faithful must be used in favor of what economists call a distributist rather than a capitalist or socialist society, that is, one in which the tax and other public instruments work to favor independent, small, free enterprise and especially the family farm."[70] Some comment on such affirmations are in order.

According to the theory of socialism, the community as a whole—that is, in practical terms, the state—would own the means of production and would control exchange. In contrast to this, capitalism is the economic system in which

---

[67] For a delightful description of such a village by William Allen White, see "The Restoration of Innocence," 74–75.

[68] Senior, *The Restoration of Christian Culture*, 63.

[69] "History and the School," 1. It is only fair to note that this quotation from Senior was written in a non-published document, although one well thought out and carefully written. Senior habitually spoke in this vein.

[70] Senior, *The Restoration of Christian Culture*, 92.

chiefly individuals or private corporations would own the means, and the market would be free. By capitalism, however, Senior is thinking, in particular, of a society in which big business and accumulation of wealth dominate, with the result that the means of production are in the hands of only a few, who in turn pay others to do the work. Distributism proposes to distribute ownership, to decentralize. Its immediate goal is to keep the common man from being treated like another cog in the machine, to render him satisfaction in his work, to stimulate initiative, generosity, responsibility and independence. The attendant benefits are the strengthening of family bonds, the placing of relationships on a more local and personal level, and the cultivation of personal growth through work. In short, distributism facilitates all the humane values we would like to find through our labor.

The Church has constantly and definitively condemned socialism, especially for denying the right to private property,[71] but her position toward capitalism is much more nuanced, partly because of the ambivalence of the term. The Church promotes economic initiative and a substantially free market; she even accepts the means of production in the hands of a few and the accompanying wage system as not unjust in themselves. Nevertheless, against what can be called an unbridled capitalism, where competition and personal profit are the only rules, she recognizes the need

---

[71] See Leo XIII, *Rerum Novarum*, May 15, 1891, para 7–23; see also Pius XI, *Quadragesimus Anno*, May 15, 1931, para. 44–45; and John Paul II, *Centesimus Annus*, May 1, 1991, para. 13.

for some control, some protection, some harmonization through public institutions for the common good.[72]

Popes have never used the term distributism. Nevertheless, Belloc, who won over Chesterton, among others, to his views, was inspired to develop the distributist theory by the thrust of much of Leo XIII's encyclical *Rerum Novarum*. Leo XIII, Pius XII, and John XXIII encouraged fostering the family farm and small businesses. More deeply, the goals of distributism correspond to principles that guide Catholic doctrine in the domain of economics, notably, that man is the subject and end of work, that there must be solidarity, subsidiarity, and moral responsibility. The popes remind us of the human dimension of work and economy. Nevertheless, the Church takes into account the contingencies of human history and recognizes in our day that matters of economy have greatly evolved in the last few decades. We do not see the popes today setting an essentially agrarian society before us as a point of reference. It is misleading, then, to affirm, as Senior does, that the popes favor a distributist framework and an agrarian economy.

Still, Senior's economic views form a beautiful ideal; favoring small businesses and family farms is quite reasonable, and proposing an agrarian economy as being most suited to man's nature a perfectly legitimate thing. He is not too concerned with financial progress, for example: "'Philosophical happiness,' said Edmund Burke, 'is to want little'—that is, less of things and therefore more truth, beauty, mirth,

[72] See Pontifical Council for Justice and Peace, *Compendium of the Social Doctrine of the Church*, April 2, 2004, para. 335.

merriment and friendship."[73] He would have agreed with John Ruskin, who observed:

> There is no wealth but life. Life including all its powers of love, of joy, and of admiration. That country is the richest which nourishes the greatest number of noble and happy human beings. . . . The final outcome and consummation of all wealth is in the producing as many as possible full-breathed, bright-eyed, and happy-hearted human creatures.[74]

Within the framework of Church doctrine, always our guiding light, Senior's call for a return to reality is very compelling. "Work itself must be in harmony with God's plan, which is nature's plan too because God is the author of nature. We will never find economic, domestic or political and social security *contra naturam*, in a society contraceptive of children and of everything natural and real."[75]

What do we do with machines, then, since they are a major factor in man's separation from nature? We need to take a last look at this subject of machinery to see what Senior proposes in practice.

Technological Violence

At every turn, Senior has struck out against machines. They blunt our senses, cut us off from reality and lead the imagination to fantasy; they breach family life and relationships;

---

[73] Senior, *The Restoration of Christian Culture*, 70.

[74] Quoted in Van Steere, *Work and Contemplation*, 62–63.

[75] Senior, *The Restoration of Christian Culture*, 93–94.

they weaken our mindfulness in work. In chapter two of *The Restoration of Christian Culture*, "The Air-Conditioned Holocaust," which is a diatribe seemingly against technology as such, affirmations such as this are common: "Technology—the new or the old; there isn't any difference whatsoever in the philosophical basis; a computer is a complicated abacus—technology is the inevitable consequence of Epicureanism; it is the dedication of our lives to the pursuit of happiness defined as pleasure."[76] Authors Senior read in his formative years, whom we have mentioned previously—Coomaraswamy, Guénon, Carlyle, Ruskin, Karl Marx—criticized Western man's use of machines, especially as the main component of factory labor, but none of them proscribed machines to the extent that Senior does.

It would seem that Senior would have us imitate the Amish and abandon machines altogether. Here, however, is a slightly more nuanced position: "Machines (as opposed to tools) are, if not intrinsically, at least commonly, evil, to be tolerated only because in a machine society there is no viable option short of heroic virtue (which God counsels but does not command)."[77] "Intrinsically" means essentially, necessarily; "commonly" denotes that the evil is accidentally, but usually, attached to something because of circumstances.[78]

---

[76] Joseph Fessio, e-mail to James Conley, April 9, 2009.

[77] "History and the School," 13.

[78] Fifteen years earlier, Senior had written that television was "intrinsically evil" (*The Restoration of Christian Culture*, 27), and the reason given was its dulling of exterior and interior senses. Senior could not have meant by this expression, as one does in moral theology, that it is always a sin to use television. He did want to say that use of television is always in some ways damaging.

Senior is thus proclaiming that the use of machines generally harms us and, thus, should only be "tolerated." In his opinion, those who have the courage and opportunity should put machines aside, which would simply mean living apart from ordinary society to some measure, since mechanization is part of the fabric of our world. Senior indeed admired the Amish from this point of view: "Virtuous people such as the Amish are trapped by a narrow theology but not by their honest way of life."[79]

By no means was Senior the distant intellectual sitting at the comfort of his desk, asserting on his blog that all should plow their fields with horses, while himself having never touched a tractor. On the contrary, he had known labor in tough, primitive conditions. And he was indeed speaking about real and important problems. Industrialism—that is, a highly mechanized society—has in fact brought on ruinous effects upon community life, in replacing beauty with ugliness, by polluting the land, air, and water. With its colossal means of production, industrialism practically demands that these be property of the state or the rich, thus making it more difficult for small businesses and the family farm to exist.

While we must at least recognize that technological progress brings challenges, often dangers, and even some losses, there are obvious difficulties with Senior's views. He used to give lectures against the use of cars. They went well until the day someone asked: "How did you get here tonight?" The professor, of course, had driven there like everyone else. For a

---

[79] Philippe Maxence, "Des Leçons á méditer. Entretien avec John Senior," *La Nef,* May 1995, 18.

while, he rode a bicycle instead of driving to town, but at last admitted this just took too much time—which is precisely the point! Machines do bring possibilities of real good. They can take away what is most burdensome in toil. John Paul II wrote that of itself the machine is "man's ally" because "it facilitates his work, perfects, accelerates and augments it."[80]

Senior seemed to think that the very notion of machines was linked to the germs of materialism in the Renaissance and the positivism of that age; he saw them as a disorder produced by the perversion of thought of that time. However, even without the help of modern materialist orientations, machinery would doubtless have eventually emerged, although in a more orderly fashion. Benedict XVI criticized those who "deny *in toto* the very idea of [technological] development" because that view proceeds from "a lack of trust in man and in God." As to the lack of trust in man: "It is . . . a serious mistake to undervalue human capacity to exercise control over the deviations of development or to overlook the fact that man is continually oriented towards 'being more.'" Refusing technological development is also a lack of trust in God and His providence because "technology . . . is a response to God's command to till and to keep the land that he has entrusted to human beings."[81]

We cannot hold man back from learning and from wanting to progress in instrumentation. Mankind is always advancing in knowledge and mastery of the world. Cultural dynamism is habitually accompanied by some technological

---

[80] John Paul II, *Laborem Exercens*, no. 5.

[81] Benedict XVI, *Caritas in Veritate*, June 29, 2009, no. 14 and 69.

progress. While it is true that our powerful instruments have become a threat, even fallen man can use them properly; he can critique what he has done and ameliorate the situation. For that, however, we must first step back a moment, slow down and take stock of things, to avoid being caught in the mad, downhill rush of technology.

Senior's reflections certainly remain a helpful starting point for a thoughtful discussion of modern technology. First, they impress on us the importance of such an analysis. Although Senior's romantic idealism and his habit of rhetorical exaggeration color his bold statements, a book review of *The Restoration of Christian Culture* remarked that his affirmations awaken us and make us sensitive toward the degree to which technology affects our lives:

> Even if you find [Senior's] contempt for modern technology somewhat extreme, I would recommend reading his ideas in order to make yourself aware of how significantly our lives are impacted by technology today. Although it's not often talked about, I think it's vitally important for parents to understand that problems with television for children go beyond simple concerns with regard to morally offensive content. People were not designed to sit in front of a box (be it a computer or a television).[82]

Second, he provides the basic principle of order for the analysis. Even in that hard-hitting chapter, "The

[82] Alicia Van Hecke, "The Restoration of Christian Culture," July 8, 2000 (accessed February 26, 2006), http://www.love2learn.net/node/923.

Air-Conditioned Holocaust," one can find at one point the essential nuance to his position: "Technology must be regeared to the proper dimensions of the human good."[83] This substantially puts all of Senior's sweeping affirmations in right order. Technology is a means, not an end; it should serve man's authentic good. We make ends out of means when, for example, "industries are organized for the efficiency of their administration and not the product or the job to be done, where we are served tasteless meals under conditions beneath the level of the feeding-trough in fast-food shops because they can get us in and out faster with a greater cash return and fewer dirty dishes."[84] We must give primacy to human values, to all that Senior argued for: beauty, relationships with other human beings, groundedness in reality, and, in work, quality and excellence rather than quantity, speed, and money.

Third, he shows that this refocus requires a profound and extensive transformation of our approach to nature. The proper attitude toward nature should fundamentally be that poetic gaze Senior so advocates—seeing the visible world as a clothing, as it were, of the spiritual world, and thus approaching it with a contemplative reverence. Then we would no longer consider sensible reality as a simple source of pleasure, power, and comfort. We would seek to collaborate with nature rather than crush it. We would strive to cultivate its beauty and worth.

---

[83] Senior, *The Restoration of Christian Culture*, 62.

[84] Senior, *The Restoration of Christian Culture*, 62.

If Senior were to have it his way, we would all be riding horses. But it must be admitted that, in practice, he did endeavor to simplify and discipline the use of technology in his immediate milieu and family. As we know, his house had no television. He lived in the country. He walked, rather than drove, or rode, when he could. He exhorted others to practice simplicity. We have examined some of his practical suggestions. Indeed, each person should reflect for himself on how best to use technology without becoming a slave to it, how to compensate for losses.

He should judge what is the best means for the human good in the circumstances at hand. We are to use machines according to God's will, for His glory and man's good. I would add that, if we use them, we ought not to curse them but give thanks to God for them.

A former student of Senior's wrote a book about his experience of a year in an Amish type of society. Its concluding passage reads:

> There really is no end to the possible uses of technology, nor are there limits to finding a way around it; but in all cases it must serve our needs, not the reverse, and we must determine these needs before considering the needs for technology. The willingness and the wisdom to do so may be the hardest ingredients to come by in this frenetic age. Perhaps what is needed most of all, then, are conditions favorable to them: quiet around us, quiet inside us, quiet born of sustained meditation and introspection. We must set a time aside for it, in our churches, in our studies, in our hearts. Only when

> we have met this last requisite, I suspect, will technology yield its power and become a helpful hand servant. Mary and I still turn on the kerosene lamp and read by the fire on a cold winter's eve. By switching off the electric light, I think we see a bit better.[85]

Senior has no secret, magical solution for reestablishing an environment of truth, or initiating the restoration of realism through gymnastic and music. What he does in his writing is mainly describe the healthy, natural bases from which culture would grow. He encourages a return to normal family and community life in a natural setting, with poetry, stories, songs, and conversation; he proposes the taking up of inspiring, honest work, preferably close to nature and with some use of the hands.

Conclusion

Senior himself had always sought the stars. He was at least seeking adventure, something beyond comfort and security, when as a scrawny thirteen-year-old New Yorker, he ran off to become a cowboy. He was reacting against immediate pleasure and egotistical pursuits, he was seeking some sort of absolute, when he desired to help establish the earthly paradise of Marxism or when he turned to the spiritual world with Plato, symbolist poetry, and Eastern thought. He one day ascertained, however, that his journey was leading nowhere, finding nothing; the stars seemed to be fading. He

---

85 Eric Brende, *Better Off: Flipping the Switch on Technology* (New York: Harper Collins, 2004), 233.

feared that life had no meaning, that it was not an adventure after all. Providence eventually led him to St. Thomas Aquinas and to a path out of the dark labyrinth. He perceived the stars once more, felt a renewal of their call, and soon had the presentiment of a love whispering to him through their beauty. He grasped that the meaning of man's life was to seek Someone who was already seeking him.

Senior therefore saw that his task was to reconnect his students to reality—beyond the mathematical schemas of modern science—with *being*, with the existence of things. The obstacle to this was not only the pseudoscientific, materialist imagination with which they were imbued, whereby quantity is the only reality. Just as fundamental was the artificial and sensational world the students lived in. Their senses first had to be connected to reality before the remainder of their faculties could delve into it. A full sensible connection to reality would not be accomplished by some sort of positivism that severs sensation from the rest of one's powers. It would only be achieved in a normal, human, integral way, where what is sensed reverberates in our whole being, where sense, memory, imagination, emotions, mind, and will function together. Senior, therefore, cultivated the sensitivity of the human person, with its natural dynamic ordered to the spiritual, to *being*.

Senior thus focused on the first two steps in education—on gymnastic, and on music and the poetic mode of knowledge. He encouraged delightful experience, and cultivated, through wonderful music, what experience his students might have. Through a poetic type of knowledge, he helped them recognize in an experiential way that things were really real, that they had substance and depth. Even though the students could not grasp the fact clearly in thought, or prove it in a syllogism, they perceived their own communion with things, their correspondence to them as they tasted the sweetness of beautiful mysteries that touched their souls. They discovered that, somehow, they were part of a whole, that they participated in something greater than themselves. Thus fixing their roots in the soil, they were also stimulated to an ascent to the stars.

Works Cited

Benedict XVI. *Caritas in Veritate.* June 29, 2009. https://www.vatican.va/content/benedict-xvi/en/encyclicals/documents/hf_ben-xvi_enc_20090629_caritas-in-veritate.html.

Brende, Eric. *Better Off: Flipping the Switch on Technology.* New York: Harper Collins, 2004.

Hecke, Alicia Van. "The Restoration of Christian Culture." July 8, 2000. http://www.love2learn.net/node/923.

John Paul II. *Laborem Exercens.* https://www.vatican.va/content/john-paul-ii/en/encyclicals/documents/hf_jp-ii_enc_14091981_laborem-exercens.html.

Lindquist, Kempton. "Professor Senior." *University Daily Kansan*, August 21, 1974.

Maxence, Philippe. "Des Leçons á méditer. Entretien avec John Senior." *La Nef*, May 1995.

Senior, John. "History and the School." Mss., 1995.

———. *The Death of Christian Culture.* New Rochelle, New York: Arlington House, 1978.

———. *The Remnants: The Final Essays of John Senior.* Forest Lake, MN: The Remnant Press, 2012.

———. *The Restoration of Christian Culture.* San Francisco: Ignatius Press, 1983.

———. "The Restoration of Innocence: An Idea of a School." mss 1994.

———. "The Thousand Good Books, or, What Everyone Should Have Read." Appendix to Senior, John. *The Death of Christian Culture.* Roman Catholic Books, 1994.

———. "The Uses of Education." *Wyoming University News*, June 1967.

———. *Pale Horse, Easy Rider.* Lawrence: Shakespeherian Rag Press, 1992.

Van Steere, Douglas. *Work and Contemplation.* New York: Harper and Brothers, 1957.

Thomas Storck

Thomas Storck, a convert to the Catholic faith, has been writing on Catholic social teaching, economics, and culture since the early 1980s. He received his undergraduate education at Kenyon College in Ohio and took an MA at St. John's College, Santa Fe, in 1980. He is the author, editor, or translator of thirteen books and of numerous articles and book reviews. Storck is also a contributing editor of *New Oxford Review*, a member of the editorial board of *The Chesterton Review*, and the host of the WCAT radio/TV program, the Open Door.

CHAPTER 6

AMERICAN CONSERVATIVES, TRADITION, AND LOCALISM

Thomas Storck

Almost any attempt to discuss something intelligently requires that one make clear at the outset the meaning of the terms one is using. So even as common a term as *conservative* warrants an attempt at definition—or at least a discussion as to the difficulties of defining it. For although the term *conservative*, like its counterpart or opposite, *liberal*, is in daily use, in fact the meaning of both terms is hardly as clear as is generally supposed.

To begin such a discussion, we certainly should acknowledge the obvious fact that in the United States today, and for some time past, there have existed two large cultural-political blocs calling themselves conservatives, or the Right, and liberals, or the Left. I say "*cultural*-political" rather than simply political because at bottom neither of these blocs have a coherent or consistent political philosophy. Indeed, membership in each is defined as much by where one lives, how one dresses, what food one eats, the kind of car one drives, the kind of entertainment one consumes, and so on, as by any explicit political commitments. As a matter of fact, it sometimes seems as if the actual views of either of these blocs are defined as much by a desire to oppose the other bloc as by any positive ideas of its own.[1] Of course these two groups do not comprise 100 percent of the population, even 100 percent of the population who are politically aware and engaged. For there are those whose ideologies and ideas transcend either group and who seek to define themselves by older or better-grounded philosophies. But our national discourse simply assumes that every person and even every idea or policy proposal can somehow be located on a left/right spectrum and makes no attempt to ascertain if there are any consistent philosophical concepts underlying them.

Now in fact there is ideological diversity in both of these blocs, especially, I think, in the conservative bloc. Conservatives differ among themselves on the role of government, on economic and foreign policy, on religion, on nearly every matter upon which there can be ideas or policies. And very recently there has arisen a school of conservative thought that rejects or questions the broad liberal consensus that has obtained approval in the West during the last nearly three hundred years. But despite this, speaking broadly, one can say that the conservative bloc or movement as a whole, certainly

---

[1] Two interesting examples of this are the changes that occurred in views toward alternative medicine and free speech. Thirty or forty years ago, these were both espoused mostly by liberals. Today, they have to a great extent been embraced by conservatives and are rejected in practice by liberals.

in its generally accepted leaders and probably in a majority of those who call themselves conservatives, adheres to more or less quasi-libertarian political and economic views. It is held that the role of government should be strictly limited, ideally to a mere guardian of law and order, and even if it is usually recognized that this goal is unattainable in practice, something like this remains the ideal or standard by which the workings of government are judged.

As a necessary corollary to this, conservatives tend to regard economic life as an activity separate from the other activities of mankind, operating almost as a self-regulating machine with its own principles, and that to the extent that anyone, especially the government, attempts to interfere in the workings of this machine, the overall economic well-being of the nation will suffer. A free market, regulated only by competition among the various free economic actors and with prohibitions against only force or fraud, narrowly defined, is regarded as the ideal, even if it is admitted that a totally free market will never be achieved. But to the extent possible, that is the ideal to be sought and maintained, the standard, again, against which any regulation of the economy is to be judged.

Now when looked at in terms of the historic trends of political philosophy, such a policy stance is nothing but nineteenth-century liberalism, as any student of political theory is well aware. How did such a viewpoint become known as *conservatism* in the United States? The reasons are complex, but the framework for such a development was well stated by the Catholic historian Christopher Dawson.

> The United States achieved their independence in the heyday of the European Enlightenment, and this ideology of the Enlightenment was the foundation of their national existence. The peoples of Europe, in spite of their revolutions, were committed to the past and to their separate national traditions. But Americans were committed to the future. They saw the Revolution as the dawn of a new age and a new civilization which was destined to be the civilization of a new world. . . .
>
> In Europe there was a general conflict between Liberalism or the ideology of the Enlightenment and the traditional forms of religion, especially Catholicism, which has divided Latin Europe down to our own days. In America the universal acceptance of the Liberal ideology precluded any such conflict. It was essentially non-controversial and was accepted as common ground by all the different sections of American opinion, whether religious or non-religious.[2]

It was classical liberalism, then, "the ideology of the Enlightenment," that was the traditional or founding philosophy of the new nation. And the Enlightenment thinker most influential in America was not Voltaire or Rousseau but the Englishman John Locke. Locke's ideas on the social order, the state, and the place of religion in society continue to exercise immense influence in this country. The historian Louis Hartz wrote that in America, Locke is a "massive national cliché" and that he "dominates American political

---

[2] Christopher Dawson, *The Crisis of Western Education* (New York: Sheed & Ward, 1961), 182–83.

thought, as no thinker anywhere dominates the political thought of a nation."[3]

Although Locke was a man of the Enlightenment, he did not write against religion; in fact, in a superficial reading of his political philosophy, he appears very favorable to religion. But in fact, he assigns religion an entirely private and subordinate place in human society; it is now simply a matter of individual *opinion*, and although religious *belief* is to be entirely free, religious practice or conduct is subject to regulation by the government whenever it contravenes a law made for some secular purpose.[4]

Locke's entire political philosophy is based on his atomistic understanding of human nature, which he held to be essentially solitary and a-social.[5] Solitary human beings enter into society for the sake of the material advantages which this brings about, but men always retain their original a-social natures. Society, therefore, is to that extent unnatural insofar as it limits our native freedom.

Locke, of course, was not the only intellectual influence on the American colonies and the nascent republic. Many of the colonial settlements, and especially those of New England and the Middle colonies, were founded for

---

[3] Louis Hartz, *The Liberal Tradition in America* (New York: Harcourt, Brace & World, 1955), 140.

[4] Locke's (first) *Letter Concerning Toleration* of 1689 is the best source for understanding the place of religion in his polity. See also my article, "John Locke, Liberal Totalitarianism, and the Trivialization of Religion," *Faith & Reason*, vol. 26, no. 3, autumn 2001, 227–48.

[5] Locke's understanding of human nature is in turn based on his nominalistic metaphysics. See, for example, his *Essay Concerning Human Understanding*, in particular, book 3, chapter 3, no. 11.

religious reasons, so that, in addition to Locke, another inheritance was present, that of Protestant Christianity, and in its most intellectually influential form, the particular brand of Puritan Calvinism. Although the influence of Calvinism has been strong in the United States, it has not been so much the actual doctrines of Calvin, already waning in their dogmatic emphasis and increasingly justified as merely a force for morality,[6] but what one might call the spiritual atmosphere created by Calvin. There existed an interesting resonance between the secularized version of Calvin's individual soul chosen for either eternal life or eternal damnation and Locke's solitary inhabitant of the state of nature, for in both cases the individual person enjoyed a unique and ultimately unfathomable relationship with what was held to be absolute, either, with Locke, a-social personal freedom, or with Calvin, the inscrutable will of God. In both cases, these absolutes simply existed, but understanding them or their purposes was beyond human capacity.

American religious ideas as they developed during the eighteenth century found themselves in broad accord with Locke's conception of religion and of the role it should play in political and social life. Moreover, even as these ideas played out in society, the predominance of small farmers and craftsmen (at least in the north) gave a certain reasonable

---

[6] At the end of the eighteenth and beginning of the nineteenth centuries, many of the old Puritan congregations of New England found it an easy transference to become Unitarian, or at least to blur or ignore the doctrinal tenets that were the original founding theological principles of Puritanism. Cf. Conrad Wright, *The Unitarian Controversy: Essays on American Unitarian History* (Boston: Skinner House, 1994).

color to this individualism, for there were as yet no large corporations with the power to dominate economic and political life.

As long as there existed a rough economic equality in the new nation, along with a residual Protestant ethical consensus, the implications of Lockean individualism were not yet apparent. The important point, however, is that the "ideology of the Enlightenment was the foundation of [American] national existence" and was accorded a "universal acceptance . . . as common ground by all the different sections of American opinion, whether religious or non-religious."[7] Hence it *was* American tradition, and what was a revolutionary and anti-traditional viewpoint in Europe became in the United States the national ideology. And as a variety of liberalism, what became American conservatism held a concept of the state and of social authority very different from that of European conservatives or of European tradition generally.[8] Frank S. Meyer, one of the architects of the post-World War II so-called fusionist conservative movement, wrote:

> Nineteenth-century [European] conservatism defended values based upon a fundamental moral order and

---

7 Dawson, *Crisis of Western Education*, 139.

8 Above I asserted that neither conservatism nor liberalism "has a coherent or consistent political philosophy." How does that statement square with my claiming that American conservatism represents nineteenth-century liberalism? In its main lines of thought, this conservatism does carry on the political and economic doctrines of classical liberalism, but it has associated with it numerous other ideas which either do not follow from or are even opposed to that liberalism, e.g., hostility to advanced liberal ideas about sexuality, gender, and so on. And even to such wholly contingent and accidental matters as vaccines. See also note 2 above.

> the authority of tradition, standing firmly against the corrosive attack of utilitarianism, positivism, and scientism. But it did not recognize as a truth corollary to its defense of moral values that acceptance by individual persons of the moral authority of objective standards of the good must be voluntary; when it is a mere surface acceptance imposed by external power, it is without meaning or content. Nineteenth-century conservatism was all too willing to substitute for the authority of the good the authoritarianism of human rulers, and to support an authoritarian political and social structure.[9]

A careful reading of the above quote will show that it is essentially based upon a Lockean or classical liberal understanding of man. Human beings are so much individuals "that acceptance by individual persons of the moral authority of objective standards of the good must be voluntary; when it is a mere surface acceptance imposed by external power, it is without meaning or content."[10] This argument, however, ignores several crucial points: first, that *any* laws, even those designed to establish a libertarian society, always impose standards and rules upon citizens, whether they agree with them or not. Law cannot operate otherwise, and in fact, the establishment of the liberal order in nineteenth-century Europe did involve the forcible overturning of innumerable

---

[9] Frank S. Meyer, "Conservatism," in Robert A. Goldwin, ed., *Left, Right and Center: Essays on Liberalism and Conservatism in the United States* (Chicago: Rand McNally, 1965, 1967), 11–12.

[10] Dawson, *Crisis of Western Education*, 117.

laws, customs, and practices that had existed since the Middle Ages and even before. Second, that the promotion of the common good is the task ultimately of the state, and that it is not dependent upon voluntary acceptance by each and every person of that program. Certainly any reading of the corpus of papal social encyclicals, for example, will make clear that the establishment of a just social order cannot be simply a voluntary project. And thirdly, that it is a false dichotomy to contrast "voluntary" with "a mere surface acceptance imposed by external power." As Aristotle taught centuries ago, law is a teacher, and good laws can lead citizens to virtuous ideas and promote virtuous conduct. Most citizens will not be in a position to intelligently evaluate such matters, and their acceptance of the ruling ideas of society will usually be somewhere in-between purely voluntary and "a mere surface acceptance."

When we look more closely at the conservative movement today in the United States, which traces its origins to the period immediately after World War II, more questions arise. Frank Meyer in the essay already cited, sees American conservatism as "based upon [a] commitment to the recovery of a tradition, the tradition of Western civilization and the American republic, which has been subjected to a revolutionary attack in the years since 1932." And he credits its origins to

> a delayed reaction to the revolutionary transformation of America that began with the election of Franklin Roosevelt in 1932. That revolution itself has been a gentler, more humane, bloodless expression in the United States of the revolutionary wave that has swept

> the globe in the twentieth century. . . . Everywhere, however open or masked, it represents an aggrandizement of the power of the state over the lives of individual persons.[11]

But in the first place, we are entitled to ask if the election of Roosevelt in 1932 and the subsequent New Deal really represented something essentially opposed to Western tradition. Allan Carlson has powerfully argued that in fact the New Deal in many respects fostered and upheld a very traditional family policy, one based upon the idea of the father as the family's breadwinner and which respected the unique place of mothers in the family and their important role in caring for children. New Deal family policy was rooted in the group that Carlson calls the maternalists.

> They supported the idealized domestic status quo—the bread-winning father, the stay-at-home mother, and children enjoying a true childhood—while attacking the "industrial evils" that threatened to undermine this system.[12]

"The most representative and influential" of the maternalists was Frances Perkins, Secretary of Labor during all four of Franklin Roosevelt's administrations. She wrote:

> The poor people have a right to their homes the same as the rich, and we should not be allowed to enslave them to a form of industry which refuses them not

[11] Meyer, "Conservatism," 3–4.

[12] Allan C. Carlson, *The "American Way": Family and Community in the Shaping of the American Identity* (Wilmington: ISI, 2003), 57.

> only their liberty, but the wage which they ought to have in return for the labor they perform.[13]

Interestingly, it was big business, especially as represented by the National Association of Manufacturers, that opposed the maternalists' vision of the family and:

> welcomed the remodeling of the family along industrial lines. The "new" family would look outward to the market-place for its values and human bonds. Industry, rather than family and father, would provide sustenance and meaning. Family autonomy and parental authority would give way to universal adult employment and a consumption-oriented lifestyle guided by advertising, one compatible with feminist ambitions.[14]

The family wage, so bitterly opposed by corporate interests, was a centerpiece of New Deal policy, as was the settlement of families on the land.[15]

Hence one is entitled to ask whether the fulminations during the 1950s and thereafter of Frank Meyer and other fusionist conservatives against the alleged "revolutionary transformation of America" was anything more than griping about the economic restrictions that American big business

---

[13] Carlson, *The "American Way,"* 61–62.

[14] Carlson, *The "American Way"*, 61. See also Carlson's book, *Third Ways: How Bulgarian Greens, Swedish Housewives, and Beer-Swilling Englishmen Created Family-Centered Economies—and Why They Disappeared* (Wilmington: ISI, 2007), for more on the pro-family policies of the New Deal, especially pp. 31–32.

[15] Carlson, *The "American Way,"* 46–48, 63–68.

had to accept, restrictions which at bottom were simply a turning away from the nineteenth-century economic liberalism that continues to be so marked a feature of so many American conservatives.[16]

The adherence by most American conservatives to nineteenth- century liberal policy ideas gives rise to an almost instinctual opposition to limiting the corporate power that has itself promoted a truly "revolutionary transformation of America" by restructuring the family to serve the interests of corporations and promoted the hollowing out of the countryside. Nor do the corporations hesitate to use their economic power to promote their own financial interests in the name of claims to individual freedom and rights. The deliberate intellectual confusion they have created was well described close to a hundred years ago.

> The owner of the small farm, of the small factory, of the village store, owns a distinct kind of property. It is the familiar, historical kind. The reason why the "little man" confidently identifies his interests with the big interests is that he cannot imagine another kind of property than his own. He thinks that there

[16] Of course, the regulation of the economy need not, and most often should not, be undertaken directly by the central government. In Catholic thought, it was intermediate groups, such as a system of revived and modernized guilds, who were to conduct most immediate economic regulation. This Catholic approach is usually ignored in our sterile debates about how and how much the federal government is to regulate the economy. The papal social encyclicals, beginning with Leo XIII's *Rerum Novarum*, offer a framework and wealth of ideas on such intermediate groups. Cf. especially Pius XI's encyclicals *Quadragesimo Anno* and *Divini Redemptoris*.

> is just "property," and that he has been less successful in accumulating it than Mr. Mellon. Of course, the corporations know better. . . . There could not be a more grotesque proof of this intention of Big Business than the Liberty League, which uses liberty and property as slogans in a campaign to deprive the American people of what little liberty, what little property, they still have.[17]

Depriving the small holder of his property has been a feature of economic liberalism since its rise in the eighteenth century. In what will be seen as a paradox of intellectual history, Friedrich Engels described the results of the action of the French revolutionary government in abolishing the guilds and other remnants of the medieval Christian economic order in words that any traditionalist would surely applaud:

> The antagonism between rich and poor, instead of dissolving into general prosperity, had become intensified by the removal of the guild and other privileges, which had to some extent bridged it, and by the removal of the charitable institutions of the Church. The "freedom of property" from feudal fetters, now veritably accomplished, turned out to be, for the small capitalists and small proprietors, the freedom to sell their small property, crushed under the overmastering competition of the large capitalists and landlords, to these great lords, and thus, as far as the small capitalists and

[17] Allen Tate, "Notes on Liberty and Property" in Herbert Agar and Allen Tate, eds., *Who Owns America? A New Declaration of Independence* (Wilmington: ISI, [1936] 1999), 112.

> peasant proprietors were concerned, became "freedom *from* property."[18]

Nineteenth-century liberalism, in championing economic freedom, which in practice always means the freedom of the rich, finds itself facing a diverse set of opponents, with very different views of the ideal society, but united in their realization that freedom is no more than a means to an end, but never an end in itself. But since American conservatism is implicated in the worldview of nineteenth-century liberalism, philosophically and politically, its understanding of freedom is univocal. Freedom is simply freedom; it simply exists, it has no purpose other than the private purpose each single political or economic actor wishes to ascribe to it. If one person is richer and is therefore able to command greater political power, we do not question either his right to his property or his ability to use his economic power to undermine the common good. Indeed, to follow the logic of economic liberalism, who is even to say there *is* such a thing as the common good, for is it not merely the sum total of the individual private goods of individual private actors, all striving against each other according to each one's desires?

This inability therefore to see that freedom divorced from purpose is at bottom simply a disordered assertion of will is linked to a larger inability to understand purpose, rooted in the empiricism of Locke and modern thinkers in general. There is no *inherent* purpose in things or practices, only

[18] Friedrich Engels, "Socialism: Utopian and Scientific," in Karl Marx and Friedrich Engels, *Basic Writings on Politics and Philosophy* (Garden City, N.Y.: Doubleday, 1959), 72.

the private and individual purposes which each individual invests them with. Today, the Left exemplifies this view with its ideas on sexuality, the Right with its ideas on economics, for both of these blocs are simply manifestations of different stages of liberalism.

Before discussing specifically the question of rural life and policies designed to foster it, we need to look at an objection that can be raised to my characterization of American conservatism. In fact, am I correct in saying that it is historically little more than nineteenth-century liberalism? Am I ignoring important aspects of its thought and some of its most important spokesmen? Let us look at this more carefully.

In the essay I have already cited, Frank S. Meyer acknowledges "stresses and strains within the conservative movement [which] center around one fundamental clash of emphasis, that between what can be called the 'traditionalist' and the 'libertarian' elements within it." Meyer's approach is to downplay any real differences between these tendencies and to emphasize whatever common ground they have or seem to have, as well as to claim that it was influences from Europe that were responsible for these stresses, "from the naturalization in the United States, during this century and the last part of the nineteenth century, of the nineteenth-century conflict between European conservatism and European liberalism."[19] But let us turn to another thinker who is often regarded as the embodiment of conservatism, or at least of what is called traditional conservatism, Russell Kirk. Kirk's 1953 book, *The Conservative Mind*, is indeed widely regarded

[19] Meyer, "Conservatism," 10, 11.

as a classic in this respect. But that book was written long before anything like a conservative movement existed, so let us look instead at a set of lectures Kirk delivered in the early 1980s when the conservative movement has just achieved its first major electoral triumph.[20]

Kirk writes scathingly of libertarians, but he defines them rather narrowly as "those doctrinaire libertarians who stand ready to sweep away government and the very moral order," those who would "abolish taxes, military defense, and all constraints upon impulse."[21] The thinker that Kirk sees as the intellectual ancestor of today's libertarians is John Stuart Mill, and in particular his work *On Liberty*. However this may be, I think that Kirk fails to see that there are really connections between libertarian or quasi-libertarian ideas on economics, whether ultimately stemming from Mill or Adam Smith, and that of a predominant number of American conservatives. These conservatives may not be as doctrinaire as the libertarians whom Kirk assails, they may not advocate for the abolition of government itself, but in their championing of a free market, they approach to the idea of

[20] Collected in *Reclaiming a Patrimony* (Washington: Heritage Foundation, 1982).

[21] Kirk, "The Conservative Movement: Then and Now" in *Reclaiming a Patrimony*, 8, 9. In insisting that the term *libertarian* applies only to those who would "abolish taxes, military defense, and all constraints upon impulse," Kirk seeks to deny altogether the division in the conservative movement which Frank Meyer acknowledged. Kirk writes that "now and again one reads of two camps of alleged conservatives: 'traditionalist conservatives and libertarian conservatives.' This is as if a newspaperman were to classify Christians as 'Protestant Christians and Muslim Christians.' A libertarian conservative is as rare a bird as a Jewish Nazi." "Libertarians: Chirping Sectaries," in *Reclaiming a Patrimony*, 30.

an economy with a minimum of regulations, ideally, regulated only by so-called economic laws and prohibitions against force or fraud, as I noted earlier.[22] Despite Kirk's no doubt sincere strictures against libertarians, conservatives tended and most often still tend to champion an idea of economic life at odds with that of historic Christendom, where economic activity was conducted within a strict framework of guild regulations and local customs. As Christopher Dawson wrote:

> Thus the medieval city was a community of communities in which the same principles of corporate rights and chartered liberties applied equally to the whole and to the parts. For the medieval idea of liberty, which finds its highest expression in the life of the free cities, was not the right of the individual to follow his own will, but the privilege of sharing in a highly organized form of corporate life which possessed its own constitution and rights of self-government. In many cases this constitution was hierarchical and authoritarian, but as every corporation had its own rights in the

---

[22] In the interests of clarity, I note that what I mean by a free market, or a free-market ideology, is (in the words of Pope Pius XI) the notion that "in the market place and in unregulated competition [there may be found] a principle of self-direction more suitable for guiding them than any created intellect which might intervene." And Pius goes on to say that, "Free competition, however, though justified and quite useful within certain limits, cannot be an adequate controlling principle in economic affairs. This has been abundantly proved by the consequences that have followed from the free rein given to these dangerous individualistic ideas." *Quadragesimo Anno*, no. 88.

> life of the city, so every individual had his place and his rights in the life of the guild.[23]

Here can be found a conception of freedom in both economic and civic life at odds with that of Lockean individualism. Although some conservatives profess a respect for Dawson, it is doubtful that the conservative invocation of ideas such as tradition and place has ever achieved much concrete application when conservatives who held political power came to legislate. Such notions made for colorful nostalgia in their historical and literary tomes, but in practical politics, it was cutting taxes and deregulation, pursued seemingly as ends in themselves, that have generally characterized actual conservative governance. Indeed, when Kirk himself recounts the development of the fusionist conservative movement, he celebrates periodicals, organizations, and individuals of a decidedly free-market cast, whose ideas would have made short work of any determined effort to assert the primacy of family, tradition, or place.[24]

How does all this apply to localism and rural life? The transformation of rural America into a vast network of corporate "farms" and decaying towns and villages is largely the result of the power of those who hold economic sway. In the interests of their profits, both the quality of food and the health of countryside suffer. For,

> as industrialism finally destroys the cities it creates, industrialism is now destroying agriculture. It

[23] Christopher Dawson, *Religion and the Rise of Western Culture* (New York: Sheed & Ward, 1950), 206.

[24] Kirk, *Reclaiming a Patrimony*, 4, 6.

> is destroying our farm homes and their owners, our broad acres and their fertility.
>
> The soil is not a machine for producing cotton, as the loom is a machine for weaving. Raw materials and typewriters and automobiles are not the same as animals and crops. Animals and crops are living things and they follow laws of nature that we must respect. We too are living things, spiritual as well as material living things, but rather than adjust ourselves to the laws of life in our material and spiritual being, we have in recent years spent most of our time in destructive efforts to reduce ourselves to machinery.[25]

Such a distortion of rural America is fundamentally opposed to a balanced understanding of society which recognizes the necessity for both rural and urban life in a healthy polity. And a rural life that consists of strong families on their own land, with all the institutions, religious, cultural, and economic, that such a society requires and fosters. For without families on the land, there will be no rural parishes or schools, few craftsmen or other small businesses, nothing but a desert employing as few hired workers as the corporations can get by with.

The laudable efforts to reestablish healthy rural life are not something that can be accomplished by merely voluntary action. The forces arrayed against such efforts are too powerful. Wealthy corporate interests have a considerable financial

---

[25] Luigi G. Ligutti and John C. Rawe, *Rural Roads to Security: America's Third Struggle for Freedom* (Milwaukee: Bruce, 1940), 102–3. If this was the case in 1940, what can one say more than eighty years later?

stake in driving people from the land and making American agriculture chiefly a factor of big business. And such corporate interests have an outsized voice in determining governmental policies which have no interest in addressing the root causes of the decline of rural life. A concerted plan, backed up with government power, will be needed to overcome corporate power.[26]

But aside from the mere desire for riches and power, the corporate vision of such a rural desert, which bases itself upon arguments rooted in the political atomism of Locke, is an equally potent enemy of healthy rural life, for ideas ultimately rule in human affairs. Mere greed will not carry the day, but greed hidden behind an apparently plausible philosophy. For if Locke and the entire liberal economic tradition are correct, we do wrong even to speak of society as more or less healthy, for society is nothing more nor less than the collective free choices of atomistic individuals.[27]

---

[26] The distributists of the 1920s and '30s recognized this, which is why Chesterton, and especially Belloc, did not hesitate to invoke the power of the state as a necessary means to foster well-distributed property. Cf. Belloc's *The Restoration of Property* for a considered program of how to achieve this.

[27] And ultimately in Locke's nominalism, as noted above, for if only individual things have reality, then it is hard to argue against a political and economic order in which only individuals and individual motives count. As Fr. Denis Fahey wrote, "For Locke . . . the State, instead of being the well-ordered organization of a natural society, is merely an artificial creation of autonomous individuals. It is an artificial association which human beings set up in order to emerge from a previous non-social 'state of nature,' and safeguard their civil interests, especially their property and their ownership of lands and money. It has no duty to God." *The Church and Farming* (Hawthorne, Calif.: Omni/Christian Book Club, [1953] 1988), 72.

In this case, there is no common good, only a multiplication of private goods, and absolutely no one has the right to choose among these private versions of the good and impose that upon society.[28] Unfortunately, due to its adherence to nineteenth-century liberalism, there is an inescapable contradiction at the heart of American conservatism between its ingrained economic liberalism and any other values it claims to hold, such as an affection for tradition, place, or family. But is there a way out? Can we escape this philosophical confusion?

I am afraid that the solution I will recommend will sound too drastic for most people. For it involves nothing more than an abandonment of the very term *conservative*. For given the often-conflicting ideas and policies held by those who cling to the term, what is it that these varying groups are trying to conserve? Just as one might ask a self-identified progressive what it is that he hopes he is progressing toward, so one might ask anyone who identifies as a conservative what he hopes to conserve. And I venture to say that in doing so, one would get many different and often opposed answers. But I will end with some comments by G. K. Chesterton

---

[28] As I noted above, the establishment of a classical liberal order is just as much an imposition of one particular vision of the good as would be any other idea of the good society. Just as medieval Christendom embodied its version of the good in a body of law and custom, so did nineteenth-century liberalism, often overturning long-established customs in a ruthless imposition of the political and economic ideas of eighteenth-century deism. Nor were these efforts to forcibly impose a new economic order confined to the nineteenth century. In England, they began in the sixteenth century with the deliberate transformation of rural life.

about the desirability of using precise labels for our ideas, taken from an interesting essay of his, "The Futurists," in which we may be able to glimpse a way out of our dilemma. Now futurism, little known except to specialists today, was an originally Italian literary and artistic movement that began in 1909. It exhibited some features in common with other irrationalist movements of that era, including Dada and early fascism. Its original manifesto proclaimed, "We intend to glorify the love of danger, the custom of energy, the strength of daring," and "we will glorify war—the only true hygiene of the world—militarism, patriotism, the destructive gesture of anarchist, the beautiful Ideas which kill, and the scorn of women."[29] And so on. Does this have anything to do with our discussion of conservatism? Not directly, but as usual, Chesterton zeroed in on what was essential about the whole matter. After some witty remarks detailing the silliness and false bravado of the futurists, he goes on to state that the "flower and finish" of their manifesto "consists ultimately in this statement: that it is bold and spirited to appeal to the future." To which Chesterton replies:

> Now, it is entirely weak and half-witted to appeal to the future. A brave man ought to ask for what he wants, not for what he expects to get. A brave man who wants Atheism in the future calls himself an Atheist; a brave man who wants Socialism, a Socialist; a brave man who wants Catholicism, a Catholic. But a

[29] Quoted in Herschel B. Chipp, *Theories of Modern Art: A Source Book by Artists and Critics* (Berkeley: University of California, 1968), 286.

> weak-minded man who does not know what he wants in the future calls himself a Futurist.[30]

In other words, if I may venture an analogy: Let those who want to conserve freedom call themselves liberals, let those who want to conserve capitalism call themselves capitalists, let those who want to conserve the Constitution call themselves constitutionalists, and let those who want to conserve Catholicism, call themselves Catholics, with all that that implies here for our vision of life upon the land and our rejection of the ideological constraints imposed by conservatism. For God forbid that anyone of us should simply call himself a conservative, for there are almost as many things to conserve in this world as there are people, and if we are to have any intelligent discussion, we had best be clear about what we think, what we want to conserve and why we want to conserve it. The notion of conservative has at its heart a mass of confused and often opposed ideas. It is not a help to our thinking or even a shorthand way of speaking, but a hindrance to clarity. I recognize that the term *conservative* has an immense appeal to many. But as well as being more clear, will we not be more honest, and indeed more brave, if we simply state what it is that we want, and, indeed, not only what we want to conserve but to renew, to extend and to share with all of mankind?

---

30 Gilbert Keith Chesterton, *Alarms and Discursions* (New York: Dodd, Mead, 1911), 126.

Works Cited

Carlson, Allan C. *The "American Way": Family and Community in the Shaping of the American Identity.* Wilmington: ISI, 2003.

Chesterton, Gilbert Keith. *Alarms and Discursions.* New York: Dodd, Mead, 1911.

Chipp, Herschel B. *Theories of Modern Art: A Source Book by Artists and Critics.* Berkeley: University of California, 1968.

Dawson, Christopher. *Religion and the Rise of Western Culture.* New York: Sheed & Ward, 1950.

———. *The Crisis of Western Education.* New York: Sheed & Ward, 1961.

Engels, Friedrich. "Socialism: Utopian and Scientific." In Karl Marx and Friedrich Engels, *Basic Writings on Politics and Philosophy.* Garden City, N.Y.: Doubleday, 1959.

Fahey, Denis. *The Church and Farming.* Hawthorne, Calif.: Omni/Christian Book Club, 1988.

Hartz, Louis. *The Liberal Tradition in America.* New York: Harcourt, Brace & World, 1955.

Kirk, Russell. *Reclaiming a Patrimony.* Washington: Heritage Foundation, 1982.

Ligutti, Luigi G. and John C. Rawe. *Rural Roads to Security: America's Third Struggle for Freedom.* Milwaukee: Bruce, 1940.

Meyer, Frank S. "Conservatism." In *Left, Right and Center: Essays on Liberalism and Conservatism in the United States*. Edited by Robert A. Goldwin. Chicago: Rand McNally, 1965.

Pius XI, *Quadragesimo Anno*, https://www.vatican.va/content/pius-xi/en/encyclicals/documents/hf_p-xi_enc_19310515_quadragesimo-anno.html.

Tate, Allen. "Notes on Liberty and Property." In *Who Owns America? A New Declaration of Independence*. Edited by Herbert Agar and Allen Tate. Wilmington: ISI, 1999.

Samuel Shephard, PhD

Samuel Shephard, PhD, is from the Isle of Skye in the Scottish Highlands. He currently serves as a Professor at Ave Maria University (AMU) in Florida. Having a lifelong passion for environmental stewardship, his work focuses on sustainable fishing, farming, and other outdoor practices that connect people to nature. Dr. Shephard directs the AMU minor in Agriculture and Catholic Environmental Stewardship and oversees the university farm and garden, blending the theory and practice of sustainability in a commitment to caring for the earth, our common home.

CHAPTER 7

THE VIRTUOUS HUNTER AND STEWARDSHIP OF THE LAND

Samuel Shephard

When I looked at the news this morning, one of the headlines proclaimed, "the first recreational astronauts to walk in space." There are all sorts of reasons why this extra-terrestrial expedition is relevant to a book on the Catholic land movement. For a start, researchers at the University of Cypress have found that the first 165 seconds of a rocket launch emits around 116 tons of CO_2 into the atmosphere.[1] In other words, it is difficult to jump off the Earth without leaving some mucky footprints behind you. The whole concept of space travel as entertainment is compelling, but what struck me most about this expedition was a widely reported comment from the primary client. Speaking from orbit, he

[1] Ioannis W. Kokkinakis and Dimitris Drikakis, "Atmospheric pollution from rockets," *Physics of Fluids* 34, May 2022, https://pubs.aip.org/aip/pof/article-abstract/34/5/056107/2847501/Atmospheric-pollution-from-rockets.

apparently said, "Back at home we all have a lot of work to do, but from here Earth sure looks like a perfect world."

Seeing our planet from the outside must be an awe-inspiring experience. I can only imagine how one's grasp of creation might be spontaneously expanded to the wonderful scale of the solar system. Of course, what you *cannot* see is the people or any of their works; Chinese astronauts report that the Great Wall of China is not in fact visible from the moon! The absence of humans is relevant, because the idea of a perfect world with minimal input from *Homo sapiens* underlies a powerful strand in the environmentalism of modern America.

An important early thinker in this mode was John Muir, the Scottish-born naturalist and California mountain wanderer. Muir spent a youthful summer working as a shepherd in Yosemite,[2] where his ecstatic encounter with natural beauty was tempered by the ecological harm imposed by his trampling and overgrazing flock. This tension introduced an enduring quandary for a man who recognized transcendent spiritual significance in nature and wished to share this glory with others. St. Bonaventure referred to the created order as "God's First Book," capturing the perspective that we can meet and learn about our Creator by spending time in the garden that He has made. Ralph Waldo Emerson said of this formative process that "the moral influence of nature upon every individual is that amount of truth which it illustrates to him."[3] John Muir was a self-professed disciple of Emerson

---

2 John Muir, *My first summer in the Sierra* (Houghton Mifflin Company, 1911).

3 Ralph Waldo Emerson, *Nature* (Liberal Arts Press, 1948).

and dedicated great energy to the preservation of natural systems, especially Yosemite. He wanted eastern modernites to engage with nature, because he believed that it would be deeply beneficial, but he felt that this interaction should (in modern parlance) "leave no trace." Muir's vision was strongly influential in the establishment of the US National Parks Service, but he also founded the Sierra Club, which retains as its primary mission statement the need "to explore, enjoy, and protect the wild places of the earth."

John Muir takes a place of honor in the evolution of the American outdoors, but his perspective was enriched by another iconic figure. Enter the (self-proclaimed) red-blooded cowboy gentleman and hunter Theodore Roosevelt. President Roosevelt was a great admirer of Muir and visited him at Yosemite in 1903. National Parks Service legend has it that he wrote ahead to California proposing a camping trip and said, "I do not want anyone with me but you, and I want to drop politics absolutely for four days and just be out in the open with you." The two men shared a deep awareness and love of nature, and a strong desire to protect the wild, but their participation in natural systems differed markedly. Roosevelt's engagement was built substantially around the "roughrider" tradition of the American West—herding Texas steers, hunting animals for food, and sleeping under the stars.[4] Despite spending most of his time in the sophisticated and socialite East, he owned two ranches in the badlands of North Dakota and considered the challenges of

---

4 Theodore Roosevelt, *The Wilderness Hunter* (Review of Reviews Co, 1893).

this rugged outdoor lifestyle to be a profoundly formative path to virtuous American manhood. Roosevelt's writing counters the wildflower soliloquy of Muir with campfire tales of grand landscapes, memorable rifle shots, and the triumphant kill.

Muir and Roosevelt differed in their approach to the use of nature: one skipped about the meadows with a long beard and a pocketful of bread, while the other rode his faithful steed "Manitou" and ate elk steaks. However, a powerful common strand in their thinking was the former's recognition that "wildness is a necessity" and that it is very vulnerable to human impacts. Both men could say with Henry David Thoreau that "the West of which I speak is but another name for the Wild; and . . . in Wildness is the preservation of the world."[5] Both also witnessed the end of an American West that had shifted rapidly from representing all the drama of wild nature and apparently infinite natural "resources" to a fragile system that needed careful management and protection. Roosevelt was writing only "a score of years" after the extirpation of plains buffalo, and reported the words of a cowboy who rode for nine days and was "never out of sight of a dead buffalo, and never in sight of a live one." Muir lamented similarly of the central valley of California that "in the noblest forests of the world, the ground, once divinely beautiful, is desolate and repulsive."[6] Each of them lived through a threshold moment of accumulating negative

---

[5] Henry David Thoreau, *Walking*, in *The Making of the American Essay*, ed. John D'Agata (Minneapolis: Graywolf Press, 2016), 167–95.

[6] John Muir, *Our National Parks* (Houghton Mifflin and Company, 1901).

anthropogenic impacts on the places that they loved deeply, and which were fundamental to their personal identity.

The latter decades of the nineteenth century thus raised novel and pressing "land use" questions in North America. The overlapping practical and theoretical responses of Muir and Roosevelt persist strongly today in our divergent environmental philosophies and practices. The two men have sometimes been set against each other as advocates for "preservation vs. conservation" approaches to nature, in which curated protection is set against sustainable use. However, their legacy is much more coherent than that. This chapter introduces both schools and argues that caring and sustainable *use* by humans who are embedded in their natural systems is the framework most fully oriented to the common (social and ecological) good. Indeed, the second line of the Sierra Club's mission statement reads "to practice and promote the responsible use of the earth's ecosystems and resources."

Having said that, there is a certain logic to the preservationist perspective elicited in John Muir by threats to his beloved mountains. Humans continue to cause widespread loss of ecosystems and species, and periodic assessments by the Stockholm Sustainability Institute suggest that these impacts cross planetary boundaries for biodiversity and ecosystem function. Many of us experience troubling evidence of environmental harm on a daily basis: there might be invasive insects in our garden, toxic algal blooms at our favorite lake, or layers of plastic on the beach. Serious environmental harm has occurred since the industrial revolution, but the current pace and scale of anthropogenic change appears unprecedented. It also has profound personal implications, especially for the poor. Pope Francis has consistently emphasized that "the human environment and the natural environment deteriorate together."[7] Worrying ecological trajectories and associated feelings of powerlessness lead many people to question "what's left?" of Earth's remaining wilderness, when, as the English poet Gerard Manley Hopkins suggested,

> . . . all is seared with trade
> bleared, smeared with toil
> and wears man's smudge and shares man's smell.[8]

The frequent conclusion is that if humans are the problem, then the wild—whatever that is—might be better off without us. The inevitable policy outcome is human exclusion, either by population control or the establishment of terrestrial or aquatic "closed areas" in which human use of nature is limited. Such negative approaches can seem to make sense but feel uncomfortable to people, including Christians and other religious believers, who have an intuition that we are in some way special and bear unavoidable responsibility to *care* for the Earth. This perspective of human uniqueness and leadership often extends beyond recognizing our unique cognitive and linguistic capacities, to accepting various dimensions of spiritual transcendence. Such glimmers of human significance and belonging on Earth suggest that societal calls for anthropogenic retreat demand rigorous reflection. We are compelled to pivot for a moment from reactive and mechanistic management tools to more

---

7 Pope Francis, *Laudato Si',* encyclical letter, 2015.

8 Gerard Manley Hopkins, *"God's Grandeur" and Other Poems*. (Dover Publications, 1995).

profound questions about who we are, how we fit into the system, and how roles, rights, and responsibilities might (or should) be parsed across non-living systems, plants and animals, and us.

Answering each of these intimidating existential questions comes down to figuring out what a human being actually *is*. In other words, a fundamental requirement for meaningful discussion of environmental issues is a right model for the position or role of the human person with regard to other aspects of the natural world. This framework can be specified as what St. John Paul II called an "adequate anthropology," or a construct which is capable of capturing the fullness of what it is to be human, with any practical or moral implications that might follow.

A superficial attempt at this anthropological exercise appears to present a gradient of options from anthropocentric to ecocentric. The former model specifies all of nature as a set of potential resources, which may be freely assimilated for human use. In other words, the world is a sort of passive platform in which we can implement our *a priori* ideas of art and architecture, culture and industry, unhindered by any inconvenient inherent role or value in the stuff that we accumulate. Conversely, ecocentrism understands humans as simply one species among many; we are essentially a single node in the complex ecological and energetic dynamics of nature and have no more objective significance than a newt. Perhaps no-one believes unequivocally in either construct, although Christians are often accused of an insidious anthropocentrism. Ecocentrism in practice is usually tinged with spiritual and pantheistic overtones, as well as discordant feelings of care which are frustrated by the lack of a philosophical platform from which to intervene in the system. In the other direction, anthropocentrism breaks down with the suspicion that a tree might be more than just a potential fence post: maybe maples matter.

Such unsatisfactory renderings of person and nature can be countered by a Catholic interpretation that recognizes certain unavoidable truths. Pope Benedict XVI referred to an "ecology of man," recognizing that "man too has a nature that he must respect."[9] Exploring what this human ecology might comprise, *Laudato Si',* observes that "our body itself establishes us in a direct relationship with the environment and with other living beings," such that "we are part of nature, included in it and thus in constant interaction with it." It seems that an adequate anthropology can incorporate ecological dynamics, placing humans firmly within a complex interacting web of human-nonhuman processes. However, Pope Francis then emphasizes that "this is not to put all living beings on the same level nor deprive human beings of their unique worth and the tremendous responsibility it entails."[10] In other words, humans are an integral part of the system, but also set apart in some anthropocentric mode, to occupy a unique role in caring for the rest of nature. Such a "situated anthropocentrism" endows humans with particular dignity but accepts that other living components of the system also have substantial inherent value.

---

9 Benedict XVI, "Address of Pope Benedict XVI to the German Parliament," *The Chesterton Review* 37 (2011): 616–22.

10 Pope Francis, *Laudato Si'*, 90.

All this indicates that humans are called to act responsibly from *within* the system, but it doesn't necessarily grant the authority to *use* other species for our benefit. For our current purpose, we will have to assume that sustainable use of nature is acceptable, and we will not look far beyond the biblical injunction "to till and to keep." Suffice to say that human life is not possible without judicious consumption of other earthly life forms, and this is the appropriate end purpose of tilling the earth. Our question will therefore not be *whether* the use of nature is acceptable but *how* we should go about it rightly. The answer will focus on the concept of environmental stewardship.

The *Catechism of the Catholic Church* states that "God entrusted animals to the stewardship of those whom He created in His own image" (*CCC* 2417). Sustainability scientist F. Stuart Chapin and co-authors defined stewardship as the "responsible use and protection of the natural environment through conservation and sustainable practices to enhance ecosystem resilience and human well-being."[11] This phrasing recapitulates the Sierra Club mission statement, but it is also very close to a summary from Pope Benedict XVI, who noted that "the environment is God's gift to everyone, and in our use of it we have a responsibility towards the poor, towards future generations and towards humanity as a whole."[12] Key common components in these parallel perspectives are *use*

---

[11] F. Stuart Chapin, Stephen R. Carpenter, Gary P. Kofinas, Carl Folke, Nick Abel, William C. Clark, Per Olsson et al., "Ecosystem stewardship: sustainability strategies for a rapidly changing planet, "*Trends in Ecology & Evolution* 25 (2010): 241–49.

[12] Benedict XVI, *Caritas in Veritate,* encyclical letter, 2009.

of nature through *sustainable or responsible actions* with some *orientation to flourishing and the common good.* The emphasis on sustainable practice, which implies deliberate intervention or manipulation, introduces a departure from the preservationist "hands-off" philosophy that has been linked here to John Muir. Instead, we find a mode of human existence in the world which is more coherent with Roosevelt's perspective that people are situated within an ecosystem and have a position in the complex predator-prey relationships from which it is constituted. Nonetheless, given our unique cognitive and spiritual capacities, we are expected to occupy and practice this role virtuously.

The link between practice and virtue has a long tradition that was exemplified quite early by Aristotle in his *Nicomachean Ethics*. The basic notion is that striving for excellence in practical tasks—that is, those involving a high level of embodied skill or muscle memory—helps a person to develop parallel intellectual and moral virtues. For example, learning to do something very difficult like riding a horse or carving wood or fly fishing (more on this later) might have collateral benefits in building patience and fortitude. Alisdair McIntyre elaborated how practice in this sense is not menial labor but "involves standards of excellence and obedience to rules as well as the achievement of goods."[13] The practitioner becomes subject to the authority of the best standard achieved in their discipline so far. The bar is set, whether you like it or not, such that "human powers to

---

[13] Alasdair MacIntyre, *After Virtue: A Study in Moral Theory* (University of Notre Dame Press, 1984).

achieve excellence, and human conceptions of the ends and goods involved, are systematically extended."

An important aspect of practice and virtue is the place of wise mentors. The difficulty with attaining excellence in multidimensional embodied tasks is exactly that it is difficult, but also that there is a limit to how far one can learn without being shown. This is evident from the popularity of visual YouTube tutorials relative to earlier self-help manuals, but also in why we still look for person-to-person training. Wise and experienced mentors can help highlight subtle details of practice that open new territory for discovery and learning. They can also judiciously share their own trials and triumphs in a way that is inspiring or reassuring. Roosevelt said in his outback memoir *The Wilderness Hunter* that "it is well to be with some old mountain hunter, a master of woodcraft, who is a first-rate hand at finding game, creeping upon it, and tracking it when wounded. With such a companion one gets much more game, and learns many things by observation instead of by painful experience."[14]

This series of components structure a system in which just use of nature through complex tasks within a local community of practice can help form a virtuous person. It can be added briefly that sustainable practice also invokes the dignity of work. Again, this is a whole topic in itself, but we should remember that our primary role on Earth is practical work: "the Lord God took the man and put him in the garden of Eden to till it and keep it" (Gn 2:15). The United States Conference of Catholic Bishops summarize how

[14] Roosevelt, *The Wilderness Hunter*, 178–79

"work is more than a way to make a living; it is a form of continuing participation in God's creation."[15] Thus, outdoor practices are not or shouldn't be simply drudgery but can aspire to leisure. German philosopher Josef Pieper declared that "the absolutely meaningful activity . . . must needs happen . . . in the contemplating awareness of the world's ultimate and intrinsic foundations."[16] This dimension is more obvious with the crafts, but all meaningful work can be a good and ennobling undertaking.

The work being "meaningful" is also significant when we remember that environmental stewardship is oriented towards ecosystem "resilience and human well-being" or "towards future generations and towards humanity as a whole." This deliberate end means correspondingly that work "must be structured and governed in an ethical manner." For our purposes then, outdoor work engaged with the use of nature is personally fruitful when it is rightly ordered toward the common good. Critical to this teleology is that it approaches consumption of natural goods sustainably, or in a way that does not compromise the ability of future generations to access and enjoy those goods.

The requirement for sustainability highlights a second class of mentor contribution, which is the introduction of moral imperatives, or the "obedience to rules" mentioned by McIntyre. Students must learn about the behavioral norms applying to their new discipline—that is, expectations about how they should act while pursuing a particular practice in

---

[15] USCCB, "Themes of Catholic Social Teaching," 2011, https://www.usccb.org/resources/themes-catholic-social-teaching.

[16] Josef Pieper, *Leisure: The Basis of Culture* (Faber and Faber, 1952).

its associated community. There are obvious links to environmental stewardship here because outdoor work typically relates to finite and/or shared resources that need to be used justly and sustainably. This constraint invokes social imperatives for moderation and equity, and these requirements are often formulated in some way, from club rules to cultural taboos. Interestingly, we tend to be quite good at making such legislative structures work, given certain conditions. The gloomy scientist Garret Hardin suggested in the 1960s that human societies would trend inevitably toward a "tragedy of the commons,"[17] because individuals would always be incentivized to cheat in their use of a shared natural resource such as common grazing grounds for cattle. He suggested that this inevitable rule-breaking would result in overexploitation, followed by ecological and then social collapse. Hardin's predictions were later convincingly disputed by Elinor Ostrom, who won the Nobel prize in economics for her groundbreaking work on so-called "social-ecological systems." Ostrom demonstrated empirically that human communities could usually manage common pool resources sustainably if they maintain community ownership of natural assets, meaningful management authority within their boundaries, and the capacity to sanction cheats.

These required conditions for sustainable social-ecological systems are obviously pertinent to care for the land in Western societies. They are the factors that impart institutional "agency," or the freedom and capacity of participants to act as

---

[17] Garrett Hardin, "Extensions of 'the tragedy of the commons,'" *Science* 280 (1998): 682–83.

they deem appropriate to manage their system in a way that conforms to the common good as they perceive it. However, jurisdiction (agency and power) can shift upward from local to external actors or be devolved back down depending on policy. Furthermore, it is all too possible to have the necessary power but still to act selfishly. This uncertainty raises the critical question: Who is most likely to be a good steward of *our* place? Elinor Ostrom famously suggested that "there is no reason to believe that bureaucrats and politicians, no matter how well meaning, are better at solving problems than the people on the spot, who have the strongest incentive to get the solution right."[18] In this context and following our argument, we might assume that the most likely steward is someone who has acquired relevant virtue through striving for excellence in outdoor tasks within a local community of practice that has management authority and maintains robust behavioral norms for participants in the system. This person has the power to act and is likely to act justly. Such a framing is consistent with the Catholic principle of subsidiarity, which holds that nothing should be done by a larger and more complex organization which can be done as well by a smaller and simpler organization.

Grassroots management agency is evident in effective local authority along with functioning social norms, which can form and support the virtuous actor. However, sustainability scientists have highlighted two further fundamental dimensions of successful environmental stewardship. These

[18] Elinor Ostrom, *Governing the Commons: The Evolution of Institutions for Collective Action* (Cambridge University Press, 1990).

aspects are closely linked to practice and virtue, and comprise *knowledge* and *care*. To be a good caretaker of a natural system, you need to care enough to act, and you need to know what the right thing is to do! It is with regard to knowledge that the multidimensionality of embodied outdoor practices becomes more evident. In order to succeed at tasks like veggie growing or pig raising or foraging for mushrooms, a practitioner needs to become a lay expert in their environment. Prescriptions for when to plant and how, or where to find wild foods, will only get you so far, but expertise comes with prolonged and committed effort. The wise mentor constantly surprises his student with an apparently magical ability to assess a situation and anticipate what is likely to work and when, or why things might be going wrong. Importantly, attaining this local ecological intuition is the key to achieving those highest standards yet achieved in a practice that we highlighted above. Attaining this degree of knowledge and skill takes a long time, but it is the core requirement for success and peer recognition, and is thus strongly incentivized both internally and socially. Vitally, this environmental insight then becomes the route to sustainable management because it is the person having the most intimate knowledge of a social-ecological system who knows best *how and when* to intervene appropriately and constructively to reorient that system to the common good.

Given agency and knowledge (and knowledge is obviously part of agency), the final dimension of environmental stewardship is care. There is a utilitarian element here, because it is expedient to conserve the place and community upon which you rely for work and welfare, but care is also a profound emotional and psychological phenomenon. In our context, it is intricately tangled up with sense of place and personal identity, and emerges almost inevitably from the process of learning and pursuing a challenging and communal outdoor task in a specific natural context. There is good experimental evidence that care for nature and propensity to pro-environmental behavior starts with personal encounters. This link makes sense if we can only "love what we know and only know what we behold." For example, if you tend a piece of land alone for a year, you can only glimpse superficially how it works, and perhaps it is still quite easy to walk away. After a decade, you might start to anticipate the cycle of the year; when the first crocus buds appear, when the swallows return, the primroses and the rains, ploughing, sowing, harvest. This fluctuating sequence will become predictable and intuitive, to the extent that shifts caused by external factors like climate or pollution are experienced almost physically—it "feels" colder or wetter or drier than it "should" be, and where have all the songbirds gone? Populate this framework with the people that you learn from and work with through the slow passage of time and repetition and you are highly likely to become embedded in your place and community. This is care—to love the land and its people like and through your own body.

The British anthropologist Tim Ingold describes this slow people-in-nature process in terms of "dwelling."[19] This dwelling perspective expresses a situated anthropology which contrasts the dualist notion of a human and their

---

[19] Tim Ingold, *The Perception of the Environment: Essays on Livelihood, Dwelling and Skill* (Routledge, 2000).

passive landscape with a relational and embodied dynamic in which place and person emerge together. In this model, the landscape is reinterpreted as a "taskscape" within which outdoor practices repeated in place and time become "constitutive acts of dwelling" like well-trodden pathways. Catholics can take this model a step further by understanding that their taskscape is not just a relational environment but a created order. Pope Francis highlighted in *Laudato Si'*, that "the word 'creation' has a broader meaning than 'nature,' for it has to do with God's loving plan in which every creature has its own value and significance."[20]

Ingold famously expressed his ideas through an exegesis on a well-known sixteenth-century painting called "The Harvesters" by Pieter Bruegel the Elder. You may have noticed the strong and corresponding pastoral atmosphere of the preceding paragraphs of this chapter, a tone which seems appropriate in a book about the Catholic land movement! There is nothing new here. Some of this thinking is already evident in the ponderings of Henry David Thoreau as he pottered around his "Bean-Field" on the shores of Walden Pond in 1845.

> What shall I learn of beans or beans of me? I cherish them, I hoe them, early and late I have an eye to them; and this is my days' work. [21]

Ralph Waldo Emerson had already asked in 1836, "What is a farm, but a mute gospel?"Although this pronouncement is somewhat undermined by his peculiar pantheism. Given

---

[20] Pope Francis, *Laudato Si'*.

[21] Henry David Thoreau, *Walden* (Macmillan Collector's Library, 2016).

this history, it is significant that the dominant philosophies in American nature conservation emerged not on the homestead but out in the wilderness. Thoreau's whimsical bean plot profoundly influenced John Muir, but the poetic Yosemite wanderer perpetually irritated his family by insisting that his real home was a solitary bower in the mountains. Similarly, Roosevelt clearly felt most deeply fulfilled while wrapped in a damp blanket by his campfire in the Dakota Badlands.

The ambiguous concept of wilderness is still extremely important in North American culture, but there is no doubt that the leave-no-trace approach of John Muir now dominates corresponding environmental discourse. Trendy outdoor corporations like Patagonia make millions of dollars selling an organic and fairly-traded hempster lifestyle that is "welcoming" to political allies of every progressive constituency. There are enormous positive elements here and numerous people of integrity and goodwill. However, the underlying philosophy seems to be that humans are slightly inconvenient visitors to nature and should be careful to take their litter home.

In contrast, the situated anthropology of sustainable use has been much less successful in capturing modern approval. Roosevelt's legacy remains evident in the numerous conservation-oriented hunting and fishing organizations of rural North America. However, claims that these practices can underpin environmental stewardship are becoming progressively less acceptable among the urbanized populations of most Western countries. Hunting and fishing are commonly perceived as cruel, unnecessary, and characteristic of outdated anthropocentric worldviews that celebrate the dominion of humans over nature. Many people accept that certain types of small-scale farming can accommodate care for the earth, but they see exactly the opposite of care in the deliberate recreational killing of wild animals. John Muir and his "myriads of fuzzy catkins," yes. Teddy Roosevelt and "the finding and killing of the game," certainly not.

In this social context, we will conclude by exploring how hunting and fishing under certain conditions can exemplify our stewardship model. First, it is worth quickly rehearsing the argument so far. We have suggested that stewardship of a place is based on social-ecological care, local knowledge, and the personal and institutional elements of agency. Knowledge and care emerge from sustained and repeated sensory experience with nature. The best mode of nature experience is learning place-based and embodied tasks that operate within an outdoor community of practice and are intrinsically embedded in the dynamics of a specific natural environment. This community can mentor new entrants, reorienting their attention to subtle but pertinent aspects of the system. Mentors also impart social norms for behavior, such as sustainable and equitable use of natural goods. Striving for clearly evident standards of excellence at practical tasks in this setting helps build virtue such that the participant acquires personal agency, comprising motivation and ethical and technical capacity to act for the common good. Personal agency becomes efficacious when the "institutional" context imparts corresponding communal agency.

The first step, nature experience, is critical. This experience must fulfill the embodied encounter or sensory engagement of our proposed relational or situated anthropology. It means allowing the body to witness what is going on in an ecosystem. Maybe we touch the bark of a tree or smell the wet earth. We learn to recognize the call of certain common birds or pick apart an owl pellet to see which prey it has been eating. Farming and gardening can be very fruitful here, but these systems are necessarily modified (to varying extents) from the wild state and shaped by ongoing human activity. Hunting and fishing are potentially more appropriate because they can offer prolonged periods in wilder environments. Trying to catch and kill a wild animal strongly incentivizes acquisition of ecological knowledge, especially relevant to target species. Where is the prey at this time of day? In this season and weather? What about this abundance and location of its food resources and refuges?

The tasks of hunting and fishing can also be multidimensional and extremely challenging to learn, often holistically engaging body and mind. Such practices fulfill the Aristotelian model of virtue development. Becoming a good fly fisherman, for example, requires patience and persistence and benefits strongly from the support of wise mentors. Eventual attainment of the highest possible level of skill is likely to be attended by the greatest piscatorial and social rewards. Sustainable hunting and fishing also require temperate and prudent use of available resources and opportunities. There will be temptations to greed and dishonesty, but these vices can be offset by social norms imposed by a user community such as an angling club that has achieved management agency through jurisdiction over their private waters.

This experiential and communal process is highly likely to develop a sense of place and identity in participants; this is *my* forest, *my* river. Such feelings might seem dominionistic, but they often entail a strong component of human-nonhuman embedding and personal meaning, in which the predominant feeling is not top-down ownership but something like dwelling in a taskscape, in the sense of Ingold. Almost inevitably, the emotional-psychological outcome is care for the system that is so profoundly significant to personal well-being. In this way, hunting and fishing act to break down the social and sensory barriers that our society has built to domesticate the wilderness. Just as modern American man is obsessed with the numeric minutiae of football, so we often try to parameterize nature. The awe of John Muir at the wonder and beauty of nineteenth-century Yosemite oriented his attention to the Creator. The farmer and amateur philosopher Wendell Berry commented a century later that until modern times, a man "returning from the wilderness" could become a "restorer of order, a preserver." This outcome is still available through properly structured outdoor practices, but Berry has lamented that wilderness has now morphed into "scenery" and our awe has become "statistical," such that "dizzy with numbers" we focus on "how high we stood or how far we saw."[22] The YouTube focus on ten-point bucks and trophy bass suggests that hunting and fishing are dangerously susceptible to statistics. However, recreational catch of wild animals is not intrinsically oriented to production and competition, and most people emphasize the experiential dimensions that can develop the components of environmental stewardship. This pro-environmental outcome

[22] Wendell Berry, *The Unsettling of America: Culture & Agriculture* (Sierra Club Books, 1996).

is evident in organizations like Ducks Unlimited, whose (self-interested) activities generate broad collateral benefits for nature conservation.

The obvious challenge to this experiential framework is that stewardship can be achieved without hunting. Why kill a wild animal when environmental virtue can be developed by growing beans or in wildlife photography? I have written about this issue in high-level scientific journals, and my answer is this: Yes, many of the same skills and experiences apply, but the definitive aspects of hunting and fishing occur at and after the kill. The kill can constitute a relational boundary point at which the hunter or angler may enter more deeply into embodied participation (a situated anthropology) than is possible through other outdoor activities. Hunting and fishing also comprise complex practices that are coordinated through body and mind and which require sensory encounter with nature. The virtuous kill is not an isolated moment but must be linked to a situated series of activities starting with preparation, finding, and killing an animal, and followed by butchering, sharing, and consuming self-caught food. Further, these processual components are colored by pressing moral imperatives to kill responsibly—the right animal at the right time in the right way.

I would like to ask Theodore Roosevelt about all this, and I suspect he would agree in general. John Muir and his environmentalist successors much less, although ongoing interest in hunting and fishing hint at a perennial desire for raw encounter with the wild. Every year, so-called adult-onset hunters pick up a bow or a gun for the first time and head out to kill a living creature. Along with wilderness, a common motivation is the desire to eat consciously. There are strong and obvious links here to localvore movements which emphasize grounded, healthy, responsible (etc.) food production. Shooting a wild deer and killing your home-raised pig are significantly different processes, as are picking suburban lettuce and foraging for wild nuts. However, these tasks and contexts link the American wilderness and its early integration into modern culture to how we might think about stewardship of the small-scale domestic taskscapes of the twenty-first-century homestead.

The point of this chapter was to recall the history of contemporary land-use philosophy in North America. I wanted to show that nineteenth-century thinking on sustainable use is fundamentally consistent with a Catholic understanding of stewardship of creation, and probably valuable to a renewed and informed Catholic land movement. A situated anthropology embeds humans intrinsically in their ecosystems but also sets us apart by the unique capacities of intellect and will. Among all animals, only we have the capacity to decide what is the right thing to do and then commit to doing it. The proper approach is therefore stewardship, or use of nature through sustainable practices with an orientation to the common good. We care for what we behold, and as Pope Francis said in *Laudate Deum*, "The world sings of an infinite love: how can we fail to care for it?"[23]

---

[23] Pope Francis, *Laudate Deum*, encyclical letter, 2023.

Works Cited

Benedict XVI. "Address of Pope Benedict XVI to the German Parliament." *The Chesterton Review* 37 (2011): 616-622.

———. *Caritas in Veritate*, https://www.vatican.va/content/benedict-xvi/en/encyclicals/documents/hf_ben-xvi_enc_20090629_caritas-in-veritate.html.

Berry, Wendell. *The Unsettling of America: Culture & Agriculture.* Sierra Club Books, 1996.

Chapin, F. Stuart, Stephen R. Carpenter, Gary P. Kofinas, Carl Folke, Nick Abel, William C. Clark, Per Olsson et al. "Ecosystem stewardship: sustainability strategies for a rapidly changing planet." *Trends in Ecology & Evolution* 25 (2010): 241–49.

Emerson, Ralph. *Nature.* Liberal Arts Press, 1948.

Hardin, Garrett. "Extensions of 'the tragedy of the commons.'" *Science* 280 (1998): 682–83.

Hopkins, Gerard Manley. *"God's Grandeur" and Other Poems.* Dover Publications, 1995.

Ingold, Tim. *The Perception of the Environment: Essays on Livelihood, Dwelling and Skill.* Routledge, 2000.

Kokkinakis, Ioannis W. and Dimitris Drikakis. "Atmospheric pollution from rockets." *Physics of Fluids* 34, May 2022. https://pubs.aip.org/aip/pof/article-abstract/34/5/056107/2847501/Atmospheric-pollution-from-rockets.

MacIntyre, Alasdair. *After Virtue: A Study in Moral Theory.* University of Notre Dame Press, 1984.

Muir, John. *My First Summer in the Sierra.* Houghton Mifflin Company, 1911.

———. *Our National Parks.* Houghton Mifflin and Company, 1901.

Ostrom, Elinor. *Governing the commons: The evolution of institutions for collective action.* Cambridge University Press, 1990.

Pieper, Josef. *Leisure: The Basis of Culture.* Faber and Faber, 1952.

Pope Francis. *Laudate Deum.* https://www.vatican.va/content/francesco/en/apost_exhortations/ documents/20231004-laudate-deum.html.

———. *Laudato Si'.* https://www.vatican.va/content/francesco/en/encyclicals/documents/papa-francesco_20150524_enciclica-laudato-si.html.

Roosevelt, Theodore. *The Wilderness Hunter.* Review of Reviews Co, 1893.

Thoreau, Henry David. *Walking.* In *The Making of the American Essay.* Edited by John D'Agata, 167–95. Minneapolis: Graywolf Press, 2016.

———. *Walden.* Macmillan Collector's Library, 2016.

Jason M. Craig

Jason M. Craig writes from a small dairy farm in Western North Carolina. He is the co-founder of Faternus, founding editor of Sword&Spade magazine, and author of *Leaving Boyhood Behind.* He holds a master's degree from the Augustine Institute and is known to claim his family invented bourbon.

CHAPTER 8

WENDELL BERRY AND THE REMEMBERING OF COMMUNITIES

Jason M. Craig

One can hardly engage agrarianism in the United States without coming across Wendell Berry. And for good reason. The essays in this book trace threads of Catholic intellectual and spiritual motivation when it comes to the land, but there is also the plain history of it. Wendell Berry knows these threads firsthand—how they come apart and come back together. And, although he isn't Catholic, American Catholics greatly benefit from his writings because his insights come from a distinctly American tradition, but they also challenge that tradition—in its corruption or foundational errors—in ways that correspond surprisingly well with Catholicism.

Few, if anyone, have told the story of our country's change from an essentially land-based economy to an industrial and post-industrial one other than Berry. Born in 1934, he has been publishing his writings since the 1960s, and his influence has been increasing since then. His own history is one of leaving his rural home for the big world—and then his return. Through a budding academic career, he found himself in Italy for a couple years and then teaching at NYU at the Bronx campus. But he famously went back home to Kentucky, and the prodigal son returning home is a consistent theme in his writings, both his fiction and his essays. He has stayed put in Henry County to live out the love of his people but also, in a sense, to remain with a place on its deathbed, to comfort it as it dies from a cancer that won't stop growing and is foreign to the body it feeds from. It is essentially his program for society's restoration and health.

Berry is not only notable because he saw the changes from horses to tractors in the fields, nor because he has forced people to see the decimation of local culture in his own community at the hands of industrialism. I think those that take interest in Berry should do so especially because he witnessed, and to this day has defended, one of the most successful attempts at preserving an agrarian community in the midst of such changes: the Burly Tobacco Cooperative. The cooperative was overseen and utilized by his own family and something that had, for a period, stayed the hand of the so-called "progress" that has consolidated farming into larger and larger holdings and also, by necessity, eradicated farming as a shared and stable way of life.

I would like to propose that the tobacco cooperative as well as the thread of "membership" in Berry's writing are something akin (or kin, as we would say in the South) to the American version of the Catholic guilds of Christendom. I also propose that they represent that illusive ideal of practical and practiced distributism. But, before that, it might be worth noting why Wendell Berry has found so many open ears in the Catholic world.

Catholic Love

Many Catholics have embraced Wendell Berry for his agrarianism, his realism, and even his sacramental imagination.

His agrarian writings and what they bring together in the American experience—from Thomas Jefferson to Aldo Leopold—represent an unquestionably consolidated storehouse of thought unique to this land, but it is also wholly and uniquely his own. In other words, Berry is a true and faithful inheritor of his ancestor's wisdom and experience, a faithful son. This easily places him as a man of tradition, that "democracy of the dead," as Chesterton put it. His agrarianism is unwaveringly human, meaning he cares for the people that live by farming because they are his people, and he believes in their goodness even as he knows their sins.[1] He's known to point out that you "can't take culture out of agriculture," which is why he loathes that agriculture has become "agribusiness," the industrialization of something that simply cannot survive with the logic of efficiency and profit alone. For those that aren't farmers or close to farmers, he reminds them that "eating is an agricultural act." In the documentary about him called *Look and See*, he is shown debating Earl Butz, former secretary of agriculture in the 1970s, and he notes that they are arguing for different

1 See his work *The Need to be Whole* where he deals explicitly with the history of racism and his people.

things. Butz wanted "quantity," says Berry, and he was arguing for quality—not of product, but of life. In some ways, Berry has been carrying on the debate since then. This is because Berry sees a human and even spiritual quality in the life of the land, and therefore, separating a nation from their farming way of life destroys something sacred that will not be recovered by other means, especially by what he calls the "industrial formula" of "Science + Technology + Political Will = The Solution."[2]

His realism is refreshing in that he "calls 'em like he sees 'em," as we say in the States. This makes him embraced and rejected by both the right and the left, which tend to be just different sides of the same coin of modern liberalism. The American left, for example, might be happy to engage him in ideas about conservation and his hard-headed passivism, but they likely won't follow him down observing the results of "sexual liberation" and even his questioning of artificial contraception. He calls environmentalism in the form of "green" this or that a "fad." Those on the American right will find all sorts of difficulties in Berry simply because he places finance capitalism and industrialism (i.e., economic liberalism) as an enemy of the very things that most conservatives claim they are conserving, like family, community, and tradition. "The 'conservatives' promote the family as a sort of public icon," says Berry, "but they will not promote the economic integrity of the household or community, which are the mainstays of family life."[3] It is no secret that Catholics have tended to

---

2 Berry, *The Art of Loading Brush* (Catapult, 2019), 104.

3 Berry, "Sex, Economy, Freedom, and Community" in *Sex, Economy, Freedom, & Community: Eight Essays* (Counterpoint, 2018), 122.

silo themselves more with these political wings than their Church when it comes to the consistent ethical teaching of the Church, embracing the liberalism of sexual "liberation" or the liberalism of unbridled economics. Those who grasp and embrace the Church's teaching on economics, environmental stewardship, the openness to and protection of life, sexual ethics, the obligation toward our neighbors' good (i.e., love), and even a form of thriftiness we might call "poverty" find a uniquely consistent friend in Berry.

As to Berry's "sacramental imagination," he has consistently spoken with more attentiveness to a Protestant sense than Catholic. But he has declared in different places his faith and how it shapes his writing:

> I take literally the statement in the Gospel of John that God loves the world. I believe that the world was created and approved by love which subsists, coheres, and endures by love, and that, insofar as it is redeemable, it can be redeemed only by love. I believe that divine love, incarnate and indwelling in the world, summons the world always toward wholeness, which ultimately is reconciliation and atonement with God.[4]

He speaks of food as a "sacrament" even, perhaps exaggerating what a Catholic might call it, yet also linking the spiritual with the physical, which is not something common

---

[4] Berry, "Health is Membership," delivered as a speech in the conference "Spirituality and Healing" in Louisville, Kentucky, October 17, 1994, https://www1.villanova.edu/dam/villanova/mission/faith/Readings/fall-2020/Health%20is%20Membership%20by%20Wendell%20Berry.pdf.

in Protestant America. He questions the idea of being a "Christian nation" because he thinks that the very act of "destroying the family farm," which our economic policies have done, is precisely because "we are *not* very religious."[5] He wants to inspire his Christian readers to see their place on the land as one of care and not exploitation, a spiritual and not merely functional or financial matter. Some have accused Berry of a sort of pantheism in his love of the land and a clear sense that it is holy. But I think he sees it as holy because he thinks God made it. He seems to propose—rightly, I think—that the country's Protestant ethic has misread the Scriptures into thinking that we can use and abuse the land and excuse ourselves with the biblical imperative to "subdue the land." He greatly dislikes such interpretation of Genesis 1. Many verses, Berry says, "even taken out of context, require humans to take the best possible care of the earth and its creatures."[6] He also echoes regularly that the abuse of land and the abuse of people often go hand in hand, and that this reveals a certain spiritual sickness, a deficient vision of the dignity and "given" nature of creatures.

These threads, as I said, make Berry a favorite among many Catholics, especially in the American literary and scholarly world. Well-known Catholic homesteader (and contributor in this book) John Cuddeback regularly blogs from a quote or two of Berry. Alan Cornett, host of the popular podcast Cultural Debris (which links itself with things like distributism and the inklings), is a regular visitor and

[5] Berry, *Bringing it to the Table* (Counterpoint, 2009), 39. Emphasis added.

[6] Berry, *The Art of Loading Brush*, 107.

friend of Wendell Berry. The popular website Front Porch Republic, which publishes the journal *Local Culture*, has so many sympathetic Catholic authors and readers that there is a recognized need to make sure Protestants can be at the table too.[7] Many Orthodox and Catholic thinkers, including William Fahey, Patrick Deneen, Rod Dreher, Jason Peters, and Anthony Esolen, contributed to the collection *Wendell Berry's Humane Vision*. Berry is a haunting spirit in Catholic magazines like *Sword & Spade*, which I co-edit, as well as *Hearth and Field*, which publishes online and in print about agrarian living. Whenever I have attended an event related to Berry, I have run into Catholic friends, intellectuals, and priests. For his part, Wendell Berry has clearly not inherited at least one thing common in America, especially in academia and the south: anti-Catholicism. In many places, he engaged with Catholic authors, but perhaps this is seen most acutely in the donation of his farm, which is nestled in a community cared for by nine generations of his family, to the Dominican Sisters of Peace.

I would argue that a father could hand volumes of Berry's essays to his homeschooling Catholic kids and only find the need for an asterisk here or there to clarify it in the light of Catholic faith. The truth sets us free, and Berry has honestly and earnestly held up a mirror to the country, forcing us to take stock of the results of both sexual and economic liberalism upon family and community life, which is always the "bottom line" by which he measures an idea or practice.

---

7 See some of the editorial statements as well as articles like *Do Protestants Belong?* by Darryl Hart.

Overall, Berry is clearly prepared and open to bringing back into union our understanding of practical life and the soul, and see how we have violated spiritual principles as well as our own national values like democracy, the family, and a (formerly strong) mistrust of financiers: "We must see that it is foolish, sinful, and suicidal to destroy the health of nature for the sake of an economy that is really not an economy at all but merely a financial system, one that is unnatural, undemocratic, sacrilegious, and ephemeral."[8]

One Place, One Story

With so many books, one might think that Berry has covered a variety of issues. But, as an avid reader of his finds out, every book is eventually about one place. In his non-fiction, the place is his own, which is Henry County, Kentucky, which is mirrored in his novels that happen in and around the literary painting of Port William. This extreme focus, if you call it that, might seem limiting, but I would argue it is what makes him so potent an apologist against many of the changes and cultural decay of the last century.

The complexities of massive social, cultural, and religious shifts are nearly impossible for people outside of "the story" to grasp. For many of us, these changes are long done and we're living in all the "post" realities—post-industrialism, post-liberalism, post-agrarianism. This is why the best understanding often comes by the most precise and "on the ground" story possible. The facts are not enough.

---

[8] Berry, "Conservation and Local Economy," in *Sex, Economy, Freedom, & Community: Eight Essays*, 13.

One Story, Many Places

As to Berry's contribution to re-telling a history and reconsidering the outcomes, I would point analogously to the massive change in land ownership and community that happened in England through and after the reign of Henry VIII. It was Henry's confiscation of monastic lands that began unraveling Christendom's coherence and gave rise of the massive powers of governments today.[9] Perhaps Henry's linking of religious and secular authority had the ironic backfiring of making England one of the least religious "Christian countries" in the world. A not uncommon presentation—much the contrary of the above—is that Henry ushered in the blessedness of secularism and "freedom" that we now enjoy. But, most importantly, Henry liberated the poor peasants from their popish superstitions. The strongest rebuttal of such a telling is *The Stripping of the Altars* by Eamon Duffy, which tells the detailed story of religious "reform" through the eyes of peasants and priests alike. But, even more telling perhaps is the follow-up book, *The Voices of Morebath: Reformation and Rebellion in an English Village*, that focuses even further in on one single village and its experience. Duffy, perhaps more than any other historian since the English "Reformation," was able to completely recast the blatantly anti-Catholic telling of Henry and his successors' takeover of the religion of their country, and he did this by homing in on the village of Morebath.

This is what Berry has done by writing about his real place in Kentucky and the literary place of Port William—he has recast the story of the suburbanization of America from an

---

9 See, for example, Christopher Dawson's *The Dividing of Christendom.*

inevitable "progress" to an intentional dismantling.[10] No one can read Eamon Duffy and maintain the simplistic story that Henry and the powers around him were merely liberating peasants from corrupt monasteries, and no one can read Wendell Berry and maintain that freedom and progress is what moved people off the land. Says Berry: "What we have called agricultural progress has, in fact, involved the forcible displacement of millions of people."[11] In a subtle nod to some sort of evolutionary theory, it is often proposed that families left the land and joined in the industrial society of the modern world because it was better, more "grown up" and enjoyable than the drudgery of toiling over fields. And, because this is a matter of progress and freedom, we cannot believe that there is a relationship to the economic and household changes of suburbanization and our loss of our families and our faith.[12] We didn't "do" this, we tell ourselves. We just organically found ourselves in a place of material abundance, degraded land, and spiritual vapidity. We didn't kill it—it just died. Berry's writings don't absolve us so easily and require a closer self-examination.

---

[10] For the historic details that show the policies and practices that caused suburbanization, see Allan Carlson's book *From Cottage to Work Station: The Family's Search for Social Harmony in the Industrial Age.*

[11] Berry, *The Unsettling of America* (Counterpoint, 2015), 41.

[12] For a more detailed analysis of the effects of suburbanization on the family, see *The Liturgy of the Land* by myself and Thomas Van Horn, which relies heavily on *From Cottage to Work Station* by Allan Carlson.

Traders and Traitors

Berry's writings also call into question the movement of the economy to a wholly money-based economy, of what Thomas Aquinas and Aristotle call an "artificial economy," one organized by and for "trade," the making of money from money, when money becomes the end and no longer the means to engage in the "natural economy" of work and exchange. As I quoted above, he often says that what we call an economy is actually just a financial system. In the artificial economy, everything must be turned into money because that is not only the measure of things or a token of value but the very point of it all. The natural economy described by the classical philosophers shows up in Berry's novels in the dedication to preserving and maintaining relationship before money (an important point as we continue) and making sure to remember money is the "token" and not the point, as the regular character Andy Catlett muses in a story where he remembers being allowed to accept dinner in exchange for helping on a farm, but never money:

> This uneasiness about money Andy recognizes from much else that he has known of the people of Port William and similar places. Free exchanges of work and other goods they manage easily, but transactions of money among friends and neighbors nearly always involved an embarrassment that they had to alleviate by much delay, much conversation, as if to make the actual handling of cash or a check incidental to a social occasion. . . . [They] held a certain distrust against money itself, or the idea of it, as if a token of

> value were obviously inferior to, obviously worse than, a thing of value.[13]

Andy comes to believe that "buying and selling for money is not simply a matter of numbers and accounting but is a dark and fearful mystery."[14] Aquinas, similarly, allows for *some* trade to sustain a place but is sure to keep it in check because in a city based entirely in trade, "civic life will necessarily be corrupted."[15] Similarly, Berry is very skeptical when "the economically powerful are not those who produce the surplus, but the ones who gather it up and control it."[16]

When we say "the market" today, we refer to the increasingly globalizing practice of "buying and selling" not "making/doing/serving and selling." Those that make the most money and wield the most power are the "middle men" of buying and selling, not the "grounded" men like farmers, tradesmen, etc. Berry includes the government in this "middleman" problem in the way they get into the business of people in ways that refuse reality in regulation, like when the fictional barber Jayber Crow shuts down because, among other reasons, he heats his water with a woodstove instead of a water heater (no one measures if the water is actually hot). His humorous solution to this and other headaches is to move out of town to a friend's cabin where he gives away haircuts for free to friends and they make donations. There's a deeper idea than a loophole, however, in that Berry

---

[13] Berry, *The Art of Loading Brush*, 232.

[14] Berry, *The Art of Loading Brush*, 233.

[15] Quoted in George H. Spetz, *The Importance of the Rural Life* (CreateSpace Independant, 2011), 96.

[16] Berry, *The Art of Loading Brush*, 94.

clearly presents the mutual care of Jayber and his community as an icon of how economics should work, and which direction we should be moving. In some ways, Berry's vision of economics is like that of the early Christians, where the necessary exchange of the things we need—which includes everything from food to affection—is freed from the limitations and corruptibility of buying and selling and becomes the art of giving and receiving.

Aquinas and Aristotle point out that an economy based in trade inevitably harms society because the purpose of economy—which is household management—disappears and degrades. Berry affirms this from a disappearing and degrading place. He always writes, he says, "in sight of the progressing decline of my home countryside and community."[17] Many American Christians (Protestant and Catholic) have had a hard time recognizing and criticizing the consolidating economy, believing America had cracked the code, being able finally to love God and mammon at the same time without consequence. Often, because we are so saturated and formed by industrialism, we think that any critique is some sort of hypocrisy or a lack of gratitude. "Since I have air conditioning, I can't be a critic." But there seems to be a reckoning at this point if for no other reason than our grand experiment in living so far from the land in a world totally of our own making is undeniably damaging to our humanity, totally chained to consumerism, and does not maintain the integrity of the household without great effort. Those ready to look harder at the problem can pull up a seat

[17] Berry, *The Art of Loading Brush*, 104.

to Wendell Berry.[18] And I would argue that it is necessary because industrialism lacks the spiritual principle of honest examination. "I long ago hatched out of the egg in which I could believe that industrialism is capable of competent judgments of its effects," says Berry, "let alone competent solutions to problems it has caused."[19]

Seeds Are Slow

For all of his love for agrarian life, if wannabe back-to-the-landers read Berry, they might want to brace for a cold shower. Ryan Hanning, a homesteading contributor to this book, has recounted to me that he wrote to Berry at one point to declare his intention to move to the land from the city only to receive a letter back telling him not to bring his problems to the land—it didn't need him. This is not surprising to those that have read his essays because Wendell Berry knows better than to believe that one can simply relocate and plant a garden and, in one fell consumerist swoop, recover a lost tradition. The reason Catholics ought to engage with Berry's thought is that he, like the Church, thinks in lifetimes and principles and not solving problems with purchases. He focuses his agrarianism not merely on technical implementation but on the tradition and philosophy of farming and

[18] If one wanted to see how it was actually government tactics and corporate greed that caused this "progress," and not an experiment in liberty, Berry's primary engagement with those powers is in *The Unsettling of America*. But, as C. S. Lewis's arguments for God are likely more seen today in the Narnia books than in his apologetical works, so too Berry's contribution to an agrarian defense is likely to be preserved in his stories.

[19] Berry, *The Art of Loading Brush*, 105.

what I would call the *communion* of it—the *relationships* that sustain around and through a productive household and local community.

As to the tradition of farming, Berry's message to those that want to start a family farm is, basically, you can't. This isn't because you don't know how, but he makes what should be an obvious observation that being a family farm requires generations. A newly bought farm is "*potentially* a family farm" after about three generations.[20] This isn't because you have to "prove" yourself but simply that you have to learn and actually find yourself bringing health and provision to land and people beyond your personal enjoyment. The truth of this observation was the inspiration of the first *Liturgy of the Land* book. Anecdotally, in my experience with friends "moving to the land," I have seen more failure than success. His goal is not to discourage but to admonish you to be humble and self-examining, accepting that recovering an agrarian life will require a conversion away from the disorders we don't even recognize yet, and a multi-generational commitment and vision, not a piece of land and a YouTube channel.

These observations simply remind us that destruction is easy and fast; cultivation and growth is slow and hard. The former is usually a matter of purchasing something, and the latter is a matter of patience, faith, and tending. The dismantling of small, rural agrarian communities happened rather quickly from a historic perspective, but the speed of it is further proof that it was in fact an act of destruction. Therefore, in humility, we must recognize that the seeds of a

[20] Berry, *Bringing it to the Table*, 32. Emphasis added.

new agrarianism will necessarily grow slowly. Too often the deserved praise for the integrity of a Catholic village from the past is studied and proposed as a model, but those that do this often find themselves disappointed to the point of disillusionment, sometimes even to the point of apostatizing. We forget too easily that Christendom took centuries to build from the decay of a dying empire. We, therefore, have a long road ahead (or a long row to hoe) if we are to enjoy it again. In other words, we cannot "build" the society we want any more than we can "build" a tree. It is simply going to take time and a growing root mass.

Re-Membering

This brings us to what I think is one of the most important insights of Berry for the modern Catholic. As John Cuddeback argues in this book, most Catholics are pulled toward life on the land from a spiritual motivation. But grace builds on nature, and it is important to know that enthusiasm and even piety is not enough if we're not also prepared for the "conversion" that is necessary to actually move to the land, or to live in a way consistent with Church teaching and an agrarian ethic (what might be called living more in accord with nature) in a way that moves from just single households to community. As Berry has pointed out, the abuse of the land is but another symptom of our abuse of one another, and the communal/relational aspect is certainly a corrective to the errors and outcomes of modernism and suburbanization. Therefore, along with understanding the need for patient tending when it comes to conversion toward an agrarian life, so too we must dedicate ourselves—perhaps firstly—to the necessity and life of *communion*, or what is called "membership" in the literary world in and around Wendell Berry.

Berry's idea of "membership," the name he gives to the bonds shared in his literary communities, might at first resemble something like a club or team. This is not only wrong but reveals the extent of our dis-membered society, when our first (and often only) thoughts of community are toward a voluntaristic engagement with one another. Many people use the word *community* to speak almost solely of social life of our own choosing and for our enjoyment, but for Berry, it is much more, it "is a locally understood interdependence of local people, local culture, local economy, and local nature."[21] In a world without "membership," our choice and preference really are the primary option for most of our relationships, perhaps iconically culminated in the tech-enabled brutality of "friending and unfriending" people with a click. You "join" a team or club. You can even "join" a Protestant church. You can "join" Hallow. And you can leave all of these too, probably from your phone. But when Berry says "membership," he means it the way that the Church does when she refers to her members, which is that of a *body or family*.

Therefore, the re-membering of society in Berry's eyes is not a matter of nostalgia or volunteered bonds but of putting together the parts of a body that belong to one another so that they can function properly. Membership is not a matter

---

[21] Berry, "Sex, Economy, Freedom, and Community," in *Sex, Economy, Freedom & Community: Eight Essays*, 120.

of dues and brands but a matter of family—that is, it is something begotten not made. When Berry challenges us on our use and abuse of one another and our land—which is how we harm the membership—it ought not be hard for us to recall the convicting question of Saint Paul to the Corinthians when, in the light of their quarrels and immoral living, Paul asks if they realize that they are "members" both of Christ and of one another (a singular reality).[22] This belonging is so powerful precisely because it is not solely predicated by our own choosing but by our openness and willingness to love—and by birth.

The Ideal

The membership of Berry's telling does not easily exist today. The modern form of liberalism takes its ideal from the self-made man, whether we mean that to be the cutthroat billionaire, the self-absorbed celebrity or sports star, or the self-mutilation caused by gender confusion. Each of these examples likely requires that the limits of things like family and community be transcended, membership made optional. Berry, by contrast and alongside the Church, takes the image of *marriage* as the ideal and pattern for life and the soul of membership. Catholics have the common image of our membership in Christ being akin to a mystical marriage, but Berry speaks to and challenges our American attitudes by charging that we are merely "cohabitating" with one another instead of being fully committed, and this is the great sickness causing dismembering. The Church in recent

[22] 1 Cor 12:27.

decades has found herself against distortions of marriage, and this often shows itself in having to refuse to conduct or even allow attendance at some "weddings." She finds herself thus defending the community's role and connectedness in protecting and even governing marriage, and this is in direct contradiction to the modern ideals where the only job of the community is to affirm the choices and love of the two individuals going into the "union" they choose. Once again, Berry does not allow for us to so easily remove ourselves as communities from "private" marriages, because marriage by its definition is communal, even beyond itself:

> Lovers must not, like usurers, live for themselves alone. They must finally turn from their gaze at one another back toward the community. If they had only themselves to consider, lovers would not need to marry, but they must think of others and of other things. They say their vows to the community as much as to one another, and the community gathers around them to hear and to wish them well, on their behalf and its own. It gathers around them because it understands how necessary, how joyful, and how fearful this joining is. These lovers, pledging themselves to one another "until death," are giving themselves away, and they are joined by this as no law or contract could join them. Lovers, then, "die" into their union with one another as a soul "dies" into its union with God. And so here, at the very heart of community life, we find not something to sell as in the public market but this

> momentous giving. If the community cannot protect this giving, it can protect nothing.[23]

For Berry the experiment in cohabitation has followed the worldly analogy in couples and has become full-on divorce.[24] I think he uses this word intentionally to speak of how bad the breakup of communities has been and how hard the reconciliation will be. Yet, if something is broken, the only way forward is to put it back together, to reconnect communities through shared life. "Only by restoring the broken connection can we be healed," says Berry. "Connection *is* health."[25] To use the words *health* and *connection* is to directly correct an underlying definition of *freedom* as "disconnect" from things that bind, restrict, and hold. Unlike most spiritual methods and "programs" today, he does not have in mind that it is even possible to keep the connection "merely" spiritual or social, which lends to the compartmentalization of faith as a private matter and drains it from the potency of its public form. This is because he sees these different parts of life—social, economic, religious, agricultural—as inseparable because insofar as they are divided, they are at war. Today's society "fragments the Creation and sets the fragments into conflict with one another," says Berry.[26] Our spiritual eyes are quite free to see this as demonic, since the very root of the word *diabolical* means "to divide." Berry even offers a sort of order of destruction, which begins

[23] Berry, "Sex, Economy, Freedom, and Community," 137–38.

[24] This wording may be in other places, but it comes out in the documentary *Look and See*.

[25] Berry, *The Unsettling of America*, 138.

[26] Berry, *The Unsettling of America*, 138.

in harming the soul, moves through family and community, and ends in harming the soil:

> The modern urban-industrial society is based on a series of radical disconnections between body and soul, husband and wife, marriage and community, community and the earth. At each of these points of disconnection the collaboration of corporation, government, and expert sets up a profit-making enterprise that results in the further dismembering and impoverishment of the Creation.[27]

And he's right, these "points of disconnection" are the very places of most profitability for corporations and excuses to grab power for governments. The act of industrializing— of drawing in natural human needs and the means of filling them as families and communities and making them into a "market"— is the very means by which Berry thinks the family and the community are divided and conquered. Massive industries of "care" now replace the work of parents caring for children, children caring for elderly parents, families cooking and cleaning with and for one another, and this is not even related to the industrialization of almost all forms of work and production. Many politicians want to keep shoving childcare to younger and younger ages, subsidized and regulated by the government, as a way to help more people enter the workforce unencumbered by childbearing (i.e., as if the family can free itself from itself).

---

[27] Berry, *The Unsettling of America*, 137

Families Are Inadequate

Without a broader idea of culture and community, one not connected to the body and the soul, there is little to be done against the darker powers so palpable today. I think many are mistaken in pulling in too much toward the family alone in trying to push back against these powers, because the family is inadequate to confront the challenge. This is certainly something Berry would point out for the simple fact he cannot and does not separate the idea of family stability from community stability. It must start at home, but we have to understand the family and the surrounding community as a sort of double helix of activity, of ascending and descending together.

That the family is "inadequate" is not to say it isn't foundational to the human person and society. What the Church teaches is that the family is "imperfect" in nature, meaning it doesn't have within itself everything it needs to be itself. One sees this most clearly in the lives of young men and women who may have the natural vocation to marriage but cannot find a spouse within the family itself. And, even if we branch out into the reality of spouse-finding, we immediately find other needs for communities to understand themselves as belonging to one another in support, care, and shared culture. For example, a conservative family can have all sorts of traditional ideas of courtship for their daughters, but unless the suitor does too, it doesn't really help much. It really does take two to tango. And, of course, a father that needs to make an income won't have many customers for his shop in his own home. The family, therefore, naturally and necessarily forms community. This is why Berry sees the disconnectedness and division of family and community as done primarily through destroying local culture and economics, or of replacing the work of mutual care by extracting the work of caring for one another by providing and serving: "If you destroy the economies of household and community, then you destroy the bonds of mutual usefulness and practical dependence without which the other bonds will not hold."[28] This thesis and observation only becomes more obvious as time goes on: that without the bonds of productivity, homes and communities "will not hold."[29] This is not a thesis of something that may happen but the reality of what has happened. Without mutual dependency, communities and families stay strong only by strained effort.

When these bonds no longer "hold"—when members of a family and of a community are not intertwined in a living culture and economy—then you end up with individuals alone looking up at the big powers that provide the goods and services we need to survive. Ultimately, in our post-industrialized and liberalized world, we recognize essentially two entities: the individual and the broader public. Each person alone then must face the powers that be. This is, of course, Marxism's explicit teaching, that there should be no power between the individual and the state, not even the family. But this isolation of the individual is also a byproduct of the finance capitalism of the last half century. However we

---

[28] Berry, "Sex, Economy, Freedom, and Community," 125.

[29] Robert Nisbet's book *The Quest for Community* makes this argument as well and calls into question the value of the volunteer associations like clubs, scouting, etc. that sprang up in urban centers.

label the grand forces today, we feel relatively isolated and impotent as individuals against such massive powers.

Intermediary Bodies

Berry's observations of this problem and prescriptive remedy align quite closely to that great champion of the natural economy, Pope Leo XIII. Specifically, they both recommend an explicit and even legal recognition of both the place of the family *and* the local community. Both Berry and Leo recognize the family as the foundation of society, but they also note that the family and the local community are mutually dependent bodies that need one another and, strictly speaking, cannot exist without the other. Whereas the public lexicon now allows "community" to mean everything from a group of college students with shared sexual preferences (or deviancies) to a pickleball club, Leo and Berry mean the fruitful interdependence of the village as commonly understood through history. From observation, study, and his own realism, Berry has seen this to be true. From an even broader observation, from the storehouse of the Magisterium and the realism of Saint Thomas Aquinas, Leo knows this to be true infallibly. I would argue that anyone who wants to "recover the family" as the foundation of society cannot do so without a recovery of the community that both binds the family together and defends it against powers that would cannibalize it. It is the community—properly understood—that can fight against the displacing powers of big government and big business. The community can do what the individual and even the family cannot do alone.

Pope Leo XIII's *Rerum Novarum* gives a historical, theological, and legal defense of associations like cooperatives and guilds as the parting (and I think most unrealized) recommendation to remedy the excess of industrialization. Leo warned of the centralization of power in the hands of government or business and recommended that intermediary bodies exist to protect what is smaller from what is bigger, to stand in between the larger powers and individuals and their families. These he called "lesser societies," not in the sense of simply being smaller or inferior, but of being closer to the lives of those they serve and their needs in the spirit of subsidiarity:

> These lesser societies and the larger society differ in many respects, because their immediate purpose and aim are different. Civil society exists for the common good, and hence is concerned with the interests of all in general, albeit with individual interests also in their due place and degree. It is therefore called a public society, because by its agency, as St. Thomas of Aquinas says, "Men establish relations in common with one another in the setting up of a commonwealth." But societies which are formed in the bosom of the commonwealth are styled private, and rightly so, since their immediate purpose is the private advantage of the associates.[30]

Recalling the Church's view of membership being a bodily reality, we know that Leo here is referring to taking care of

[30] Leo XIII, *Rerum Novarum*, no. 51.

what we would now call your local community, a distinction that would have been somewhat unnecessary in the past before such absurdities as "online communities," but more in line with what Berry means. Along with the guilds of old, Leo says he is "reminded of the confraternities, societies, and religious orders" of the past that grew into local, integrated wholeness that protected and cared for specific places and people. These intermediary societies that exist between people and large powers are "real societies," says Leo, and therefore afford logically the "sanction of law and nature." Berry likely uses the word *community* because it in some way retains the air of free association, but we might note that Christendom did not leave mutual charity and care to chance and was quite happy to bind people together more explicitly. From the Rule of St. Benedict to the charters of an English guild, Catholicism tends toward tangible commitments that order people's lives toward God and one another.[31]

Berry is a little less deferential to "public society," by which Leo means something more like the state. But Berry is helpful in defining the "public" as the broad alliances of big business, big government, or simply "public opinion." Unlike his later translators like G. K. Chesterton, Leo did not foresee in the encyclical the merging of these powers into the bloc we see today. But, like Leo, Berry sees his definition of *community* as the only bulwark against consolidated powers that operate on a different logic than that of the family.

[31] See Gervase Rosser, *The Art of Solidarity in the Middle Ages: Guilds in England 1250-1550* for an excellent overview of the spirit and law of the guilds.

This is where I turn to Berry's wisdom in proposing Burley Tobacco Growers Cooperative Association and how it might help American Catholics see how "practical" things like distributism and the ancient network of guilds can be.

The cooperative's history is inseparable from the Berry family. It was Wendell Berry's grandfather who told the story of returning from the market where he sold his crops with exactly nothing. The year of zero profit was an intentional strategy of James B. Duke of the American Tobacco Company to drive down the prices of tobacco and force farms to "consolidate," which means to displace many small farmers in favor of fewer bigger ones. This so scandalized his son (Wendell's father) that he dedicated his entire life to the creation and sustaining of the cooperative. In its simplest form, it established production limits for its members and opened ways for them to sell directly to manufacturers. (Berry tells the story of facing Mr. Duke's statue at Duke University in his famous essay *It All Turns on Affection*.) Cooperative farming is not only the basis for civilization but also good for the economics of farmers since—as Berry writes in many places—they tend to be their own worst enemy when it comes to production. If a bushel of corn sells for a good amount, the next year they plant more, which then drives the price down, and this very process has been exploited by corporations to bring more and more production into control. When farming imbibes industrialism's logic, the two options are "down and out," when debt and depressed prices force them out, or "up and massive" when the scale jumps from agriculture to what John Senior called "factories in the field" or just the name "agribusiness." Because industrialism does not have an inner logic of self-preservation, farmers have only successfully carried on the culture and tradition of farming by a certain communal limitation, a focus and care for more than money and a dedication to one another and standing together against larger powers that would overtake them, in this case a rapidly consolidating market. The result of the cooperative, ironically if we are conditioned to think only in certain economic terms, is that more farmers are better paid over longer periods of time.

The Burley Tobacco Growers Cooperative did what it wanted to do and preserved the viability of farming, the craftsmanship of it, and culture in the "burley belt" states like Ohio, Kentucky, West Virginia, Missouri, and Indiana. Once it was finally and fatally defeated by big tabaco, that burley belt broke and the communities and the generational farms started going away. The argument against the cooperative was the same as other industrializing arguments—the limitations of it made them less competitive in the globalizing industry. Like other industries that followed the same argument—"we must adapt and change our ways, or we can't compete"—the end result seems to always be the same: steady decline, consolidation, and finally exportation. Today, the largest grower of tobacco is China.

Although the cooperative was clearly an economic form of preservation, it also carried with it the preservation of culture, a shared and stable way of life. The guilds of Christendom had similar goals and a similar effect, if for no other reason that they allowed in more human considerations than profit, and even did the unconscionable and considered the good of the soul over that of the wallet. This re-situates "community" in its more grounded and dependent sense, in a truer and more binding connection that is the primary defender of individuals and homes against powerful domestic and foreign threats. The cooperatives and the guides were a localized power that could mediate between individuals and their families and the broader world of trade and governance. The primary difference between them and the industrialist arguments like that of Duke's is that the cooperatives and guilds used economics to preserve and sustain community, but the corporations would use communities to preserve and grow the economy—and they would "use them up" if needed.

Limits to Freedom or Freedom through Limits

What Leo and Berry are recognizing and presenting is a truth that grates against our more libertarian leanings: we need the binding limitations of attachment to actually be free. In answering modernism's slow march through Christian societies, too many have been contented with getting the argument right. It is true that things like relativism turn truth on its head in the name of freedom—are we set free by the truth or free to set the truth? But we fail to recognize how important the context—the ecosystem—is for things like faith and family. We forget the soil true freedom needs to grow in. Like the sin of gluttony, we want to enjoy something without acknowledging the consequences. Baked into modernism and liberalism is the central tenant of individual autonomy, and it is this very autonomy that we have labeled "freedom" and let loose without question. By accepting this definition of freedom, we have allowed for the dis-membering of our communities, our families, and even our own bodies—all in the name of and excused by "liberty." Our communities have been dis-membered first by industrialization and then by globalization and the consumerism these things depend on. Our families are dis-membered by dissolving the vows and commitments of love and family as well as losing any practical economic bonds within the household. And our bodies have even been dis-membered by not only allowing in the poison that comes from much of what is sold as food, but by consciously rejecting the biological reality of them.

In other words, in the name of freedom, we have cast off all *limits.* A family, after all, limits itself when it marries, has children, and contains itself in a shared household. A local community is also limited in where it procures its needs and directs its energies. These are the very limitations that liberalism—often in the sexual and economic iterations of it—promises to free us from so that we can thrive. If we reject this promise, this offer, the implications are that we accept and even embrace the limitations of membership, of belonging to one another in a binding way. This will not be easy, and the stories and writings of Wendell Berry serve less as roadmaps as they do destinations, but as such they clarify what we're really after: communion and a clarity of belonging.

Theological Advantage

Catholics just might have the edge in this sense, this understanding of membership and communion, if for no other reason than we take communion seriously. The source and summit of our life is the supreme act of communion with God and with each other. Through the sacraments, we are truly made into a family—not symbolically but truly. This bond, in fact, transcends even the familial bonds of earth since our family, the Church, will be our family now and into eternity. To offend this family requires reconciling not only with God but with the community, both of whom are mediated through the priest in confession. To lose this communion, to be severed from the family and the membership, is to jeopardize our present and eternal happiness. Dis-membering from the Church has different forms—mortal sin, apostacy, heresy, schism—and each is perilous. And, although the Church is universal, she isn't globalist, meaning we know exactly who "our people" are. It's our neighbor, those closest to us, bound as family at the birth of baptism. And while we know we are called to love everyone, Scripture is quite clear that we are to first love and serve "the household of God," our family. In other words, unlike the rest of the liberal world, Catholicism has an internal logic that holds things together, that keeps the membership.

Yet, we are clearly not immune to the unraveling of this communion through the temptations and ways of the world. For us to come together in the type of communal belonging of an agrarian village is nearly impossible, for the simple reason that the economic reality of most households is not what we would call "rooted." We share a transient and temporary bond with our own places, and the weights of debt and the allure of ambition calls a lot of the shots. At this point, we have an understandably difficult time with staying put and staying together. We shop parishes, and in today's ecclesial environment, that becomes more excusable. In the age of collapsing and consolidating parishes, many who hold to the membership are doing so heroically, and it is made all the harder because the bond is *only* spiritual, and the "practical" realities of life do not flow from or mirror our privately lived faith. This causes us to compartmentalize our faith, our family and household decisions, and economic reality into the private and individual space.

For her part, the Church in the United States quite intentionally broke up the so-called "ghettos" of Catholicism in many places that had held to old-world customs and traditions particular to their country and were a help at maintaining "membership" (Germany, Italy, and so on, with possibly the exception of Mexico that still maintains its cultural and Catholic identity parallel to the "regular" parish). The reason for this was unashamedly to become "more American," accepted and respected in a country founded on Protestantism and, perhaps more so, on the liberal creeds that flowed from the Enlightenment. The side effect is clearly that we have absorbed identities from the world that are proving harmful to faith and orthodoxy. One sees this especially in the tension in places like politics, academics, and public opinion, where "inner feelings" of Catholic faith must be made subjective and non-threatening—that is, private and relative—to a hostile public.

If there was a time that it seemed prudent to please and participate in "the public," whether for the sake of assimilation into culture or evangelization, perhaps that time has passed—or has been taken away. We must also allow for the thesis that it was always a mistake to try to make too much peace with a world built on something other than the Kingship of Christ. To "start afresh," however, is not a matter of reclaiming something older by imitating it (which will likely just look a lot like re-branding an essentially liberal lifestyle), but of building up in small, local ways. The excitement around books like Rod Dreher's *The Benedict Option* and other well-branded localism proposals shows there is a hunger for it. Some propose a grand return to a former civilization itself by leveraging what's left of Christian culture and building a large-scale push back against the tyranny of techno-globalism and the woke ideologies that accompany it. But this actually doesn't seem to be the way historic Christianity (at least the sort that makes a lot of saints) works—at least not when the cultural decay is this advanced. As Rodney Starke showed in *The Rise of Christianity*, strong local attachments not only stabilize our own lives as Christians, but they also tend to be the source of rapid and profound conversions. Starke shows that while theology and the presentation of truth are important, conversion is not just about accepting a truth but "about bringing one's religious behavior into alignment with that of one's friends and family members."[32] If the world is as dark as it seems, then localism is not merely a practical reality but an evangelical imperative.

The writings of Wendell Berry can help Catholics grasp and situate their practical answer to this hunger in something

[32] Rodney Starke, *The Rise of Christianity* (Princeton University, 1996), 17.

beyond a shared theology to an actual shared way of life, which must include both a counter-culture *and* a counter-economy, and we must be contented and focused on the same place the Gospel asks us to focus—our proximate neighbor. Here's how Berry puts it in his latest iteration of it after years of effort and reflection:

> So far as I can see, and I have been looking hard for a long time, the only defense of land and people against the predatory or colonial economy . . . is a reasonably self-sufficient and self-determining local economy. This would have to be consciously and conscientiously a counter-economy. A counter-culture would be necessary also, but it had better come as a part or a consequence of the effort to make and continue the counter-economy.[33]

Our "counter-culture" is clearly our faith, and it will be strengthened as we take care of one another, which is a much better definition of "economy" than making money. Wendell Berry has helped us take note and notice of the decline of local community and health. May we be able to tell the story of new growth from new seeds of faith.

---

[33] Berry, *The Art of Loading Brush*, 84.

Works Cited

Berry, Wendell. *Bringing it to the Table.* Counterpoint, 2009.

———. "Health is Membership." Delivered as a speech in the conference "Spirituality and Healing" in Louisville, Kentucky. October 17, 1994. https://www1.villanova.edu/dam/villanova/mission/faith/Readings/fall-2020/Health%20is%20Membership%20by%20Wendell%20Berry.pdf.

———. *The Art of Loading Brush: New Agrarian Writings.* Catapult, 2019.

———. *The Unsettling of America.* Counterpoint, 2015.

———. *Sex, Economy, Freedom, & Community: Eight Essays.* Counterpoint, 2018.

Leo XIII, *Rerum Novarum,* https://www.vatican.va/content/leo-xiii/en/encyclicals/documents/hf_l-xiii_enc_15051891_rerum-novarum.html.

Spetz, George H. *The Importance of the Rural Life.* CreateSpace Independant, 2011.

Starke, Rodney. *The Rise of Christianity.* Princeton University, 1996.

Ryan Hanning, PhD

Ryan Hanning, PhD, is a professor of Theology who writes and speaks internationally on education, theology, ecological ethics and virtuous leadership. Ryan currently stewards a small homestead called Isidro Acres in Tennessee with his beautiful wife Rebecca, and their ten well-socialized homeschooled children.

CHAPTER 9

THE CULT OF HYPER-MOBILIZATION AND THE LOSS OF PLACE IN THE AMERICAN HOME

Ryan Hanning

One of my professors in graduate school was a polyglot whose encyclopedic knowledge of medieval history and philosophy bordered on the absurd. At times we questioned if he was just making stuff up or if he actually knew St. Bernard's Pentecost homily from 1116 by heart. Or if he accurately described the annual grain production in Bavaria in 1565, its impact on monastic brewing, and influence on local culture. Luckily, he informed us, "the grape production in Bavaria was not affected during those years, so there was sufficient wine for the Sacraments." Oh, what a relief to our worries. In addition to teaching us history, he wanted to impress upon his students, specifically his American students, just how at odds the modern world was with the rest of human history in regard to place. For nearly all human history, the time and geographical location of one's birth set into motion generally inescapable relationships. Even if you were to leave your birthplace, for marriage, for work, from famine, war, or fear of war, it was generally understood your previous place, as well as your new one, made certain demands on you. These demands were understood as the ordinary effects of being a corporeal being in a material world. The Christian faith elevated our sense of dignity to be sure, but it did not make us so arrogant as to think we could or should live without regard to our corporeal existence in the world—a world, though fallen, still good and charged with the grandeur of God.

Those series of lectures on medieval philosophy, and the conversations over dozens (possibly hundreds) of pints between dinner and compline, started an intellectual curiosity which eventually led me to leave my place of economic comfort in the city and live in closer proximity to the land on a small homestead in Tennessee. Needless to say, it was a horrible idea. Like many good bad decisions, it has allowed me to think more deeply about place and whether the hyper-mobility worshipped by our modern age is good, or even neutral to real being and living in relationship with God and with others in the places we find ourselves. I do not pretend to offer easy solutions but can at least provide the questions we ought to be asking of today's idol of mobility and whether it's not just really a lack of commitment. Our desire to cohabitate with the world around us limits our ability to marry the land, so to speak, and enter into the fecundity which can only come from being in a real relationship with the places we live. Here, I offer the questions that should be asked and provide some guides who have had immeasurable impact in helping me understand the importance of place, and what still needs to be corrected in me if I will ever be meek enough to inherit the earth.

Let us begin with a quick analysis of what life was like for most of human history regarding place. You were born in a particular time and place, into a culture largely based on the language, religious beliefs, agriculture, and climate. You learned at a young age the nuances of your place: what could and could not be eaten, what could and could not be said. You knew your place was special and different and, like all youth, wanted to explore and discover new places. This description is not altogether different from today, except that for most of human history, the intimacy of your knowledge of place was deeper and tied to more tangible things. Even in more modern times, cities have a feel, a personality, based on the collective history of how people lived in that place. The "personality" of a place is nearly inescapable. Sadly, most modern cities today are breathing the fumes of the culture preceding them and losing what has made them unique. Big cities today feel less distinct and less a result of the place and more a result of the placelessness of the people who occupy them. Chesterton, with his customary and acerbic wit, reminds us that the "modern city is ugly not because it is a city but because it is not enough of a city, because it is a jungle, because it is confused and anarchic, and surging with selfish and materialistic energies." Chesterton is right, as he often is, the issue with the city is not in the principle of a large, centralized population gathered for the possibility of economic or material prosperity or at least comfort, but with the transience, lack of commitment, and injustices often accompanying them.

In the past, to be cosmopolitan meant you knew the world and appreciated the various cultures and places in relationship to your own. To be cosmopolitan meant to be citified, so to speak, and a cultured member of the world in all its variety. As a good member, you were able to enter into new places with equal parts fascination and reservation. Entering in with a knowledge that these other places had something to offer, but ultimately, they were not your own. Today, to be cosmopolitan means to be worldly, to be equally comfortable in any place because you aren't committed to any one of them. In the past, to be cosmopolitan meant to be an explorer; now it more likely means you are lost.

In a similar way, to be a good citizen used to mean to belong to a place (large or small, a nation or township), to protect and advocate for its ideals and attempt to live up to them the best you could. Today, being a citizen is often reduced to a legal status, without the inherent reciprocal commitment it requires. Can we be good citizens if we have lost how our identity is connected to place or arrogantly rejected the physical limitations in favor of more abstracted existence? As Wilfred McClay in his introduction to an excellent anthology of *Why Place Matters* reminds us, "one cannot be a citizen without being a citizen of some place in particular; one cannot be a citizen of a website or a motel."[1]

---

[1] Wilfred M. McClay and Ted V. McAllister, eds., *Why Place Matters: Geography, Identity, and Civic Life in Modern America* (New York: Encounter Books, 2014), x.

Our digital age enhances and encourages our placelessness, but it cannot solve it.

In 1956, Romano Guardini, a priest and philosopher, provided a philosophical and theological reflection on man's current state in the so-called "modern world." His book *End of the Modern World* (1956) provided piercing insights about the trajectory of modern "mass" man disconnected from the world and theorized on the anthropological and theological effects of being dislocated from your time and your place, on being a consumer of the world rather than a participant in it, on watching people live as opposed to living with people. His follow-up to this work, *Power and Responsibility*, provided additional insights about our increasingly disjointed relationship with nature. In these texts, he asks whether we are more free or less free when unmoored from the traditional anchors which have grounded our human experience and orientation in our place and time.

Similarly, and less theoretical, Wendell Berry's seminal work *The Unsettling of America* (1977), along with many of his subsequent essays and fiction, reflect with equal insight on the practical impact of the forcible displacement of millions of people from the land and a more agrarian subsistence. This unquestioned exodus to the city impacted not only man but the land and places he left behind. It can be argued we have become more urbanized, more mobilized, and in the process less grounded. It is a sad irony in the "communication age" we have lost the ability to form community. We are more "connected" but have less meaningful connections. Increasing rates of anxiety, confusion over our purpose and even existence, the artificiality of economic systems more abstracted from reality, the cult of progress, and the rise of reactive pantheism are in no doubt related to the effects of being two and three generations removed from agriculture. While not the point of this article, it's worth noting that less than 3 percent of today's jobs are in agriculture, which seems remarkable since we don't all need streaming services, but we do all need to eat. Even more remarkable considering even up until WWII, agriculture was the single largest component of the US economy (second was manufacturing). Similar trends can be found throughout "industrialized" modern countries, where financial services and retail sectors have a workforce ten times larger than agriculture. It is only in a society so far removed from the land and places sustaining it that there could be recommendations to abolish private farming and centralize agriculture, as the World Bank advocated in June of 2024.

Berry reminds us that individuality is not a prerequisite for identity. Despite the proliferation of truncated fairytales (often missing the actual point), it is not true that we only find ourselves by leaving our place. Identity is not found in isolation. "According to the new norm, the child's destiny is not to succeed the parents, but to outmode them. . . . He or she is educated to leave home and earn money in a provisional future with nothing to do with place or community."[2]

I hadn't realized at the time, but those evenings in the pub were forming more than my intellect. I was being initiated

---

2 Wendell Berry, "The Work of Local Culture," in *What are People For? Essays* (Catapult, 2010), 163.

into a deeply Catholic vision of place. A vision the Christian worldview is based upon. How we interact with our place is directly connected to how we receive the gifts God has given us and participate in bringing them to serve ourselves and others. In my own life, I had failed to discern whether I should stay in a place or go to another in light of my vocation and mission. Whether I was being a good member of the community and the land I occupied or if I was making good on the commitments required of me in that place never really entered my mind or, for that matter, my prayers. Rather, the assumption was that economic gain and mobility were necessary prerequisites, with acceptable "goods" always taking unquestioned priority.

One night, we opened the small humble closet holding the power of transforming the college's parlor into a proper pub. In the closet was a small glass-doored fridge, a stainless-steel sink, and the necessary glassware and accoutrements to make a decent cocktail. Among the selection of local beers and lower- to mid-shelf whiskeys was something special. One of our professors had brought some beer and liqueur from a small monastery in Switzerland. The clearly non-commercial label on the bottles indicated, at least to us, these were something special. We also wondered if this was an indication we had made good progress during our presentations early in the day.

The beer was unique in its effervescences and lingering bitter taste, as if they roasted their hops along with coffee beans. Our professors watched with a level of delight and annoyance as we tried to impress upon them the quality of our palates. They explained this beer had been brewed in the same place for over a thousand years, and in the '60s, they tried to commercialize it without success. The monks brew the beer in open containers before final fermentation. The result of the open containers is that a strain of wild yeast, specific to the area, which has developed organically in concert with the farming practices over the centuries, suffuses the beer. The wild yeast and subsequent fermentation that ensues imparts a quality and taste specific to this one place and cannot be replicated elsewhere. In a quite literal way, the culture (in this case, the yeast) is a direct product of the relationship between man and his environment. I like to think the prayer of the monks also has something to do with it. In a similar way, the lime content of water from local springs impacts the specific taste of whiskey. Less prayer, but you get the point.

Hypermobility and placelessness are attractive in the sense that they are convenient, in the same way cheap beer or generic whiskey is convenient. Without the bonds holding you to a place, you are seemingly freer to more efficiently accept opportunities as they come. Without limits imposed by a commitment to place, you are supposed to be disposed to a broader range of opportunities to develop your gifts and serve more broadly. These ideas are attractive, but the benefits most often articulated come from mobility in general—the type of mobility proper to beings who willfully move within time and space. St. Thomas's baptism of Aristotelian taxonomies points out our movement, and specifically our movement as guided by a rational and sensitive will, makes us like our Creator. The issue with hypermobility is that the prefix and the assumption are that more mobility maximizes its potential fruits. To be sensitive is good; to be hypersensitive is not so good. To be active is good; to be hyperactive is too much. Tension holds the bridge; hypertension leads to cardiac arrest. That humans perceive and react to their world through both compulsion, aversion, and by choice is a good thing. But compulsion and aversion are perhaps less dignified. Being forced to move for fear or lack of opportunity is different than choosing to move by the strength of reason and will.

The default expectation of modernity, claiming that the most extreme form of mobility is the best and that loose affiliations provide the necessary freedom for economic gain and human flourishing, is dubious at best. Hypermobility is the fruit of an absurd placelessness and a refusal to recognize the corporeal limits inherent in being human, and the rejection of obligations placed on us by our environment. It can only be framed as hubris arrogance, woeful ignorance, or an annoying combination of the two. Many today are looking to reclaim the rightful sense of place; however, there is temptation to oversimplify the issue and wrongly assume the decision is between accepting or rejecting technology or being urban or rural. Rather, our reimagination and reclamation of place should not be based on what we reject as false in our hypermobile age but rather how we seek to live in radical commitment to place. The goal, as I recently told a group of students who thought they were coming to a lecture about the joys of living on the land, is not to return to some never-existent golden era of the past but to enter into the place you have been called. I reminded them that one can be a thief and a banker as much as one can be a crook and a farmer (though it seems to me natural justice is quicker on the land than it is in the city). Similarly, one can be grounded in the city as much as one can be dislocated on the land. The difference between the two comes down to understanding the role of place and the discernment of our careful and attentive relationship to it.

From my perspective, the angst so many feel in relationship with the city occurs because, in the city, it is so hard to be in relationship with the land. It's hard to build a home independent of the anchors and cycles necessary to forming home life. Everywhere in the city, we attempt to avoid the rhythms and natural cycles and the sweat and toil meant to turn our eyes not downwards to the earth, or inwards towards ourselves (or more currently, to a screen), but upwards towards God. Like the parable of the plowshare, it is only by having your eyes elevated towards the horizon with a view of both earth and heaven that our work can be productive in transforming and preparing us. This has led many ardent Catholics to "flee to the land" and participate in what can be called the Catholic land movement.

On a very human level, not being in right relationship with the land becomes an obstacle to understanding who we are in relationship to each other, and ultimately who we are in relationship to God, in Whom we are utterly dependent, and uniquely called to participate in His order of creation. All this to say that any authentic community must, at its core, be in right relationship with the land. The city need not be in opposition to this, and models of cities, rightly ordered, tend to honor and uphold the trades and means of production as much as, if not more than, the apparatus helping us consume these goods. Benedictines and Cistercians are examples of movements in the life of the Church that sought to build communities living in relationship to the city while intentionally focusing on maintaining the three fundamental relationships.

The Catholic land ethos is built on the practical and theological understanding of these relationships. Practically, understand the limits and commitments of the place where you live and how you are called to participate in the thoughtful and attentive stewardship of it. Theologically, understand how God's providence shapes you in and through your place, and how well you enter it. What is too easily lost in our hypermobile age and the resulting placelessness is the ability to achieve any sense of home: to build, with others, a place to live and work and leave your family better off than you are. It is perhaps the most striking contradiction and sad irony that building a home today is often predicated on economic advantages that come from being placeless. We have forgotten how to be members who belong to one another. We have forgotten how to be neighbors, let alone good neighbors. We have ultimately become disconnected from the solid things that make us who we are: our families, towns, institutions who formed us for good or for naught. Running away indeed may be necessary, but always in search of making a home in some place while awaiting our everlasting home in eternity.

A return to the land can only exist as one option within a broader Catholic vision of place. The Catholic land movement cannot be limited to rebuilding the Eden we long for but rather to building the city of God we are made for. The restoration of Christian culture will come first from the reclamation and irrigation of Christian homelife. This begins by living in right relationship with your place, whether rural or urban. The two are not exclusive of one another, but the people who occupy them ought to discern where they are called to be. We ought to reject the idol of hypermobility for what it is: a fear of commitment or the hubris of presumption. It is the mission of every disciple to prayerfully discern where they are called. And once called, to receive their place as a gift and enter into it. We cannot subdue the land by fleeing from it, nor can we build homes without living in them.

In Alexandre Solzhenitsyn's well-known short story "Matryona's Place," the old widow was the only one who mourned the loss of the broken associations caused by sin and the brutality of communism. She knew her place, and as a result was the only one capable of building a home, even as hers was physically dismantled. "We all lived beside her, and never understood she was the righteous one without whom, according to the proverb, no village can stand. Nor any city. Nor our whole land."[3]

[3] Aleksandr Isaevich Solzhenitsyn, "Matryona's Place," in *"We Never Make Mistakes": Two Short Novels* (New York: W.W. Norton, 1996), 138.

Works Cited

Berry, Wendell. "The Work of Local Culture." In *What are People For? Essays.* Catapult, 2010.

McClay, Wilfred M. and Ted V. McAllister, Eds., *Why Place Matters: Geography, Identity, and Civic Life in Modern America.* New York: Encounter Books, 2014.

Solzhenitsyn, Aleksandr Isaevich. "Matryona's Place." In *"We Never Make Mistakes": Two Short Novels.* New York: W.W. Norton, 1996.

John A. Cuddeback, PhD

John A. Cuddeback, PhD, is professor of Philosophy at Christendom College, where he has taught for thirty years. He lectures widely on topics including marriage, fatherhood, virtue, friendship, household and homesteading. His professional writings appear in various journals, including *Nova et Vetera*, *The Thomist*, and *The American Catholic Philosophical Quarterly*, as well as in a number of academic collections. He is a regular lecturer for the Thomistic Institute and has recorded videos for their popular Aquinas 101 series. His book *True Friendship* was republished by Ignatius Press in 2021, and his book on household is forthcoming. His weekly blog posts are posted at numerous popular sites across the internet, and his podcasts, blogging, and courses at LifeCraft are renowned for applying timeless wisdom to life today.

CHAPTER 10

SPIRITUALLY MOTIVATED HOMESTEADING: AN ANSWER FOR THE TWENTY-FIRST CENTURY

John A. Cuddeback, PhD

Certain early twentieth-century Catholic thinkers in America saw clearly how the challenges the Church faces are deeply intertwined with the economic theory and practice of the day. In their 1940 book *Rural Roads to Security* (henceforth, *RRS*), Msgr. Luigi Ligutti and Fr. John Rawe, SJ, distilled and built upon several decades of agrarian thinking from a distinctively American and Catholic perspective when they issued a call for a "spiritually motivated homesteading" (henceforth, SMH). While not the entirety of their program for renewing the Church and America itself through a deeply grounded and reinvigorated rural life, SMH was certainly a central feature of it.

Hearkening back to this rich but now seldom-noticed flowering of faith-inspired agrarianism, I seek in this essay to articulate a notion of SMH for our day, along with an account fitted to current circumstances for its justification and promotion. There is already a growing movement that might be characterized as SMH, but it could benefit from a clearer vision of just what such homesteading is and what its goals are, and why and how to go about it, especially today. It is my purpose here to find in *RRS* the root principles of such SMH and then to suggest how they apply as we enter the second quarter of the twenty-first century.

I begin with a simple and challenging theological principle with far-reaching implications in human life. The great theologian St. Thomas Aquinas puts it this way:

> Now man is placed between the things of this world, and spiritual goods wherein eternal happiness consists: so that the more he cleaves to the one, the more he withdraws from the other, and conversely. Wherefore he that cleaves wholly to the things of this world, so as to make them his end, and to look upon them as the reason and rule of all he does, falls away altogether from spiritual goods.[1]

What we might call the "opposition" of spiritual goods and worldly goods is prone to be misunderstood. At issue here is not some kind of Manichean division between good and bad wherein material things are evil and to be shunned. On the contrary, Aquinas—who is especially known as an advocate for the goodness and importance of the material world—here expresses the key truth that human flourishing is all about seeing and enacting the true order of things. The problem

---

1 St. Thomas Aquinas, *Summa theologiae* I–II Q. 108, art. 4.

with things of this world is when one "cleaves" to them, putting an inappropriate priority on them. Such a disordered priority undermines not only the pursuit of the higher spiritual goods; it also undermines the worldly goods themselves. Aquinas is explicit that one "does not need to renounce the things of the world altogether since he can, while using the things of this world, attain to eternal happiness."[2]

This is not some abstract, far-away theological reflection. It takes us to the heart of human life; it also takes us to the heart of the disorder of our age and why SMH is such an important response to it. To bring this into sharper focus, here is another foundational principle from St. Thomas Aquinas:

> For an individual man to lead a good life two things are required. The first and most important is to act in a virtuous manner (for virtue is that by which one lives well); the other, which is secondary and instrumental, is a sufficiency of those bodily goods whose use is necessary for virtuous life.[3]

This is a necessary corollary and further explanation of the principle above. Bodily goods are secondary precisely because they are instrumental. To recognize their instrumentality is to discover their true dignity and importance in human life. By a divine plan they are necessary for us, and so the very shape of human life is determined in significant part by how we go about acquiring these necessary goods. And central in the great moral drama is whether we will recognize

---

2 St. Thomas Aquinas, *Summa theologiae* I–II Q. 108, art. 4.

3 St. Thomas Aquinas, *On Kingship* II, C. 4, p. 393.

their place, again therein discovering their true importance, and so seek them in a commensurate fashion.

An honest consideration of not only human history but our own lives will indicate that achieving this basic right order is anything but a given. Indeed, we might judge any age, civilization, or society by how well this right order is cultivated and lived. It is my contention that characteristic of our time is that we get this wrong. What we are calling SMH is at root a response to this problem and an effort to establish right order in human life. It is "spiritually motivated" precisely inasmuch as it stems from the intention to put first things first.

In *The Church and the Land* (1925), the English Dominican Vincent McNabb opened with "a call to contemplatives," saying that "there is a little hope of saving civilization or religion except by the return of contemplatives to the land!"[4] He pleads with his hearers to return to the land "not in order to scorn suburbia or to lead a simple life, but to worship God."[5] The radical nature of this call finds an echo in *RRS*:

> The major economic and social need in work for spiritual and cultural advancement and preservation of liberty in American life is: family-unit operation and fee-simple, family-basis ownership of land *based on religious principles and spiritually motivated.*[6]

---

4 Vincent McNabb, O.P., *The Church and the Land* (Norfolk: IHS Press, 2003), 31.

5 McNabb, *The Church and the Land*, 33.

6 Luigi Ligutti and John Rawe, *Rural Roads to Security* (Milwaukee: Bruce, 1946), 10. Emphasis added.

A return to the land is not the *only* path for families who seek to prioritize the highest things. My contention is that if it is not the path best suited to the challenges of our day (which it might well be), it is in any case an outstanding option for reasons I will unfold. This return to the land in the form of homesteading, while rooted in and having much in common with traditional household practices, will be a new kind of thing, deeply imprinted with the stamp of our times.[7]

Today when marriage, family, and home-life are threatened as never before, it is crucial that we discover the enduring natural and supernatural advantages of living on the land. I divide my reflections into two main parts: an assessment of our situation today, and then why SMH is such a fitting response to it.

The Situation Today

Much of the analysis of the situation almost a century ago by Msgr. Ligutti and Fr. Rawe is still valid today. They refer to the rise of a materialistic philosophy, which they capture under the name "Liberalism," that "saw only good in the ambitions of men, [and] demanded fullest liberty for the satisfaction of personal aggrandizement without hindrance of law, or organization, or any effort to safeguard one man against the greed of another."[8] They note the evisceration of the household that was well under way: "With

---

[7] See *RRS*, 183, "Most emphatically, we are not advocating a return to the old type of farm." and "The homestead-to-be is a modern, almost-more-than reasonably convenient farm."

[8] *RRS*, 3.

the appearance of the factory system home occupations decreased quite generally."[9] "Self-interest was created by the separate purses of husband and wife."[10] And, "Commercialized amusements, the movie, dance halls, soft-drink parlors, saloons, and the automobile assisted in drawing people out of the home."[11]

In these few quotations, Ligutti and Rawe have pointed to what other thinkers such as Wendell Berry have further articulated. "Without the household—not just as a unifying ideal, but as a practical circumstance of mutual dependence and obligation, requiring skill, moral discipline, and work—husband and wife find it less and less possible to imagine and enact their marriage."[12] Similarly:

> It is clear to me from my experience as a teacher, for example that children need an ordinary daily association with *both* parents. They need to see their parents work; they need, at first, to play at the work they see their parents doing, and then they need to work with their parents. It does not matter so much that this working together should be what is called "quality time," but it matters a great deal that the work done should have the dignity of economic value.[13]

---

9 *RRS*, 6.

10 *RRS*, 6.

11 *RRS*, 6.

12 Wendell Berry, "The Body and the Earth" in *The Unsettling of America* (Sierra Club Books, 1996), 117.

13 Wendell Berry, "Feminism, the Body, and the Machine" in *What are People For?* (New York: North Point Press, 1990), 182.

Ligutti and Rawe proceed to suggest that people were becoming increasingly aware and disillusioned, even to the extent that "armies of America's third struggle for freedom are being mobilized."[14] But for reasons that we need not now discern or enumerate, while their call surely inspired and moved many to action, and remains a rich resource for today, a widespread agrarian renewal did not follow. Rather, today many of the problems have grown more dire, while at the same time the customs and practices of agrarian life are practically unknown in most communities, making a return to them yet more difficult.

It is my contention that we have now arrived at a unique moment. We have pushed human nature to its limit. In the mid-twentieth century, though the seeds of corruption had been sprouting for a long time, basic human communities and relationships were largely intact—at least in comparison to now. Today the deepening demise of homelife goes hand in hand with the undoing of the most foundational and natural of human relationships: marriage and parent-child. When we add the loss of home as a place of meaningful work that connects us to neighbors and to the earth, we have a human crisis of the first order, one of unprecedented disconnection, isolation, and unhappiness.

People are feeling this, and many are looking or are ready to look for something different. Yet a return to the land today, and so likewise the promotion of such a movement, will be different now from in the twentieth century. A reader of *RRS* notices a focus on convincing the industrial laborer

---

[14] *RRS*, 7.

that a homestead is not only a better, healthier way of life but also a more economically secure situation, with much emphasis, understandably, on the latter. While a case for a homestead still can be made, and at times should be, from an "economic" perspective, my experience is that today the more effective and telling appeal is the deeper one to spiritual and moral considerations.[15] Families are turning their sights to the land not for economic security but for a richer, safer, and more wholesome way of life. Indeed, many such families find that one of the main obstacles to "turning to the land is the economic cost."

Land values and costs are a particularly problematic aspect of the project of SMH today. For some time, especially post-Covid crisis of the early 2020s, the movement back to the exurbs/countryside has led to an increase in cost of land there. This coming after decades of rural communities being decimated by an urban exodus, families today face something of a catch twenty-two regarding where and how to return to the land. Affordable land tends to be far from job opportunities[16] and perhaps, more significantly, from vibrant communities to which they already have or wish to establish ties. Land closer to economic centers, job opportunities, and the communities where most people's relatives and friends live tends to be expensive.

---

[15] Of course, as already indicated, the call of Ligutti and Rawe was "spiritually motivated." Nonetheless, at that time the "economic" reasons were more obvious and were understandably highlighted in *RRS*. I will return to this in the conclusion. There were also rural communities, still repositories of vast handed-down knowledge and practices, that could be tapped into.

[16] The expanded possibility of working remotely can mitigate this factor.

For some families, this is not a major impediment; some can take up SMH today with a financial/economic freedom provided by an excess of accumulated wealth. In other words, they can purchase land and live a homesteading existence wherein major expenses are covered by savings or investments. While this occurs with some regularity, a model for widespread SMH must include ongoing income from non-agricultural sources. Interestingly, Ligutti and Rawe envisioned a homesteading where industrial families relocate to the land—not far from urban centers—and they continue to work in industry and also grow their own food. Thus they "stand on both feet—one foot in industry, the other on the soil."[17] Some such two-footed approach will be the most common and achievable form of homesteading today.

Yet other problems come to the fore. The two-footed approach, which even in 1940 must have been uniquely demanding, will seem especially challenging in our age marked by busyness and over-commitment. Another challenge that is more serious today might easily be missed. To the extent that many jobs bring with them an engagement with attitudes and practices foreign to and even contrary to the spiritual motivation of homesteading, the "one foot in industry" can be a kind of trojan horse working against the other foot.[18]

My purpose in this section has been to indicate that the last century has seen at once an intensification of the need for

---

[17] *RRS*, 150.

[18] See for instance *RRS*, 191: "The psychology of the factory dominates society, government, rural and urban communities, the city and the farm."

SMH and a multiplication of obstacles to it. The realism and determination of the call in *RRS* still points the way for us.

> Let us know why—let us be firmly established in our philosophy. Then let us have the courage of our convictions. Where there is a will, there is a way. . . . Then let us take steps in the right direction, small and perhaps insignificant, but every move in the right direction is a move toward the goal.[19]

Indeed, to have such a firm will requires a clear sense of the why—why SMH is a uniquely fitting response to the challenges of our day.

Why SMH Today

In making their call for SMH, Msgr. Ligutti and Fr. Rawe follow Aristotle and St. Thomas Aquinas in their emphasis of starting with the end. The "final cause"—that for the sake of which an endeavor is undertaken—is the first of causes; it gives reason, direction, and order to the endeavor. It is important then that we think clearly about why SMH is worth pursuing. Here I will focus on four reasons: the homestead is a conducive context for marriage; it is a conducive context for raising children; it has positive moral influence on all involved; and it offers religious and liturgical formation.

Above I quoted Wendell Berry to the effect that without the traditional household, a husband and wife find it difficult to discover just what it is they do together and share in common. He also points to a better, older way of doing marriage:

---

[19] *RRS*, 150.

> There are, however, still some married couples who understand themselves as belonging to their marriage, to each other, and to their children. . . . This sort of marriage usually has at its heart a household that is to some extent productive. The couple, that is, makes around itself a household economy that involves the work of both wife and husband, that gives them a measure of economic independence and self-protection, a measure of self-employment, a measure of freedom, as well as a common ground and a common satisfaction.[20]

In play here is a fundamental truth about marriage. Marriage is not simply an agreement to live together in friendship; it is an agreement and indeed a covenant to do something specific together: to make a household, which is a community of daily living wherein a host of basic human needs—physical, psychological, intellectual, spiritual—are met.

St. Thomas Aquinas characterizes the end of marriage as "the begetting and upbringing of children."[21] This conception of marriage as ordered to procreation is often misunderstood as narrow, somehow limiting marriage to being about "having babies." In another text, St. Thomas explains how what might have seemed a narrow or limiting end is in fact quite the contrary:

> Offspring signifies not only the begetting of children, but also their education, to which as its end is directed the entire communion of works that exists between

---

[20] Wendell Berry, "Feminism, the Body, and the Machine" in *What are People For*, 181.

[21] St. Thomas Aquinas, *Summa theologiae* III Q. 29, art. 2.

> man and wife as united in marriage, since parents naturally "lay up" for their "children" (2 Cor. 12:14); so that the offspring like a principal end includes another, as it were, secondary end.[22]

Here the term *education* might better be rendered as "raising"—that is, as the complex project of attending not only to the physical needs but also the total formation of the young. What starts to come into focus is that the natural ordination of marriage to procreation constitutes it as the most complex, significant, and beautiful of natural relationships. "The entire communion of works" between spouses is necessarily a profoundly rich reality precisely because it is what it is in view of the formation of the next generation.

To go to the center of the wondrous reality of marriage is to go also to the center of human identity or human nature. Marriage exemplifies that my seeking to live a good life is never just about me; what I do or make in and of my life is at root about others. It is an enactment of love, ultimately for God and proximately about other human persons, in loving whom I love and serve God. Such is to be a husband or wife, and then a father or mother.

What does this have to do with homesteading? The "project," as it were, of marriage is always a project of making a life together, ultimately in view of being "generous" or "generating" offspring. We must see here, however, that this ordination toward offspring does not "skip over" the spouses themselves. Indeed, the very ordination toward children demands an integrity of the shared life of spouses, into

[22] S.t. Suppl. 49.2ad1.

which or in the context of which children are welcomed and formed. We rightly ask then what it means for a husband and wife to make a human life together. While a truly human life is always centered on the higher things, and indeed *because it is centered on them it also essentially includes attending to the many lower needs of persons*, beginning with food, shelter, etc.[23]

The household that springs from a marriage naturally exemplifies these truths of human nature. Put otherwise, the household has a kind of body and soul. The body is a very incarnate daily life, and the soul is the pursuit of the spiritual, moral, and intellectual human perfections, all under the operation of grace. And just as the human body should be well suited for the operations of the soul, the daily life of the household should be well suited to serve the ends of marriage and the Christian perfection of all members of the household.

A homestead forged for "spiritual" reasons aims to be just such a household—one that is well suited to the ends of marriage and the pursuit of Christian perfection precisely in and through the shared work of cultivating earth, plant, and animal.

My first two points about SMH, while distinguishable from one another, can practically be treated as one. A homestead is a conducive context for marriage and for raising children for the same reasons, since to be conducive to one is to be conducive to the other. But of course by a natural order, marriage comes first. The daily shared life of spouses is precisely the life that they then share with children.

---

[23] See again footnote 5 above on how all material goods are instrumental with regards to virtuous living.

Here an important point comes to the fore. Berry, writing in the 1980s, referred in the quotation above to healthy marriages as those that "usually" belong to a productive household. This assertion might be hard to verify empirically. In any case, it seems to me that another angle needs to complement his observation. I would assert that, whether in the 1980s or now, healthy marriages are "usually" those that understand and practice its intrinsic ordination toward procreation. Further, the reality is that at least a good number of such marriages are not in households that would qualify as "productive" by Berry's standards. Even if Berry's own observations do not take account of this point, I think it is in principle compatible with his approach. I suggest that many marriages have remained fundamentally healthy through a sense and practice of the shared work of raising children. In other words, raising children is itself a kind of "production," or in any case a genuine work that gives unity and focus to marriage life. One could say that the text cited from Berry does not take due notice of this fact; namely, that even apart from the kind of production characteristic of a homestead, a marriage can be well grounded in child-raising.

But this forces us to take a closer look. Child-raising is not some kind of standalone activity. I cannot put on my to-do list for this week that I will "raise my children." In short, we raise children primarily by doing *some kind of activities with them*. Herein, in my estimation, we come upon a central feature of the challenge of making a marriage, making a home, and of raising children today. What are the activities most conducive to doing these things? Or from the other side, we can ask: Why is it so difficult for us to do these things?

My assertion is that the work of a homestead is the most natural and conducive, even while certainly not the only, context to enact a marriage and raise children. By a natural order, what is the very first concrete thing to which a husband and wife must attend? They must make a living and provide, first for themselves, the material necessities of life. In earlier times, the primary form this took in the household transculturally was by engaging in the productive arts of husbandry and wifery. Socio-economic changes have brought us to where those arts have been largely replaced by other professions, the practice of which provides wages that can support the needs of life, and sometimes much more. For several generations now, we have assumed that this arrangement is good, and an advance over "subsistence" or other such forms of homesteading.

This is a complex issue that must not be oversimplified. My purpose here is first to raise the flag of a re-examination of this situation in view of human nature, marriage, and the Christian vocation. And as a first step in such a re-examination, I am suggesting that something answering the name of homesteading has key features that by nature are especially suited to be the daily stuff of marriage and raising children. We might say that only after economic developments made possible the almost complete separation of families from the land did we start to have occasion to see that connection to the land was not accidental or peripheral. It was the stuff of a natural plan. Ever since the demise of the basic arts of husbandry and wifery in the household, spouses and parents have struggled to find activities well suited to share with one another and their children.

In his book on governing a household, the Greek philosopher Xenophon, a contemporary of Plato, expresses the common ancient view that the complementarity of man and woman pertains not only to the reproduction of offspring but also to the normal work of the household, as exemplified in the many tasks involved in producing food and using it for nourishment.[24] Consider when Homer's Odysseus said to the princess Nausikaa this unforgettable, beautiful prayer:

> And may the gods accomplish your desire:
> a home, a husband, and harmonious
> converse with him—the best thing in the world
> being a strong house held in serenity
> where man and wife agree. Woe to their enemies,
> joy to their friends! But all this they know best.[25]

The most obvious referent of the "harmonious converse with him" is in the context of the work of an agriculturally productive household. The same is true in the "Economics" attributed to Aristotle, but probably written by a member of his school, when it says, "Some things should be attended to by the master, others by his wife, according to the sphere allotted to each in the economy of the household."[26]

A fuller consideration of the many concrete ways the work of a homestead is conducive to shared life in marriage and in

---

[24] See Xenophon, "The Estate Manager" in *Xenophon: Conversations of Socrates* (Penguin: New York, 1990), chapter 7, 313–14.

[25] Homer, *Odyssey*, trans. Robert Fitzgerald (Vintage Classics: New York, 1990) Bk VI, lines 193ff.

[26] "Economics" in *The Complete Works of Aristotle: The Revised Oxford Translation*, vol. 2, ed. Jonathan Barnes (Princeton University Press, 1984), Bk I, ch. 6, 1345a5–6.

raising children is beyond our scope. A few principles from Xenophon, however, point in a helpful direction.

"Agriculture is the mother and nurse of all other arts."[27]

"Agriculture also contributes toward training people in cooperation."[28]

"What is more . . . gratifying to one's wife, or welcome to one's children, or agreeable to one's friends [than living on the land]?"[29]

What might have seemed an exaggerated ancient panegyric to agriculture rather shows itself more and more to be true. Experience ranging from the ancients to the growing number of families (re)turning to the land today verifies that the cluster of activities involved in producing food in the household is a work at once practical, satisfying, and uniquely able to bring people together.

In turning to the third of my list of four, we see again how these four intertwine and overlap, as the aspect of moral formation—which applies not only to the young—is a key aspect of seeing how a homestead is well suited to raising children. While a general association of good character with "country folk" or "farm raised" people is proverbial, it behooves us briefly to take a closer look. Again, as SMH is an intentional project that can only provide certain limited aspects of country living, a clear conception of its specific advantages will help determine how to go about it.

Though the advantages of living close to the land are many, I think some principles in Aristotle and St. Thomas Aquinas

---

[27] Xenophon, "The Estate Manager," 307.

[28] Xenophon, "The Estate Manager," 307.

[29] Xenophon, "The Estate Manager," 306.

on "*oeconomia*," or the art of household management, take us to the heart of the matter. For Aristotle and Aquinas, the virtue of domestic prudence—which is the ability to do "household management" well—is a central virtue of the good life. It arranges or gives order to all aspects of household life in view of the true flourishing of family members. A foundational principle of its exercise is that all the *things* of life in the home are about serving virtuous living of *people*. Put otherwise, this is the virtue of doing well the great challenge we referenced at the opening of this essay—namely, that all worldly goods be used and valued precisely in view of spiritual goods.

For the vast majority of human persons, the primary locus of this challenge is in the household, and so the development of this virtue is central to all human flourishing. This becomes especially clear in Aristotle and Aquinas's treatment of the too common demise of household management, or rather household managers. Not surprisingly, this demise takes the form of a failure to seek first the higher things—namely, virtuous living. A major instantiation of this failure, or the form it commonly takes, is that those running the household lose their focus on what is most important and become more intent on multiplying wealth. What this concretely means is that they pursue wealth beyond the limit of *what they truly need*. The notion of the "limit" of what is "needed" is key.

Bodily needs are always limited; unfortunately, our desires often become "unlimited." Indeed, a key way to characterize disordered desire, or concupiscence, is desire that is unhinged from or not limited by the true good. The notion of "need" is complex and nuanced. Properly understood, the needs of a household go well beyond bare physical requirements. Again, "need" is understood in relation to virtuous flourishing, which can include an array of "things" that pertain to appropriate cultural and social manifestations. Nevertheless, these needs are limited.[30]

What does this have to do with homesteading? Much. Aristotle and Aquinas emphasize that the arts of producing food—interestingly, they use language of these arts as "receiving" what nature offers—tend to instantiate, we could even say cultivate, the right attitude toward wealth. How do they do this? Unless twisted to serve other ends, these arts—at least as practiced in a household—come to a natural completion in the fulfillment of human needs. For example, a man cultivating fruit trees tends to discover and observe the natural limit of how much fruit can be reasonably eaten, shared with neighbors, and stored for winter use. This limit can even include growing extra as a kind of "cash crop." Now yes, this man could also think to himself, "I could make my orchard bigger and bigger to make a lot of money;" but this mindset is clearly something "imported" as it were. It is even, I think we can say, "alien," though joinable, to the art of growing fruit.

The art of growing fruit, as all the parts of agriculture, find their most natural expression in the household, where

---

[30] Indeed, it is worth noting here that a Christian understanding of wealth not only honors the limits of need but also highlights the desirability of a spirit of poverty—a complex topic beyond our scope. On this point see the great book by Christopher Franks, *He Became Poor: The Poverty of Christ and Aquinas's Economic Teachings* (Grand Rapids, MI: Eerdmans, 2009).

an intrinsic ordination to the (limited) needs of people is most obvious. Aristotle and Aquinas actually call such arts a "part" of household management, in view of their natural compatibility with and service to this greater art of the home. Aquinas goes further, and speaking of agriculture and animal husbandry, he writes, "Therefore, the acquisition by which one acquires such things as belong to the necessities of life is natural."[31] Because the Author of nature intended plants and animals for human sustenance, the arts themselves of tending and harvesting such food are also clearly intended for human practice. And the most obvious place of such practice is in households.

These principles ground a clearer vision of the salutary character of homesteading. Homesteading explicitly practices the agricultural arts in view of serving human needs—needs understood in view of true human flourishing. Nobody *homesteads* as a way of making a lot of money. Such an intention would make it something other than homesteading. SMH practiced well highlights for all involved—parents, children, and anyone else—the right order of material things, worldly goods, and spiritual goods. Seen in this light, homesteading, when rightly conceived and practiced, offers to families an exercise and training in putting right order in their understanding and desire for material goods.

Homesteading as an exercise in other good moral dispositions can be seen as rooted in this pillar of its natural place in the home. The arts of tending earth, plant, and animal are

[31] St. Thomas Aquinas, *Commentary on Aristotle's Politics* Bk I, ch. 6, #8, p. 47.

proverbially associated with inculcating a sense of responsibility. Xenophon places great emphasis on responsibility; he has a husband and wife each relate that the fundamental life lesson they received in their homes was to be "responsible."[32] He sees agriculture as especially suited to form that disposition:

> The land provides the greatest abundance of good things, but doesn't allow them to be taken without effort.
>
> Furthermore, the land also freely teaches justice to those who are capable of learning; for it does people favors in proportion to how well they serve it.[33]

He goes even further. Having noted how in his experience farmers generally are more than willing to share their know-how with others, a major character states, "Do you see, Socrates, how very generous agriculture apparently makes the characters of those who are involved in it?"[34] Generosity! What better moral disposition for the household community grounded in the call to "generation."

I will mention quickly here two more points that while not directly moral formation are closely related to it. The work of homesteading is well suited to give people a deeper connection to their body and a sense of competence. Young people today, as most of the rest of us, suffer acutely from an alienation from their bodies. Working with the earth, plants, and animals, while not an automatic remedy, is a force

---

[32] Xenophon, "The Estate Manager," ch. 7, p. 313.

[33] Xenophon, "The Estate Manager," ch. 5, pp. 305–6.

[34] Xenophon, "The Estate Manager," ch. 15, p. 340.

for reconnecting with their embodiedness. Similarly, part of the younger generation's lack of security and rootedness stems from their general incompetence in the many arts of husbandry and wifery. Put otherwise, they know how to do very little with their hands. Xenophon points to the unique learnability of agriculture,[35] even while it remains an art that will never simply be mastered and so holds endless delight in learning more.

The final aspect of my account of why SMH is particularly important and appealing today is in how it serves the spiritual life by, among other ways, forming the imagination. Many if not most of the common images of Sacred Scripture as well as the sacramental and liturgical life of the Church are agriculturally based. This is a vast topic in itself worthy of close consideration. Here I offer but a couple of thoughts.

One of the most remarkable images in the Last Supper discourse is when Our Lord says, "I am the true vine, and my Father is the vinegrower" (Jn 15:1). The Vulgate rendering of the second clause is *Pater meus agricola est*. My Father is a farmer. Regardless of translation, a profound truth is expressed in identifying God Himself as a farmer. We were created in a garden, and we were told to tend it. The Old Testament is full of images of plants and animals, how they are tended or not, and how they respond to such tending. Again and again, the Lord Jesus uses agricultural images to convey who He is, how He acts toward us, and how we should serve Him. To speak only of the importance of a general "familiarity" with such things is too weak, especially today in a

[35] Xenophon, "The Estate Manager," ch. 15.

society so thoroughly separated in our daily life from these profound *human* realities.

The features of a responsible tending of the natural world, already itself a natural mode of how God reveals Himself to us through the "book of nature,"[36] take on an even greater significance as a privileged idiom of His supernatural revelation. This comes into clearer focus when we consider how the liturgical and sacramental life of the Church is similarly steeped in the rhythms, ways, and means of the natural world and the human tending of it.

Some Clarifications and Conclusion

Today SMH will be more difficult than it seems. And the primary, though certainly not only difficulty, is in the change of mindset and expectations it will demand in those who do it. Msgr. Ligutti and Fr. Rawe were deeply aware of this challenge. "If the mind of the homesteader is thoroughly imbued with the false advantages of commercialism . . . then no none can help him."[37] "We have become so money-minded,"[38] they observe, that many people are not able to recognize and appreciate naturally good things, such as living close to the

[36] St. Augustine wrote: "It is the divine page that you must listen to; it is the book of the universe that you must observe. The pages of Scripture can only be read by those who know how to read and write, while everyone, even the illiterate, can read the book of the universe." *Exposition of the Psalms* (Psalm 45).

[37] *RRS*, p. 152.

[38] *RRS*, p. 182.

land. "The desire to get something for nothing . . . cannot be the spirit of the successful homesteader."[39]

SMH requires a choice for hard work and a willingness to undertake an uncommon frugality and restraint in lifestyle. If a wealthy family moves to the country and dabbles in agricultural projects while it continues to live fundamentally as it did in the city or suburbs, this is not what we are calling SMH.[40]

The financial demands (as already noted earlier) are certainly a complicating factor in considering the practicality of SMH. Msgr. Ligutti and Fr. Rawe relate that "Adam Smith expressed the maxim that the prudent master of a family will never make at home what it will cost him more to make than to buy."[41] They note that while this maxim in itself is true enough, many have wrongly assumed that most everything can be more efficiently produced outside the home. Ligutti and Rawe counter that "the efficiency of the modern production of many things in the home unit for home use is easily demonstrated."[42] They proceed to give a list of activities of home production that "homestead studies show conclusively" to be more economical than production outside the home.[43] This raises a very important issue, which while we certainly cannot sort out here, demands to be addressed.

---

39 *RRS*, p. 151.

40 This is not necessarily to stand in judgment of such a situation. We simply must distinguish this from what we term SMH.

41 *RRS*, 189.

42 *RRS*, 190.

43 Here is the list: "Such varied activities as baking at home, milling at home, gardening, canning and preserving, the home dairy, berry and fruit growing, home laundering, sewing, weaving, knitting, spinning

As strange as it might seem, we have come to the point where it might be fitting to contradict Adam Smith's seemingly obvious maxim. In other words, in the name of the greater good, we might choose home production *even if it is not the most "economical."* Let me be clear: I am convinced that in general, a socio-economic order grounded on productive homesteads is the most stable and reliable arrangement for meeting human needs. Thus ultimately, such homesteads are most "economical" in a very important sense. Nonetheless, I think we must also recognize the reality that, as can be seen today, a socio-economic order of purchasing most everything that is needed can work[44]—at least for some people, for some length of time. And in this situation, it might well be, at least from a limited but real perspective, that home production is "less economical." It is my contention that families today need to be prepared to make some hard decisions, again, prioritizing home production and living close to the land for its many other virtues, even if not for being most "economical."

Making the choice for spiritually motivated homesteading and all it entails might just be a particular form today of seeking first the Kingdom of God. In his dramatic call to return to the land, Fr. McNabb asserts:

---

yarn, home building, woodworking, poultry keeping, etc." p. 190.

44 This presumably is the result in part of generations of economic development intent most of all on efficiency. Again, I do not grant that this "efficiency" is the only kind of efficiency, nor that it should be the ultimate criterion of economic success.

> No people has ever left the town for the land, or remained on the land when it could have gone to the town, except under the motive of religion.[45]

To the extent that one can live on the land without really living with and from the land and its creatures, then McNabb's assertion is surely wide of the mark. Some people go to the land for selfish reasons, and live there just like they live in city, suburb, or wherever else they go.

But McNabb has in mind SMH, which springs from seeking first the higher things, and so really enters and receives the gift of the land, including its demands and limitations. And lo, such homesteading can be an astounding instance of all other things being rendered to us besides.

[45] McNabb, *The Church and the Land*, 33.

Works Cited

Aquinas, St. Thomas. *Commentary on Aristotle's Politics.*

———. *On Kingship.*

———. *Summa theologiae.*

Aristotle. "Economics." In *The Complete Works of Aristotle: The Revised Oxford Translation*, vol. 2. Edited by Jonathan Barnes. Princeton University Press, 1984.

Augustine of Hippo. *Exposition of the Psalms.*

Berry, Wendell. "Feminism, the Body, and the Machine." In *What are People For?* New York: North Point Press, 1990.

———. "The Body and the Earth." In *The Unsettling of America.* Sierra Club Books, 1996.

Homer. *The Odyssey.* Translated by Robert Fitzgerald. Vintage Classics: New York, 1990.

Ligutti, Luigi and John Rawe. *Rural Roads to Security.* Milwaukee: Bruce, 1946.

McNabb, Vincent. *The Church and the Land.* Norfolk: IHS Press, 2003.

Xenophon. "The Estate Manager." In *Xenophon: Conversations of Socrates.* Penguin: New York, 1990.

R. Jared Staudt, PhD

R. Jared Staudt, PhD, works for the renewal of Catholic culture as a writer, educator, and founder. He serves as Director of Content for Exodus 90 and Director of the Adeodatus Catholic Culture Institute, an immersive program seeking to initiate participants more deeply into Christian life. He holds a doctorate in systematic theology from Ave Maria University and a master's and bachelor's degree in Catholic Studies from the University of St. Thomas in St. Paul, Minnesota. He served previously as Academic Dean of the Augustine Institute, Director of the Catholic Studies Program at the University of Mary, and Associate Superintendent for the Archdiocese of Denver. He has helped establish numerous high school programs, as well as Rosary College in Greenville, South Carolina. Staudt has authored several books, including *Words Made Flesh: The Sacramental Mission of Catholic Education* (Catholic Education Press), *How the Eucharist Can Save Civilization* (TAN Books), *The Primacy of God: The Virtue of Religion in Catholic Theology* (Emmaus Academic), and T*he Beer Option: Brewing a Catholic Culture Yesterday & Today* (Angelico). An oblate of Clear Creek Abbey, he and his wife, Anne, have six children.

CHAPTER 11

REDEEMING THE LAND: THE SPIRITUAL MISSION OF THE AMERICAN CATHOLIC LAND MOVEMENT

R. Jared Staudt

"The land is sick here. Work to heal the land. Pray that it may be healed." The intuition of a Cherokee woman in Western North Carolina points to the important task that lies ahead in the American Catholic land movement. Many Americans feel something similar, though they might express it differently. "Something is wrong. We're not living right. If we don't change, things are going to break down. Is our current path really sustainable?" Many Catholics today answer in the negative, realizing that something must change.

Like all things Catholic, the answer must be expressed sacramentality: fundamentally spiritual, though necessarily including a material instantiation. We cannot heal the land and our nation without prayer, holding our society up from within through sacrifice; yet we must also engage in the manual work needed to till the soil, making our country again a healthy, wholesome, and holy place to live. Although many people think God cares only for the soul and spiritual realities, they forget that He is the Creator of the body and the material cosmos. God cares deeply for His creation and how we, His stewards, treat it. In the book of Revelation, the twenty-four elders proclaim that God both vindicates the righteous and destroys those who destroy the earth (see Rv 11:18).

God's work of redemption, therefore, reaches beyond the soul by setting the body and the material world free from the forces that oppress them. We see this in Isaiah's prophecy of Israel's restoration from exile, as God espouses Himself both to His people *and* to their land:

> You shall no more be termed Forsaken,
> and your land shall no more be termed Desolate;
> but you shall be called My delight is in her,
> and your land Espoused;
> for the Lord delights in you,
> and your land shall be espoused. (Is 62:4)

In the modern world, Catholics have too long neglected the material implications of their redemption. But this interior crisis necessarily creates disorder surrounding it. Both must be addressed. We cannot solve agrarian and environmental problems without attending to the ultimate source of oppression that comes from within—sin.

The American Catholic land movement, therefore, cannot pursue cultural goals—the renewal of agriculture and a traditional way of life—without addressing the spiritual problems that underlie the crisis of culture. The two aspects of fruitfulness—spiritual and cultural—depend upon each other. Overcoming the spiritual challenges we face in North America requires the support of a robust culture, an entire way of life centered on God and His glory. Peter Maurin rightly said that we must aim at forming a society where it's easier to be good. John Senior spoke of it as tilling the soil of culture: "The restoration of culture, spiritually, morally, physically, demands the cultivation of the soil in which the love of Christ can grow, and that means we must, as they say, rethink priorities."[1] Proverbially tilling the soil of culture to pursue holiness will be facilitated by actually tilling the soil. But there are many thorns to overcome, and the soil itself has been exhausted.

Secularism: *The* Problem of Modern America

As we face overwhelming problems in modern America, how could we deny that a fundamental spiritual crisis undergirds them all? The deepest problem we face is the one within us, for the interior forms and shapes the exterior. The prophetic Pope Benedict XVI never tired of reminding us, "When God is eclipsed, our ability to recognize the natural order, purpose, and the 'good' begins to wane."[2] Our secular

---

[1] John Senior, *The Restoration of Christian Culture* (Ignatius Press, 1983), 24.

[2] Pope Benedict XVI, "Address at the Welcoming Celebration by the Young People, Apostolic Journey to Sydney (Australia) on the Occasion of the Twenty-third World Youth Day," July 17, 2008, in *The Garden of God: Toward a Human Ecology*, ed. *Maria Milvia Morciano* (Washington, DC: Catholic University of America Press, 2014), 25.

mentality keeps God and faith on the perimeter of life to pursue an abundant natural harvest of its own making, relying on technological savvy. Without God's sustaining grace, however, nature itself wears thin, suffering aridity because its steward has gone astray. Turning from God leads His created works to flounder: human beings first and then the rest of creation under their care.

Secularism splits the highest and lowest, breaking the integrity of life and striking at the very identity of created things. The soil descends into simple dirt, no longer the handiwork of God, the clay out of which we were made, but subject only to man's earthly dominion. Work becomes utilitarian, not an act of stewardship on behalf of God for His glory. Secularism pulls body away from soul, with the inner man subject to one's own thoughts and opinions, though more and more conditioned by media, while the body becomes subject to the dictates of science and medicine alone. This cuts at the heart of human identity, for we are the connection between earth and heaven, springing up from one and ordered to the other. They meet in us, and we must reconcile them.

Secularism, however, leads to individualism as it breaks apart the communion God intends for us, leading people to assert the meaning of their own existence rather than finding it in God and others. God created human beings to express and foster life, rooted in the fundamental tasks of procreation and agriculture, while sin undermines this life by alienating us from God, one another, and the earth. Continuing the rebellion of our first parents, the modern world fundamentally seeks independence, free of attachments to one another and the burden of labor. Communion flows from love, producing new life, which in itself creates burdens of commitment and dependence. Sin rebels against these tasks, seeking only self and refusing to pass on the life that is entrusted to us.

The end of our current crisis is infertility—in us and the land as well. C. S. Lewis's *That Hideous Strength* prophetically unmasks the demonic attempt to strip down human life from its contact with the organic and fertile, as expressed by the mad scientist Filostrato: "Slowly we learn how. Learn to make our brains live with less and less body: learn to build our bodies directly with chemicals, no longer have to stuff them full of dead brutes and weeds. Learn how to reproduce ourselves without copulation." Likewise, the doctor of the Church St. Hildegard of Bingen perceived that the work of the anti-Christ would fundamentally undermine the order of human sexuality toward the family. "He will assert that sexual immorality and other like things are not sins at all. . . . He will also assert that all commandments concerning chastity were made in ignorance. . . . And again he will say to the faithful, 'Your law of sexual restraint was established contrary to the way of nature.'"[3] As human beings go, so goes nature under its care, which is why the destruction of human fertility through technological means typifies the sterile approach to agriculture, forcing production on our own terms rather than drawing forth its intrinsic fruitfulness.

In response to our disastrous independence from God, one another, and the fertility of nature, rediscovering some

---

[3] Hildegard von Bingen, *Book of Divine Works.*

necessary dependence offers prospects for renewal. The independence valued so highly by modern Americans ironically leads to greater dependence on a global system of government and industry. Accepting our dependence on nature, working with it instead of against it, does more than simply symbolize dependence on God; it facilitates it. Putting hands into the *humus* of the soil leads to humility and wisdom, recognizing the true nature of things and how many beings fit into the whole. To fight secularism, it is necessary to overcome the divisions of life that would prevent the integration of life as a whole: body and soul, person and community, work and prayer, earth and heaven.

The task for Catholics, therefore, entails overcoming the essential problem of secularism and the isolation of individualism that follows. It is time to rediscover the fundamental mission given to us by God to be fertile in our lives and in our work, to be generators and cultivators of life, participating in God's creative action. Since we're not simply individuals, what happens in our country affects us, and likewise, our actions will influence others, spilling over into the Church and society. The actions of Catholics influence the whole for good or ill, with the potential to become a spiritual leaven for the whole, initiating a great project of reintegration.

With this consciousness, the Catholic land movement needs to act for the good of the entire nation. The economic mission of land stewardship may be clear, though we cannot take it for granted, but what about the spiritual mission? How must we relate to the land for our own sanctification, and how do we glorify God through it? Fighting back the thorns that arise in the soul and our culture will assist in our salvation, and a life of prayer will enable us to order the world properly. God did not intend the land to be approached as a secular "thing" cut off from Him. Our work can become religious in the sense that we do it to honor God, overcoming the inner dualism that cleaves our lives apart. It can become the means of ordering the land itself to God, enabling creation to realize its own goal of giving God glory. This is the original vision of life, flowing from the primal mission of Adam, and one which we must restore to the best of our ability.

A Biblical Vision of the Land's Redemption

America has fallen captive to the tyranny of spiritual slavery. The Catholic land movement must redeem it from all that has taken hold of it—on the bodily and spiritual levels, breaking out of the tyranny of modern culture. When the Israelites broke free from the bondage of Egypt, they had to learn how to live in accord with the lordship of God, struggling in the desert to order their thoughts and desires to Him. Likewise, we must accept that the land and its resources belong ultimately to God. He has given them to us as stewards who must direct all things back to their rightful owner.

Secular solutions have failed and will continue to fail because they do not offer a complete response to today's crisis that addresses the entirety of the human person. Wendell Berry describes the religious and practical importance of recovering a biblical vision of the land for America today, flowing from the story of Israel rooted in the promised land.

> What we have, then, is a story and a discourse about the connection of a people to a place. This connection is at once urgently religious and urgently practical. It is urgently religious because the land is understood, never as a human "property," but as a part of an infinitely complex creation, both natural and divine, belonging to God. It is urgently practical because of the strict conditions of gratitude and care enjoined upon its users.[4]

To return to a biblical vision of the land, man must dethrone himself as a demi-god, capable of doing whatever he desires to his "possessions," in order to return to his role as steward. Rather than acting for profit and temporary success, this will entail coming to terms with the very purpose of our lives within God's plan for His creation as a whole.

The Bible supports the understanding that the land may grow sick, becoming unclean and in need of redemption. God called the Israelites to accept the promise of the land as a mission: they were to purify the land, redeem it from its polluted state. If we follow the conquest and colonization of the promised land, we find the most complete picture of what it looks like to sanctify a particular place and to live a rightly ordered life in community.

---

4 Wendell Berry, foreword to Ellen F. Davis, *Scripture, Culture, and Agriculture: An Agrarian Reading of the Bible* (New York: Cambridge University Press, 2009), xi. Although Aldo Leopold, admired by Berry, criticized the Abrahamic concept of land as opposed to conservation, for somehow viewing land as a personal possession, we will see how the Bible upholds the opposite view, that God remains its true lord. See Aldo Leopold, *A Sand County Almanac and Sketches Here and There* (New York: Oxford University Press, 1949), viii.

The true goal of the American Catholic land movement, in response to a biblical vision, should entail ordering the land of this continent to God on behalf of all. Raising children, tilling soil, teaching the Faith, and worshipping God—these things matter and act like leaven for the whole. Ordering all things to God will liberate the land from the spiritual tyranny that hangs over it like a sickness, redeeming it from oppression and disfigurement, so that God Himself may dwell in this land for His glory.

God is the one who has entrusted the land and all created goods into our care. On the sixth day of creation, He withheld some of His dominion over the earth to give it to humanity to subdue as a mission to bring it to perfection. After the Exodus and conquest of the promised land, He allotted portions to the tribes of Israel and insisted that His people maintain their ownership as an expression of the general command of dominion: "The land shall not be sold in perpetuity, for the land is mine; for you are strangers and sojourners with me. And in all the country you possess, you shall grant a redemption of the land" (Lv 25:23–24). Even if the land is sold, this can only serve as a temporary grant pertaining to the use of the land. If it does become alienated from the family, God commands that it should be redeemed as soon as possible. If it does not, it must return to the family in the Jubilee Year, when all debts are canceled and the transfer of land returns back to the original owners.

For our utilitarian culture, God's commands act as a necessary check to productivity and profit. Work must cease one day a week on the Sabbath Day, representing the primacy of God in creation, for all the works of God are ordered toward the perfection of His rest. Years likewise follow this cycle based on the days of creation, with six years dedicated to work and the seventh a year of rest for the land.

> Six years you shall sow your field, and six years you shall prune your vineyard, and gather in its fruits; but in the seventh year there shall be a sabbath of solemn rest for the land, a sabbath to the Lord; you shall not sow your field or prune your vineyard. What grows of itself in your harvest you shall not reap, and the grapes of your undressed vine you shall not gather; it shall be a year of solemn rest for the land. (Lv 25:3–5)

This radical command often fell out of practice, as we might imagine. God is telling Israel that the land He entrusted to His people remained His own and that it could not be worked indiscriminately, and should be left to heal and for the care of the poor. Just as people need rest, so does the land.

Returning to the Jubilee Year, we see that the fiftieth year, as a sabbath of sabbath years, brought about a great restoration of property rights and the cancelling of debts.

> In this year of jubilee each of you shall return to his property. And if you sell to your neighbor or buy from your neighbor, you shall not wrong one another. According to the number of years after the jubilee, you shall buy from your neighbor, and according to the number of years for crops he shall sell to you. If the years are many you shall increase the price, and if the years are few you shall diminish the price, for it is the

> number of the crops that he is selling to you. You shall not wrong one another, but you shall fear your God; for I am the Lord your God. (Lv 25:13–17)

God lent His land to His chosen people. They could temporarily allow others to use that land, but it must always be returned to the original owner, because the family received this land in the great allotment following Joshua's conquest.

Land was so essential to the life of Israel that a family could not relinquish it, even if they wished to do so. In fact, there was an obligation to redeem the land if possible. In the ancient world, the role of the redeemer would be to pay the remittance for a family member who had fallen into slavery through debt. The same principle applied to the family's allotment of the promised land. When, due to economic hardship, it had to be sold, an obligation lay upon the family to redeem the land, pulling it out of its alienation from the rightful owners. "If your brother becomes poor, and sells part of his property, then his next of kin shall come and redeem what his brother has sold" (Lv 25:25).

This principle of the land's redemption should inspire us in America to bring this place back from a state of alienation and oppression, falling into abuse from consolidation, overuse, erosion, and toxic chemicals. America also stands in desperate need of liberation from new forces of slavery, both spiritual and economic, that exploit its natural gifts.

Pollution and Purification

Our task today is no longer the settling of the land but its purification. Catholics played a significant role in the settling of America and now can become leaders in this next stage of the land movement.[5] Though a minority within the United States, as members of the Body of Christ, they play a role in sanctifying the entire nation, both spiritually through prayer and materially as cultural leaders, acting as leaven for the whole. Catholics may focus on glorying God in prayer and work, but it is impossible to ignore the great sins of the nation crying out to God.

The Bible teaches us that the murder of children and sexual sin pollute the land, which must be overcome to fulfill the spiritual mission given to the people. Spiritual pollution leads to material pollution, because obscuring human dignity leads to a loss of man's role as guardian of creation. Discarding human life as something expendable for utilitarian purposes can only lead to viewing other things, with less dignity, also as simple means to an end that can be exploited without limitation. This desire to push beyond boundaries reaches back to the first sin, grasping after divine wisdom and power in the forbidden fruit. The enemy offers a false promise of immortality and unbounded freedom. This age-old dynamic to grasp what exceeds nature's possibilities has become more pronounced today in artificial intelligence (so-called) and transhumanism through genetic manipulation.

---

5 The colonization of America addressed real problems, similar to those of the Canaanites. It also introduced others, such as the unjust seizure of land and forced labor.

The primal vocation bestowed upon humanity in Genesis 1 appears conservative in contrast, translated variously as to "till and protect," "cultivate and watch over," or "work and keep." *Abad* and *shamar*, transliterated from the Hebrew, constituted a priestly task of preserving what God had instituted and offering it back to Him for His glory and the perfection of the work itself. Sin ruptured this task, creating alienation and even enmity where peace and communion had existed previously. The book of Genesis, in many ways, lays out two paths—that of Cain and Abel, of Lamech and Noah. Sin pollutes the land, which is why God Himself initiated a cleansing in the flood, wiping out the violence that had defiled it, but corruption returned immediately. God later envisioned a new cleansing of the promised land, calling Abraham to begin a new people who would bring about renewal, but He waited until the corruption of the Canaanites reached its fullness (see Gn 15:16).

If we have received the land and our own lives as a gift, then we cannot simply do whatever we like with it; instead, we must be responsible toward it as stewards of the Creator. There is something demonic to the view that we can subject creation to our own goals without any reference to God and the integrity of things in themselves. Losing a divine reference in our secular culture, we act as if everything is up for grabs, including human nature, and that our thoughts do not need restraint from the rational order of things or revealed wisdom. Consequently, we do not respect the land, the plants, and the integrity of our own bodies, seeking, rather, to dominate them by turning them to our own devices.

The pollution of the land reverses the role of stewardship given to man, with interior pollution overflowing to the rest of creation. God reveals this in Leviticus 18:

> Do not defile yourselves by any of these things [concerning sexual immorality], for by all these the nations I am casting out before you defiled themselves; and the land became defiled, so that I punished its iniquity, and the land vomited out its inhabitants. But you shall keep my statutes and my ordinances and do none of these abominations, either the native or the stranger who sojourns among you (for all of these abominations the men of the land did, who were before you, so that the land became defiled); lest the land vomit you out, when you defile it, as it vomited out the nation that was before you. (vv. 24–28)

And then Moses speaks to the people about this reality in Deuteronomy 19, warning them not to imitate the way the Canaanites polluted the land:

> When you come into the land which the Lord your God gives you, you shall not learn to follow the abominable practices of those nations. There shall not be found among you any one who burns his son or his daughter as an offering, any one who practices divination, a soothsayer, or an augur, or a sorcerer, or a charmer, or a medium, or a wizard, or a necromancer. For whoever does these things is an abomination to the Lord; and because of these abominable practices the

> Lord your God is driving them out before you. You shall be blameless before the Lord your God. (vv. 9–13)

The land itself will rebel against those who defile it through sin. Although we tend to think of sin as solely spiritual in nature, it disrupts the communion we have with another, leading to social consequences, and also the task that God has given us over His works. Sin disables us from fulfilling our duties properly, throwing the entire cosmos into chaos without the proper priestly stewardship it was meant to receive through us. Sin wounds us, and it wounds everything around us.

Israel was given the mission to remove the pollution of the promised land. When it failed to root out idolatry and sin completely, the people suffered the consequences of imitating the Canaanites, adding their own pollution to the land given to them by God. Psalm 106 describes how this happened:

> They did not destroy the peoples,
> as the Lord commanded them,
> but they mingled with the nations
> and learned to do as they did.
> They served their idols,
> which became a snare to them.
> They sacrificed their sons
> and their daughters to the demons;
> they poured out innocent blood,
> the blood of their sons and daughters,
> whom they sacrificed to the idols of Canaan;
> and the land was polluted with blood.

> Thus they became unclean by their acts,
> and played the harlot in their doings.
> Then the anger of the Lord was kindled against his people,
> and he abhorred his heritage;
> he gave them into the hand of the nations,
> so that those who hated them ruled over them.
> Their enemies oppressed them,
> and they were brought into subjection under their power.
> Many times he delivered them,
> but they were rebellious in their purposes,
> and were brought low through their iniquity.
> (vv. 34–43)

Even those chosen by God suffer interior and exterior consequences when they rupture the order God established for the world and for human relations. From these passages, we see that sexual immorality (incest, adultery, and homosexuality are named in Leviticus 18), the destruction of children, superstitious practices, idolatry, and murder all pollute the land and cry out for vengeance from God. These actions lead to practical consequences, particularly in Israel becoming subject to foreign invasion and losing control of the land. But God also redeems His people from their captivity and calls them back to renew the land through faithfulness to the covenant.

Often, we look back to these stories as mere ancient history, but St. Paul relates that what happened to Israel matters to us: "Now these things are warnings for us, not to desire evil as they did" (1 Cor 10:6). We view the possession of land in the modern world solely as a matter of private property upheld by modern notions of sovereignty. We know, however, that God remains Lord over His creation and that we possess our property only as a gift from Him. Collectively, as a nation, we hold the land in trust from Him. Will we forfeit our right to use this land by sinning against our stewardship? We certainly have polluted it with innocent blood, the blood of millions of babies, and have defiled ourselves through countless impurities. As we see from the life of Israel, pollution leads to displacement, a reality that gives urgency to the task of renewal.

The land, therefore, must be redeemed from this state of impurity and defilement. Catholics have been brought to this land for a reason. Even if our fathers have sinned against the land, and we too cannot stand innocently before the Lord, we must repent and begin the work of redemption. God has entrusted this mission to us now, to make reparation and to bring about healing. We can do this by consecrating the land to God and offering sacrifice in reparation for sin. We can lead the nation to return to necessary rest in the Lord, stepping back from our enslavement to profit and looking to its higher end. Catholics can unite in a common purpose of working together for the common good in a way that respects God's plan for creation. We can work to remove the obstacles, the new idols, that stand in the way of following the Lord more faithfully. Finally, we can work to restore a more human approach to agriculture, integrating it within a broader vision for culture.

Sacrifice: Combatting Idolatry

The world exists for sacrifice: to be made holy. The Sabbath rest, for instance, is built into the very structure of the created world as the completion that exists beyond it. Made in six days of work, the culmination of creation comes not from any of its works, including the one placed within it as the image of God in His temple, but from God's own rest. Creation exists for Him, and the Sabbath day reminds, anticipates, and even enacts this rest in the world. Humanity needs this participatory reminder more than ever, caught up in an endless cycle of productivity and distraction. God commanded human beings to stop the unending pursuit of sustenance and self-assertion.

God gives the land to Israel specifically as a place of rest, as we see at the beginning of Joshua: "The Lord your God is providing you a place of rest, and will give you this land" (Jo 1:13). Israel consciously enters into the Sabbath rest in the worship of God and the cessation of labor. But all things are ordered toward God and meant to share in His rest to some degree. Israel, therefore, receives the command to give the land rest. The rest also signifies freedom from any other force, earthly or heavenly, which is why no other gods should even be mentioned, signifying God's absolute lordship. The Sabbath recognizes this lordship also by enabling the land to feed the poor, showing God's intention for it to serve all of His people.

In addition to rest, the land can be sanctified directly through worship. The most effective way to redeem the land is through sacrifice, which means to "make holy." The earth bears an intrinsic order toward God as its end, but the Fall disrupted the order and harmony of creation, making it subject to futility (see Rom 8:20). Into the void created by sin, demons stepped in to dominate the land through giants, aggressive political tyrants who used the land as a means of oppression and domination. Israel had to oppose these giants through force (such as Og, king of Bashan) and to repair the damage done. Sacrifice returns the created world to right order with God, recapturing some aspect of the Garden and enabling man to return to his role as priest.

The Bible lays out a vision for the renewal of the land that Catholics can take up in modern America. Living as a minority within an increasingly pagan and hostile territory does not impede this mission from taking shape but cries out for it all the more. "Christians are the soul of the world," the ancient letter to Diognetus asserts.[6] Catholics must become the soul of America, giving life to the body of the people and the land itself. Our prayer must help to sanctify our nation, and our work must do its part in healing the land and modeling the integration we need to move forward in a truly human and Christian fashion.

Sacrifice entails turning to the Lord to make things holy. Holiness of life takes shape when we turn all things to God, sanctifying our lives and the world. Idolatry, on the other hand, inverts this order, wanting to bring the holy down into material things in a manipulative way, worshipping material things for a material return. Israel constantly turned away

---

6 See "The Epistle of Mathetes to Diognetus," https://www.newadvent.org/fathers/0101.htm, ch. 6.

from the Lord and toward the idols of the nation, often associated with fertility. God promised fertility to His people, yet they wanted to take things into their own hands, controlling them through spiritual shortcuts. Likewise, modern idols grasp after material ends, though without the hard work, labor, and sacrifice needed for things to blossom according to God's plan. By placing something out of its proper order, it is man who becomes the ultimate idol, seeking to direct things to self rather than to God.

Before entering into the Lord's rest, therefore, Joshua must remove the obstacles that await Israel in the land. Israel cannot settle there alongside the evil that pollutes it, as even the land itself would continue to be drawn under the evil influence of idolatry and sin. Fr. Stephen de Young describes the biblical vision of how sin pollutes things:

> Sin is portrayed as a force, sometimes even as a demonic creature, that Adam's transgression released into the world. Sin is less a judgment cast upon an action than a poison or a deadly disease. Individual actions are symptoms of this disease that reveal its presence and the degree of its progression toward death. Sin can pass from one person to another. Sin can intensify within a population and become a defining aspect of a community. Like a virus or bacteria in our modern understanding, sin leaves its mark and its contagion in the world. This stain left by sin poisons not only humans but animals, plants, and even the inanimate objects of God's created order. Thus, the Torah prescribes actions that are aimed at containing

> and eliminating the disease of sin. Purification was a battle with life-and-death stakes.[7]

This helps us to see why God asked Israel to enact a ban in Canaan, destroying all that had fallen under the dominion and curse of demons, which would contaminate God's people as they entered the land.

With staggering advancements in technology, Catholics face new giants that have figuratively and literally polluted the land. Like David mocking Goliath, any talk of standing up to them and chasing them off the land meets only derision. Yet, with each unchallenged step, the makers become subject to the tools, just as worshippers become subjects to the demands of their idols. The demons of old demanded blood, and the new ones seem to as well, subordinating human life more and more into a brave new world of automation. Following after idols opposed God's plans for His people centered on rest and care, and the new idols likewise create a new paradigm for humanity, a new way of life breaking beyond the limits of nature and even genetics.

Rest remains the goal, however. As God's people have become alienated from the gift of land and the task to exercise dominion over it, bound instead to an artificial, virtual reality, the solution must address this fundamental problem. The problem grows exponentially worse each year with ever greater power over the life of plant and animal organisms and the possibility of remaking human genetics. How can

---

7 Stephen de Young, *God Is a Man of War: The Problem of Violence in the Old Testament* (Chesterton, IN: Ancient Fatih Publishing, 2021), 41–42.

humanity find rest in its God-given identity in this life-and-death crisis?

Moses commands the people to go to Mt. Gerizim and Mt. Ebal when they enter the land, two side-by-side mountains representing the blessing and the curse that may await them in the land. God knows that His people will not remain faithful to the covenant and will fall into sin. Moses instructs Joshua, therefore, to build an altar on the mountain of the curse, Ebal, to atone for sin (see Dt 7:1–8). If sin reaches to the land, to pollute it, there must be a response based on the land, redirecting its goods to the lordship of God. After commanding this altar to be built, Moses reminds the people, "Be silent, Israel, and listen! You have now become the people of the Lord your God. Obey the Lord your God and follow his commands and decrees that I give you today" (Dt 7:9–10).

The sins of America must be addressed through sacrifice, redeeming the land from sin and dedicating it to God. Rather than offering animal and cereal offerings, God has given us a new sacrifice, drawing upon the work of our hands, to sanctify and perfect our lives. John Senior rightly pointed out that Christian culture *is* the Mass, the gift given to us not only for our own sanctification but as a means of redemption for our nation and the world. First Fridays and Saturdays, fasting, adoration, processions, ember and rogation days, and the feasts of the saints—these things offer us a means of combatting the new idolatry and pollution of the nation.

Reaffirming the Primal Covenant

The Catholic land movement plays an important role in this spiritual renewal by providing a means for all Catholics to return to the sources of culture. This movement should never succumb to the mentality of retreating from the problems of culture. It can spearhead an integrated response on behalf of the whole by modeling a return to the fundamental elements of the mission God has given us in relation to the created world and human community.

We cannot live without the land. Agrarians know that without some real connection to our roots, the humus from which we all derive, we remain incomplete, not taking up both the primal task to till or the penance to drive back the brambles by the sweat of our brow. Something within us impels us to the land, even if not to farm. The Bible is clear: we come from the earth and are destined to return to it, temporarily at least. The same could be said of all animals, but uniquely within the material cosmos, humans have been given the mission to bring order to the earth in which we have been placed. And this task rises up within us, urging us to return to our roots.

Our lives follow a paradigm derived from the Sacred Page: we yearn to return to a primal state from which we have fallen as we suffer through the exile of this life, cry out to God for restoration, and strive to reach some kind of settled life in communion with others. God gives us gifts to guide us, both material and spiritual, as we seek healing for ourselves and order in our communities. Yet, this work will always remain tentative, for it looks toward a city to come. That city, however, becomes a model for the partial restoration of paradise even on earth. In the meantime, the difficult labor of culture becomes a means toward the perfection of the next life. The sweat of the brow and the pains of childbirth are meant to be part of the healing process, but we sought to rid ourselves of both. Returning to the garden by destroying the effects of the Fall doesn't work; it only creates more alienation. Rather, we need to embrace the tasks of work and procreation as a means of restoring order in obedience and love.

If secularism undermines community and fertility, it is time to renew these fundamental goods that flow from our first covenant with God. This is why the Catholic land movement must play a pivotal role in the renewal of American culture. With our culture literally out of control, beyond the control of any individual or group, it is time to return to the primal goods that we can shape and develop. *The land will become a place of Catholic renewal* because it offers access to the simple goods that those in the city and suburbs lack.[8] It is a place to

---

[8] Jeffrey Marlett describes, "An oft-repeated mantra of the Catholic rural life movement—'Christ to the Country, the Country to Christ'—expressed a similar view. The two phrases captured the conference's imaginative theological appreciation of American Catholic rural life. Agriculture was not merely an occupation, but an analogy for the soul's relationship with the divine life. Farmers worked with God's natural gifts to produce food, just as Christians cooperated with God's grace to hasten God's kingdom. Like the church's seven sacraments, farming conveyed grace in a form inaccessible elsewhere." "Strangers in Our Midst: Catholics in Rural America," in *Roman Catholicism in the United States: A Thematic History*, ed. Margaret M. McGuinness and James T. Fisher (New York: Fordham University Press, 2019), 165.

gather away from the new idols, to encounter reality again, and to form bonds of friendship and economic dependence.

We cannot immediately solve America's problems, but we can begin to address the problems of family life and local community through humble steps. Catholics can connect to communities that produce food, supporting agricultural communities and establishing bonds with them, leading to friendship and opportunities for festivity. Small rural Catholic communities can become places for economic cooperation and social communion. It's beginning to happen in pockets across the country and has the potential to grow because it meets a genuine cultural need. The land can become a place for community and culture for many Catholics, addressing spiritual and economic needs at once.

A greater connection to agricultural communities also models the fundamental blessing that God intends for all people: the fruitfulness of our lives and work. Moses describes to the Israelites how the Lord will bless them when they arrive in the land:

> The Lord will send a blessing on your barns and on everything you put your hand to. The Lord your God will bless you in the land he is giving you. The Lord will establish you as his holy people, as he promised you on oath, if you keep the commands of the Lord your God and walk in obedience to him. Then all the peoples on earth will see that you are called by the name of the Lord, and they will fear you. The Lord will grant you abundant prosperity—in the fruit of

> your womb, the young of your livestock and the crops of your ground. (Dt 28:8–11)

We see the connection between the land, work, families, and the community as a whole. Critics of the land movement may claim nostalgia for a lost culture as the prime motivating factor behind its attempted revival, but we must answer with God's own plan for His people.

Like Joshua, Catholics must reaffirm the dominion of the Lord in order to oppose the new idols: "But as for me and my household, we will serve the Lord" (Jo 24:15). It may be a losing battle, but we will fight it. We will seek to follow the original covenant given to humanity and the mission that flows from it: to be fruitful and to bring the earth under the Lord's dominion.

Act 6: Redeeming America, One Acre at a Time

To some degree, we might venture to say that God drew Catholics to America to stop some serious sins that had polluted the land here, such as the horrific sacrifice of the Aztecs. But, like the Israelites of old, we have also betrayed the promise through our own sins. And now, we have returned to the same sins that the Canaanites and Aztecs practiced. But this does not justify the sins and abuses that arose in its Catholic settlement. The work of the Catholic missions ended too abruptly, and the unity that began to coalesce around the Faith and the intervention of Our Lady was thwarted. The work remains for another generation to continue in a new way.

In addition, America faces a more general agricultural crisis of biblical proportions. Rather than God's plagues striking down the land's fertility and yield, the earth has been desacralized and exploited by its steward, as it cries out for the kind of healing and redemption Israel was entrusted to bring to Canaan. Rather than distorting our claim to the land using the Bible, Wendell Berry challenges us to take its lessons more seriously.

> We Americans readily saw the parallel between the Israelites' entrance into the land of Canaan and our own westward expansion. We adopted the simple nationalism of the old story along with its "promised land" idea of ownership prior to settlement—we called it "manifest destiny." But we conveniently ignored the elaborate agrarianism and ecological stewardship implicit in that story's insistence upon the land's sanctity. The result, still continuing, has been desecration and destruction of the land, as well as the destruction, dispossession, and exile of the American Indians who, like the Israelites and unlike most white Americans, believed the land was holy.[9]

The story of the American Catholic land movement continues, giving us the opportunity to address, even in small ways, the missed opportunities of the past.

God settled Israel in the land to become a source of unity, not only for the twelve tribes, but also for the nations. Americans have often looked to this continent as a new promised

---

[9] Berry, foreword to Davis, *Scripture, Culture, and Agriculture*, xi.

land of opportunity. Even though we must be careful not to take the comparison too far, we can recognize the gift of the land that God has given to His people in America, calling them to respond with the proper stewardship He taught His people throughout salvation history.

Each Israelite family received an allotted portion of land from that which was bestowed upon the tribes (see Jo 13–19). In some cases, the land came with the burden of removing the remaining enemies and idols from the territory before the tribe could take up its rest. This should encourage us to take up the task allotted to us in the place where the Lord has settled us to sanctify it through prayer and the fulfillment of our duties. Each Catholic today is not responsible for the whole but for one particular place and one group of people. This becomes the mission field that can be redeemed in small ways by sacrifice and the overturning of idols.

The biblical vision of the land, labor, and community remains the paradigm for all time. Applying it to modern America unlocks our current opportunities, even with the unique technological challenges we face. Following the picture of Israel's settlement, we can take courage for the work ahead, not giving into anxiety about the whole problem of culture, by pulling back from consumerism and the dominance of technology, living an integrated life, and bringing healing to the earth as much as we are able.

Following the history of the American Catholic land movement, we can bring the great heritage of our Catholic faith and tradition into particularly American gifts and opportunities. This includes our agrarian heritage and strides that have been made in conservation, particularly when approached in a holistic manner.

> Catholic agrarianism's theological worldview expressed a uniquely American and Catholic appreciation of the natural world. It thus represented the first incarnation of American Catholic environmentalism. Catholic rural-lifers blended aspects of U.S. culture with the Catholic Revival motifs associated with neo-Scholastic philosophy in the 1930s and 1940s, particularly the focus on "restoring all things in Christ." The U.S. farmer embodied everything "American," while simultaneously symbolizing the dawn of a new order built on Catholic principles. God's gift of the land to the farmer supplied the basis for both claims.[10]

Like the heyday of the land movement in the early twentieth century, we, too, can bring theological and spiritual insights to bear on contemporary problems. The economic and cultural environment needs this intervention even more than it did then, for the problems have grown even more complex than during the Great Depression, with the advancements in automation and biotechnology. Who will speak to these problems and offer humane and godly solutions if not Catholics?

At the same time, ordinary, humble Catholics can do their part. America can be healed and redeemed one acre at a time. Wendell Berry, speaking of Andy Catlett, one of

---

[10] Marlett, "Strangers in Our Midst," 170.

the members of his semi-fictional community, Port William, relates how he looked back over many decades: "As a farm perhaps never better than marginal, the place in its time has known abuse, neglect, and then, in Andy's own tenure and care, as he is proud to think, it has known also healing and health and ever-increasing beauty."[11] What better description could we propose for our own ability to improve our little "acre," our place whether rural or urban? Berry further proposes that everyone have a similar focus on one place where we can love and serve and improve that place: "The primary vocation probably is the call to go home, to go where one's gifts and one's work can be offered to one's family and neighbors, to one's home place—to 'what is actually loved and known.'"[12] God does not call each one of us to bring the entire world under his dominion, but our own little place within it.[13]

---

11 Wendell Berry, *The Art of Loading Brush: New Agrarian Writings* (Catapult, 2019), 237.

12 Berry, *The Art of Loading Brush*, 79.

13 One example of this can be seen in Bishop Chad Zielinski's consecration of the New Ulm Diocese to Our Lady of the Prairie. He commissioned an icon for the occasion, which he processed throughout the diocese. During the pilgrimage, he blessed the headwaters of the Minnesota River with a relic of the true Cross, during which he prayed: "As we stand at the headwaters of the Minnesota River asking God to pour forth his blessing, we are reminded of the grace flowing from Our Lady of the Prairie. . . . I pray that as this blessing joins the Minnesota River flowing through the heart of our diocese that a new era of grace flows into the hearts, minds, homes, farms and parishes of the Diocese of New Ulm. Our Lady of the Prairie has claimed us as her children, and with great joy we claim her as Our Mother" (Quoted in Mary Farrow, "American Pope, American Lady: The story behind Our Lady of the Prairie," *The Pillar*, Sep. 5, 2025, https://www.pillarcatholic.com/p/american-pope-american-lady-the-story).

We can heal the land and allow it to heal us. Spiritual and material fertility are bound up together, and the redemption of one from oppression may just free up the other. Jesus has redeemed us from sin, and the effects of that redemption must reach all of creation. We can free it from the oppressive domination of utility and profit, fine enough when they remain within their proper measure but not as pharaohs dominating over man and the earth. All Catholics can take up the primal vocation of work, re-engaging nature and drawing forth its potential in some way. If we venture too far, abstracting from the foundation of nature to the point of breaking, we will find continual danger, becoming like Israel turning to the idols of the surrounding nations.

As Catholics, we can remind our fellow Americans that we cannot truly own the land. As Willa Cather put it in *O Pioneers*, "We come and go, but the land is always here. And the people who love it and understand it are the people who own it—for a little while." We receive it from the Lord temporarily as stewards and should make it fruitful—ordered toward the care of the community and the Lord's own glory. We are not directly responsible for other places, but God has entrusted *this* place to us as Americans. John Paul II indicated something of the spiritual responsibility for particular places when he prayed, on his first visit back to his Polish homeland after his election as pope, "Renew the face of *this* land." God will renew the entire earth in His own time, but, in the meantime, we His agents, His stewards, begin the work of renewal here and now.

Works Cited

Benedict XVI. "Address at the Welcoming Celebration by the Young People, Apostolic Journey to Sydney (Australia) on the Occasion of the Twenty-third World Youth Day." July 17, 2008. In *The Garden of God: Toward a Human Ecology.* Edited by Maria Milvia Morciano. Washington, DC: Catholic University of America Press, 2014.

Berry, Wendell. Foreword to Ellen F. Davis. *Scripture, Culture, and Agriculture: An Agrarian Reading of the Bible.* New York: Cambridge University Press, 2009.

———. *The Art of Loading Brush: New Agrarian Writings.* Catapult, 2019.

Bingen, Hildegard von. *Book of Divine Works.* Translated by Nathaniel Campbell. Washington, DC: Catholic University of America Press, 2018.

Marlett, Jeffrey. "Strangers in Our Midst: Catholics in Rural America." In *Roman Catholicism in the United States: A Thematic History,* edited by Margaret M. McGuinness and James T. Fisher. New York: Fordham University Press, 2019.

Senior, John. *The Restoration of Christian Culture.* Ignatius Press, 1983.

Young, Stephen de. *God Is a Man of War: The Problem of Violence in the Old Testament.* Chesterton, IN: Ancient Faith Publishing, 2021.

DEDICATION OF THE RURAL FAMILY TO THE DIVINE MAJESTY

Almighty and merciful Father, whom Your only-begotten Son, our Lord, Jesus Christ, has named the Husbandman, or Farmer, graciously accept our praise and adoration. All things were made by You and all that we have is Yours.

Our lives and our talents, our home and furnishings, the soil and its fruits, the animals and their abode, sunshine and rain, fruit and harvest are all from You. By their use we are to come more securely to You. For all Your gifts, O God, we offer You our thanks.

You have made us branches of Your Son, the true Vine, members of Your kingdom, and sheep of Him who is our Good Shepherd. In gratitude and love we promise to remain ever close to the divine Heart of Him who is the Way, the Truth, and the Life.

We humbly beseech You to look with favor upon this Your family and to sanctify its members. Bless also our home, our flocks and herds, our fields and labors. Keep from us all attacks of Satan and preserve us from all evil, through Your beloved Son in the charity of the Holy Spirit.

With filial affection and reverence we humbly dedicate ourselves to the Blessed Trinity, the Father, the Son, and the Holy Ghost. Keep us ever in Your love, faithful and true unto death.

We place this our dedication in the pure hands of the Immaculate Mother of God, the patroness of our beloved country. May the Most Holy Virgin Mary carry this offering of ourselves and all that is ours to the throne of Your divine majesty. Grant us through her intercession, we beseech You, the grace to pass through things temporal that we may not lose those which are eternal. Through Christ our Lord. Amen.

—*The Rural Life Prayer Book*, 1956,
National Catholic Rural Life Conference